IRISH SEA

THE WASH

DOVEDALE

Swallow Falls

R. Severn

Avon

Thames

LONDON

SELBORNE

SOUTHAMPTON

STONEHENGE

DARTMOOR

LAND'S END

ENGLISH CHANNEL

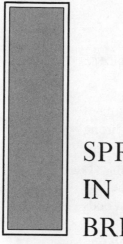

SPRINGTIME
IN
BRITAIN

by EDWIN WAY TEALE

Grassroot Jungles
The Golden Throng
Near Horizons
The Junior Book of Insects
Dune Boy
The Lost Woods
Days Without Time
Adventures in Nature
The Strange Lives of Familiar Insects
Circle of the Seasons
Insect Friends
North With the Spring
Journey Into Summer
Autumn Across America
Wandering Through Winter

edited by EDWIN WAY TEALE

Walden
Green Treasury
The Thoughts of Thoreau
The Insect World of J. Henri Fabre
The Wilderness World of John Muir

Edwin Way Teale

SPRINGTIME IN BRITAIN

ILLUSTRATED
WITH PHOTOGRAPHS BY THE AUTHOR

An 11,000-Mile Journey Through the Natural History of Britain
from Land's End to John o' Groats

Dodd, Mead & Company *New York*

TO NELLIE

The Best of Companions

on the Longest Journey of All

ISBN 0-396-06209-1
Library of Congress Catalog Card Number: 79-126294
Printed in the United States of America
by Vail-Ballou Press, Inc., Binghamton, N. Y.

ACKNOWLEDGMENTS

My indebtedness to those who aided us before, during, and after our travels through Britain extends to both sides of the Atlantic. By reading portions of the manuscript, by aiding in problems of identification, by giving me the benefit of specialized knowledge, and by providing help of various kinds, they rendered assistance for which I am deeply grateful.

In America special acknowledgments are due to Dean Amadon, Paul Brooks, Polly Calhoun, Lois Darling, Walter Harding, Marjorie Hemphill, John and Margaret Kieran, Alexander B. Klots, Elizabeth Burroughs Kelley, Marjorie Medary, Fred and Edith Nagler, Leila Ostby, Roger Tory Peterson, Harold W. Rickett, James Slater, Mark and Dorothy Van Doren, Sonia Wedge, and Farida A. Wiley. In Britain I am particularly indebted to Rev. Edward A. Armstrong, Bruce Campbell, Mrs. William A. Creeth, James Fisher, Rev. Eben Fiske, Mrs. Elsa Godfrey, Maurice Griggs, Gerald and Peggy Humphrey, John and Lois James, A. T. Morley-Hewitt, Cyril Reginald Nortcliffe, and James and Ruth Skilling.

David Ascoli, of Cassell and Company, Ltd., gave invaluable help by reading the entire manuscript from the viewpoint of an English editor. Once more, as in so many of my former books, my debt is great to Benjamin T. Richards for his copy-editing of the manuscript and his checking of the galleys and page proofs.

On both the original journey and in reliving that journey in writing the book, my wife, Nellie, has been of inestimable help.

Prior to book publication, "The Selborne Nightingale," Chapter 14, appeared in *Audubon* magazine. I wish to express my thanks to the editor for permission to include this material in the present volume.

After twenty books and more than thirty years of cordial relationship, I am keenly aware of my indebtedness to many members of the staff of Dodd, Mead & Company, particularly, as in the past, to Edward H. Dodd, Jr., S. Phelps Platt, Jr., Raymond T. Bond, Helen M. Winfield, and Mary Mc-Partland. Special help of many kinds given by S. Phelps Platt, Jr., in making our arrangements and in smoothing our way at the start and finish of our travels, is acknowledged with gratitude.

Trail Wood
March 1, 1970
EDWIN WAY TEALE

CONTENTS

ILLUSTRATIONS

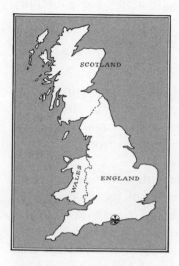

chapter 1

OUTWARD BOUND

A thousand miles of rolling ocean lay behind us—most of it still in sunshine. Another thousand miles stretched ahead —most of it now in darkness. Tilting deliberately up and down like an enormous seesaw, the 642-foot *Statendam* advanced across the great swells of the mid-Atlantic.

Clinging to the stern rail, rising and falling with the ship, we watched the sun approach and sink below the dark ruler-line of the sea's horizon. The glow faded from the sky. Dusk enveloped the waves. At the end of that March sunset, while day was giving way to night, winter also gave way to spring. We, who had encountered this transition point of the year so often on land, experienced it now for a first time on the open sea.

Three sunsets later, low smudges on the horizon grew darker. A slender, vertical column of white became visible —the lighthouse on Bishop Rock, marking the outer edge of the Isles of Scilly. With soft gray mist and gentle rain, dusk came to Land's End and the Channel coast. Far into the night, through our portholes, we could see, moving slowly by, vague pinpoints of light along the shoreline, faintly luminous patches on the sky above inland towns, the beams, steady or revolving, of lighthouses. The coast stood out black at the water's edge, the same southern shore of England that to the sailors of Conrad's *Narcissus* had appeared like the side of a ship of fabulous dimensions, "the great flagship of the race, stronger than the storms and anchored in the open sea." When dawn broke, the New Forest lay on our left. We were turning in from the Channel, riding up Southampton Water.

Three centuries ago, an old English writer admonished the prospective traveler: "Know most of the rooms of thy native land before thou goest over the threshold thereof." During nearly two decades of journeying through the four American seasons, my wife, Nellie, and I had become well acquainted with most of the rooms of our native country. We had wandered across the United States from the Atlantic to the Pacific, from Mexico to Canada. Now we had passed over the threshold thereof. In a fresh first time, we were to observe and enjoy and compare with our own the natural history of a foreign land.

In former days, naturalists from Britain explored other continents, sailed around the world, and enriched the literature of nature by their travels. But, curiously, few have been the reverse journeys. Few have been those from other lands who have crossed the sea to record in books their contacts with nature in Britain. Among North American naturalists, the last to undertake such a journey seems to have been John Burroughs. In 1884 Burroughs published *Fresh Fields,* an account of his three months in Britain and his observations of nature between Glasgow, in Scotland, and Selborne, in Hampshire. Since then, all during the more than eight intervening decades, no other American naturalist, so far as I can find, has crossed the Atlantic and returned to write a similar volume about his travels through the nature of this older land. Like our predecessor, Burroughs, we were crossing the ocean—eight decades later—"less to see the noted sights and places than to observe the general face of nature."

Ours was to be literally a pilgrimage to another *country*, to the *country* of Britain. We were looking forward to its copses and downs and moors, to its fields and lanes and villages. This was the springtime of another year, the season when, in the often-quoted line from the Prologue of *The Canterbury Tales*, "longen folk to goon on pilgrimages." All during the spring, and part of the summer, too, our pilgrimage would carry us through the beauty of nature in new forms, in unfamiliar places. The old seasonal pageant would return, but it would appear on a new stage, with a new cast of characters. Instead of arriving with hepatica and trillium, bluebird and wood thrush, the English spring would come with skylarks and daffodils, bluebells and nightingales.

The days of the previous winter had been passed in the pleasures of preparation. Happy evenings went into poring over books, marking maps, listing things to see. We practiced using pounds, shillings and pence. We spent hours streamlining our luggage to the requirements of a compact car and the air trip home. The heaviest items were our binoculars, our cameras, and the lightest-weight portable typewriter I could find. Needed nature guides, such as *The Oxford Book of Wildflowers* and *A Field Guide to the Birds of Britain and Europe*, by Peterson, Mountford, and Hollom, we could obtain after we landed. So, on a bright St. Patrick's Day, we sailed from New York and our new adventure began.

In general our plan was to start at the farthest tip of Cornwall and work northward in long, ascending strokes, zigzagging back and forth across the country until we reached the topmost coast of Scotland. The map that rode with us on the *Statendam* was measled over with a rash of red circles marking the places we hoped to visit. But our precise itinerary was left to chance. We would veer this way and that as we heard of new and interesting things to see.

The cavernous buildings where we passed through customs echoed with a sound familiar to the ancient Saxons, the chirping of house sparrows. In Southampton, with its innumerable American products, we seemed still at home. On a sidewalk in the business district, I picked up a shining coin. For a moment, I thought I had found a ten-dollar gold piece. It was a newly minted English penny. Walking through a park, on that initial day in Britain, we encountered our first jackdaw, trailing an injured leg; our first pied wagtail, flashing its black-and-white plumage among the bushes; our first blackbird, that member of the thrush family, with its yellow bill and glorious voice.

The next day, in a deluge of rain, I practiced handling a rented car, a compact blue Vauxhall. I learned all over again the use of a manual gearshift. I drilled myself in driving on the left, on "the wrong side of the road." When the lesson was over, my instructor left with a cautious: "I *think* you will get through all right." Ahead of me now stretched thousands of miles—as it turned out, 11,000 miles—of country roads, superhighways, hedge-bordered lanes, and village streets.

It was raining again the next morning when we stowed away our luggage and eased ourselves into the front seat of the unfamiliar car. Four wide-ranging months, all untouched, lay ahead; four months, free from the ordinary responsibilities of life, in which to explore a foreign spring. Our travels by water were over. Our travels by land were beginning. We turned toward Cornwall.

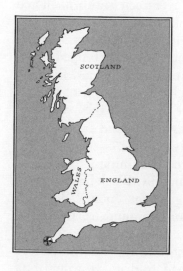

chapter 2

LAND'S END

Coming in from the sea, we had looked across the dim shapes of the Isles of Scilly toward Land's End. Now, our view reversed, we looked from Land's End across those misty islands toward the open Atlantic. Far below us, great waves swept in from the ocean and, with reverberating thunder, shattered into seething foam all along the base of the gray, granite cliffs on which we stood. Our path, centuries old, at times a hundred feet above the water, led us beside the precipice. Its thin line traced across turf that runs to the very cliff edge one fragment of a chain of ancient Coast Guard footpaths that extend almost the whole length of Cornwall's rugged shoreline. Walking here at the tip of the Cornish peninsula, standing on this stone prow of England pushing out into the Atlantic, we were at the farthest southwestern point of the land.

Close to a white stone cottage that carries on its roof in large black letters the words: "FIRST AND LAST HOUSE IN ENGLAND," we came upon a washing laid out to dry on a clump of wiry furze. In spite of the wind, the innumerable spines of this evergreen shrub anchored the garments fast. Furze—or whin, or gorse—was here already golden with the yellow of its pealike flowers. Several times, in exposed places along the cliffs, we stopped to examine curiously bisected masses of furze. Toward the land they were rich with green and yellow, the green of foliage, the yellow of flower. But toward the ocean they were dry, dead, straw-colored. Salt spray, driven inland by the gales, had blasted each clump on its seaward side.

House martins, with white breasts shining like those of our tree swallows at home, skimmed by. Black-headed gulls, reminding us of the Franklin's gull, the "prairie dove" of the Great Plains, whirled screaming around us. Before we left home, Roger Tory Peterson, whose field guides have helped millions identify the living bird in the bush instead of the dead bird in the hand, had told us we would find roughly a third of the British birds the same as our own, a third similar to birds we knew, and a third entirely different.

All across the headland turf, below the martins and the gulls, the small white disks of the English daisies were supported on stems that were often no more than an inch or two high. Bending close, we noticed the edging of rich pinkish-red that encircles these flowers when their petals are unfolding. Here, on the cliff-brink trails of Land's End, Nellie and I were beginning our long adventure with the new birds and the unfamiliar wildflowers of Britain. How many birds, how many flowers, were strangers now that would become familiar companions during our travels in the months ahead!

In the lee of one of the clumps of furze, we discovered a fleshy plant with a rosette of heart-shaped lower leaves hugging the ground. The white flowers, diminutive and four-petaled, were still weeks away. We felt the thick leaves. We ran the stems between thumbs and forefingers. For the first time in our lives, here on the cliffs of Land's End, we were examining that famous plant of sailing-ship days, the *Cochlearia officinalis* of systematic botanists, the scurvy grass of seamen.

A member of the mustard family, it grows along seashores, on clifftops, and on river banks in arctic North America as well as in the British Isles. Its leaves are rich in vitamin C. When added to the diet of sailors, on long voyages under canvas, it prevented scurvy. Out toward the sea, where we saw the waves sparkling and a sprinkling of liners, freighters, and fishing boats, an ample supply of this plant growing at our feet had ridden in the hold of the *Endeavour* when, in the summer of 1768, Captain James Cook headed away from Land's End toward the unknown world of the South Seas.

After a time, we left the clifftop paths and wandered inland, climbing amid heather and furze to higher ground. Wherever we had gone along the edge of the sea that day, during momentary pauses in the crying of the gulls our ears had caught tantalizing snatches of a wild, jumbled song, a medley, sweet and sustained. It came to us from the green expanse of the upland. As we mounted among boulders and across deep, springy carpets of heather, the singing grew louder. Gaining the summit of the low plateau, we leaned back against a huge gray boulder, splotched and seamed with gray and yellow lichens. All across the open, unfenced land about us, small birds, streaked and brownish and about the size of our song sparrow at home, hung in the air on fluttering wings. These were birds we had read about all our lives—the skylarks of England.

Climbing sometimes a hundred feet into the air, they sang as they rose, sang as they hovered in the air, sang as they descended again. We watched their forms growing tiny against the clouds. We watched them drift this way and that as they parachuted down to drop, at the end, in a swift plunging descent, often returning to the same rock or furze clump from which they had ascended. These song flights sometimes lasted for several minutes. Frequently, we observed, the singers fluttered their wings, then closed them momentarily, and fluttered them again.

And all the while they were in the air their songs came tumbling down in a shower of bright musical sound, a mingling of sweet repeated phrases and notes. They went on and on, varied, seemingly improvised, seemingly never twice precisely the same, yet always formed of the same basic song material. At times, during the ascents, the voices of the singers reached our ears with a slight buzzing quality.

During every month of the year, skylarks sing somewhere in England. Scattered over tens of thousands of open fields across the length and breadth of the country are the singing perches of these birds. For so vocal are the larks that they sing on the ground as well as aloft. It is the climbing, hovering, drifting, parachuting ascent and descent, however, that produce the ecstatic jumble of liquid, twittering, warbling notes for which these small singers in the sky are famous.

I leaned back against the granite boulder listening, thinking of the song of the bird. The song of a bird may be an enticement for a mate. It may be a warning to trespassers on its territory. But why so musical? Would not jarring notes or guttural sounds or shrill and piercing whistles achieve as well these ends? Why does the enticement and the warning have to be so melodious, so moving, so beautiful? All we can say, with our sense of wonder aroused, is that it, like the delicate perfume of the wildflower, is part of nature's endless employment of beauty to achieve its utilitarian ends.

Numerous American birds mount in brief song flights during the breeding season. But none we had ever seen climbed so high or poured forth an aerial song so extended in its range and volume and duration. There are, according to the estimate of James Fisher, three-quarters of a million skylarks in England and Wales alone. We were to hear their singing at Stonehenge, on the South Downs of Sussex, in the Cotswolds, beside Hadrian's Wall, amid the mountain pastures of the Highlands of Scotland. We were to meet the birds in greater numbers later on. We were to hear their singing all the way to John o' Groats. But here, on this initial encounter, we watched and listened as though these were the only skylarks we would see in Britain.

Following the flight of the singers with our binoculars, we noted how they lifted high their heads, craned their necks, peered about them as they hovered. Thus, no doubt, for the duration of their songs they keep track of rivals and remain on guard against hawks. Larks represent one of the chief sources of food for sparrow hawks.

Once a black-headed gull swept close beneath a singing lark. The smaller bird paid virtually no attention to it. Another time, with wings fluttering, almost translucent in the blacklighting of the sun, a skylark drifted toward the cliff edge. There it hung, descending almost imperceptibly, held aloft by the updraft. We could picture the dramatic scene outspread below it—the yellow of the furze dotting the green expanse of the headland, the great cliffs fronting the sea, the white lace of foam at their base, the sparkling water extending away beyond. So time passed. In some of the happiest hours of the trip, here, so close to its beginning, we forgot all else except our intense enjoyment of the larks.

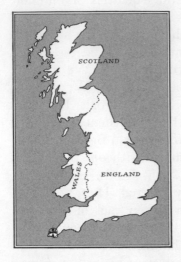

chapter 3

HIGH TOR

In a garden by the sea, some twenty miles up the Cornish coast, at St. Ives, the following day, our introduction to the flowers and birds of Britain continued. The garden was warm within the sheltering curve of a high bluff. It was filled with exciting scents and sounds. For we were in a garden of birds as well as of flowers.

All the time we were there an English robin—the Cock Robin of the nursery rhyme, the most popular bird in Britain—sang over and over its modest warbling song. So different from the larger, brighter, louder American robin, it reminded us of our eastern bluebird. It was this robin of England, not the robin of America, that the Plymouth Bay colonists were thinking of when they named the bluebird the "blue robin."

The male we saw sang always from the same dry twig. It would probably spend the bulk of its life close to this one garden. Although the females migrate—but usually no farther than the Pyrenees—the males of the British robin are largely sedentary. The sweet, rather thin, warbling phrases we heard continue around the year except from about mid-June to mid-July. The old English expression: "Tame as a robin," tells much about the fearlessness of this bird, which often chooses as its nesting ground yards and gardens close to human habitations.

The English bird that reminded us most of the American robin was also active in this garden at St. Ives. This was the blackbird. Both it and our robin have yellow bills. Both run over the ground in hunting food. Both use mud in building their nests. When disturbed, both fly away with loud notes of alarm. Both sing on into the evening after sunset. Both belong to the thrush group, having the same generic name, *Turdus*. The male American robin, with its brick-red breast and white markings, is by far the more colorful bird. Only the yellow of the bill and the eye rim relieves the uniform black of the plumage of the blackbird. However, the song of the blackbird possesses a rich and melodious, a moving and spiritual quality not found in the loud, robust and cheerful song of our robin at home.

Another encounter we made that day was with the great tit. It appeared and disappeared among the dry fronds of a palm. Once seen, it is a bird that is always remembered. Its blue-black head and neck, its white cheeks, and the vertical stripe of black that divides its yellow breast, make its plumage pattern as distinctive as that of the black-masked yellowthroat among our warblers in eastern America.

These new birds moved among new and unknown flowers. We breathed perfumes that were unfamiliar. Bushes flamed from top to bottom with brilliant orange blossoms. Wall flowers, sweet-scented and richly hued, grew in dense, ruglike masses. At times, among these botanical strangers, we came upon familiar forms—palms, bamboos, yuccas. In England the yucca blooms, but it sets no seed. For the yucca moth of the American Southwest—which, by its own elaborate procedure, fertilizes the blooms of this desert plant—

has not followed it across the Atlantic. Thousands of miles separated these yuccas from the only insect in the world able to pollinate them.

Woven through all our memories of this garden above a Cornish bay is the crying of the gulls. No wonder W. H. Hudson included in *The Land's End* a whole chapter on "The Gulls of St. Ives." It was in connection with Hudson that, on this portion of the coast, we met our first unexpected adventure of the trip. Near the little granite village of Zennor, I encountered a farmer named Maurice Griggs. With a rugged, thoughtful face, black, piercing eyes, and a thatch of white hair blowing in the wind, he was nearing seventy. As a boy of nine he had guided Hudson about the countryside when the author of *Green Mansions* and *Far Away and Long Ago* had boarded at his mother's house in the village. After leading me to the house—a curious dwelling originally built by a religious zealot and shaped like an old-fashioned coffin—he offered to show me, as he had shown Hudson, the Cornish coast from the summit of a high tor, or hill crowned with a jumble of granite rocks, that rose above his Tremedda Farm.

With Griggs in his rubber boots leading the way, we commenced the ascent. Along the winding path we followed, he stopped often to point out things of interest—here the sliding hoofmark left by fox hunters who had ridden to hounds over the rough terrain, there the bright green rosettes of the wild foxgloves, farther on shallow holes where badgers had dug in the stony soil for grubs.

We were 700 feet above the tide line when we ended our climb. My eyes, wandering over the maze of interconnecting stone walls that cut the landscape into a vast patchwork of small fields, could trace, almost from Land's End to Newquay, a distance of nearly thirty miles, the windings of the cliff-edged coast. Directly below, in a small cluster of buildings—like a fly caught in the spiderweb of the network of walls—lay the village of Zennor. Looking away from this high vantage point, I let my gaze travel, to use an old Cornish expression, "up-along and down-along" a land of ancient events. Two millenniums ago, Mediterranean merchants came to Cornwall for tin. The Spanish Armada, in 1588, sailed within sight of the cliffs on its way to meet the ships of Sir Francis Drake. In all probability, the very height on which I stood had been part of that long chain of beacon hills, stretching as far as the Bristol Channel, on which bonfires were lit at night to warn of the approach of the "Invincible Armada."

Such reflections as these were interrupted by an outcry arising from one of the pasture fields of Tremedda Farm. Looking down, we saw a gander rushing, with flapping wings, toward a group of ten or a dozen cows feeding at the far side of the field. Its strident voice reached our ears more than half a mile away. As it neared the group, a small reddish cow turned tail and bolted, with the gander floundering in clamorous pursuit. For several minutes the chase and the uproar continued. Then quiet returned to the pasture. Every day, Griggs told me, this one gander seeks a time of excitement and diversion by chasing cows.

I thought of other geese I had known. One, on a Vermont farm, had to be penned up because of its habit of pulling the tails of lambs. Another used to accompany a large and shaggy dog wherever it went. When the animal lay down, it would preen the fur around its head as though it was formed of feathers. In a village near Rochester, New York, another goose spent hours gazing at and rubbing against its own reflection in the shiny hubcap of an automobile. When I was a small boy, on a neighboring farm in the Indiana dunes a gander guarded a lane and set up an outcry whenever a visitor approached. Ever since Roman times, these domestic birds have been celebrated as sentinels.

In her charming book, *Field with Geese*, Lyn Irving tells of a three-year-old bird on a Cheshire farm that would detach itself from the flock and follow the farmer whenever he came near. It would waddle after him down the furrows when he was plowing and would accompany him when he went shooting. If permitted, it would mount on his lap as he sat by the fire in the evening, nestling close or preening the hair of his head with its bill. In time, the superstitious farmer came to believe that the unusual attentions of the bird foreboded evil. The goose, although its affectionate nature deserved a kinder recompense, was killed.

Some years ago, on a farm in New Jersey, a gander took over the role of sheep dog. It regularly rounded up the flock and drove it to the feeding trough. After it was almost trampled underfoot on one occasion when the animals bolted through a narrow gate, it developed a quick, bouncing, one-two-three sidestep whenever it came to the opening. Long-lived birds, sometimes attaining an age well in excess of thirty years, domestic geese exhibit manifold pecularities. Near Allerden, in Holland, one summer, a farmer kept finding the tires of his truck deflated. He suspected neighborhood children until he discovered a pair of geese were pecking at the valves and letting out the hissing air.

Remembering all the curious, surprising actions of these avian individualists, I recalled the canny look in the eye of a domestic goose. Who can guess what is going on in the wide-awake brain of one of these birds? Or, as the old couplet runs:

"When the rain raineth and the goose winketh,
Little wots the gosling what the goose thinketh."

As we walked among the great rocks that lay in tumbled profusion on the summit of the tor, Griggs pointed out one like a huge bench with a vertical back rising to a projecting mass that extended out like an awning of granite. A little higher than my head, cut in the upright stone, ran a line of letters about five inches high. They were dimmed by the accumulating lichens of half a century. I ran my fingers slowly down the line, making out the words. The sentence read:

"W. H. HUDSON OFTEN CAME HERE."

This eyrie-bench of stone, to which my companion had first brought him, had been Hudson's favorite spot in the region. It was his habit to climb the tor to watch the sun set over the water. To commemorate his association with the spot, the painter Arnold Forster, living at nearby Eagle's Nest, had had the words cut in granite at the top of the tor.

"The finest time of year here," Griggs told me before we retraced our steps down the slope, "comes toward the end of May. Then the bracken gets its new growth and all the hillsides are covered with brilliant green."

He pointed out a rounded opening in the earth, a mile or so away among the walled-in fields. Appearing, from our distance, no larger than the entrance of a fox or badger burrow, it marked the mouth of a now-abandoned tin mine. He had worked there for a time before going into service in the First World War.

Away to the south, pale tan smoke trailed low over the ground in several places, drawn out toward the east by a breeze blowing in from the sea.

"They are burning off the furze," my guide explained.

These fires of spring, opening new fields, clearing old pasture land, constitute an annual rite. Sixty years before, leaning back in the shelter of the same rocks where we were sitting, W. H. Hudson, as he recalls in *The Land's End*, watched furze fires burning while the dusk deepened and the billowing smoke took on an intense orange hue reflected from the running flames below.

It was Hudson's gift to preserve moments of the past like

fossils held within clear amber. The things he saw, the things he experienced, the things he felt, were set down in a lucid, moving style that attained its ends without calling attention to itself. For Nellie and me, with all of England stretching before us, innumerable places ahead held added interest because we had met them long before in Hudson's pages.

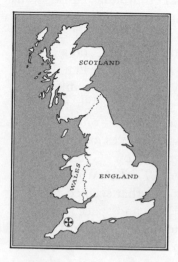

chapter 4

DARTMOOR
IN THE RAIN

"By the side of a wood, in a country a long way off, ran a fine stream of water . . ."

So begins one of the fairy tales of the brothers Grimm. Nellie and I were standing at the edge of a wood that clambered steeply out of a valley. We were in a country a long way from home. And before us flowed a fine stream of water, the River Tamar on the boundary where Cornwall ends and Devon begins.

From the gulls of St. Ives and the shore birds of the Hayle Estuary we had worked our way up the length of the Cornish peninsula—by the black, sea-eroded rocks of Newquay, past the clifftop ruins of Tintagel Castle, linked by legend to King Arthur, across desolate Bodmin Moor and among white mountains of mine waste where that ingredient of the finest porcelain, China clay, is extracted from the earth.

During a Sunday of slashing rain, we rested at the ancient hill town of Launceston. The stone arch through which we entered the White Hart Inn dates back to 400 years be-

fore the Reformation, and the crumbling castle walls
nearby halted the Norman invasion in the west. I remember we looked through windows streaming with rain over
tile roofs, where jackdaws tossed on the gusts, and a garden,
where palm trees lashed in the wind. But, when I recall
that stormy day, another memory comes first to mind. It is
the far-away sound of a piano echoing through the quiet
inn. Someone, in some distant room, played on and on for
his or her enjoyment, played classical pieces and old songs,
such songs as *Beautiful Dreamer, Flow Gently, Sweet
Afton,* and *There's a Long, Long Trail A-Winding,* the
songs of another age, simple melodies that seemed to reach
us from a great distance in both time and space.

Now, following the valley of the Tamar, beyond Launceston, we were in a region of deep side ravines cut by tribu-
tary streams. They are sheltered from the wind and lie at
such an angle that the sun penetrates them for much of the
day. Their air is warm and still. Growth and bloom and
fruit arrive early. These valleys on the Devon-Cornwall border form natural hothouses. From them come the first
strawberries in England, the earliest native lettuce to reach
the market, and precocious blooms that are hurried to the
London florists.

When we climbed out of this narrow zone of an earlier
spring, we were beyond the Devon border. We turned
south, paralleling the flow of the Tamar. In its fifty-nine-
mile course, this stream cuts across almost the entire peninsula, nearly transforming Cornwall into an island. At the
end of our descent of the river we found Plymouth, where
the *Mayflower* set sail for America and Devonport, where
Charles Darwin's *Beagle* headed around the world. All up
the Channel coast of Devon, we ran through towns that derived their names from the mouths of rivers—Dartmouth,
at the mouth of the River Dart, Teignmouth, at the mouth
of the River Teign, Sidmouth, at the mouth of the River

Sid. Many an American place name, crossing the sea from Britain, can be traced back to the end of an English stream.

We were surrounded, in Devon, by a softer, more fertile land. Left behind were the harsh, stony fields of Cornwall. They were replaced by the deep, rich soil of disintegrated Old Red Sandstone. Gone were the stone walls, and in their place rose high hedges. And now, with flowing lines and the weathered hues of their thatched roofs, the country cottages appeared to have grown where they stood. Instead of being distracting, man-made blemishes on the landscape, these most appealing of all the small houses of the world give the impression of being natural additions to the beauty of the scene.

For thousands of miles along the roads of England, in days that followed, Nellie and I diverted ourselves by noting the subtle and infinitely varied shadings of color in thatched roofs along the way. The newest, freshly installed, shone with the gold of a field of ripe wheat. The oldest, weather-beaten and smoke-stained, were so dark a chocolate they were nearly black. In between, they appeared gray, taupe, russet, the color of a mole, the rich brown of a beaver pelt. Many exhibited a smooth, glossy shine like that observed on well-stroked fur. Older thatch, grown more compact, sometimes had the appearance of being carved from yellow-brown wood.

The most prized material for such roofs is—as it has been for generations—the stems of *Phragmites communis*, the reed found around the world and, in England, harvested mainly in the broads of Norfolk. Roofs made of this material last two or three decades and even longer. Also widely employed is wheat straw. Readers of Tolstoy's *War and Peace* will recall how the starving horses of the Pavlograd Regiment were fed on straw dragged down from the thatched roofs of peasant cottages. Wheat grown with commercial fertilizer, it has been discovered, produces straw unsuitable for thatching. Apparently because of its more rapid growth, the stems are weaker, more brittle, more liable to breakage and decay. In the south of England, in recent years, farmers have begun growing wheat without using commercial fertilizer, to produce special straw for thatching. It is marketed under the name of "wheat reed."

Some day I hope someone will write a whole book on the natural history of the thatched roof. Moss and ferns and wildflowers thrive on ancient thatching. In one instance we saw hartstongue ferns leaning down over the eaves; in another, willow herb in full bloom along the lower edge of a decaying roof. At all stages, the close-packed mass of stems, each perhaps with the diameter of a pencil, provides a home for innumerable small creatures. Earwigs and spiders, particularly one small, dark species, inhabit the roofing material. Wasps find shelter in the hollow stems. Birds not only comb the roofs for living prey, but some also nest there. House sparrows pull out straws and create holes in which they even lay their eggs. Thomas Hardy, in *The Woodlanders*, tells of Marty South lying in bed and hearing the sparrows walking down their long tunnels to the exit at the eaves. I counted seven such holes on the roof of one country cottage. Starlings, taking over the openings made by sparrows, also nest in the thatch.

Some cottagers cover their roofs with wire mesh as a protection against such birds. Although many owners hesitate because the wire would interfere with tossing off burning reeds or straw if the roof caught fire, the practice is increasing. One morning, after a night of rain, I remember coming around a turn in the road and seeing the roof of a thatched cottage ahead spangled from end to end as though with glittering diamonds evenly spaced. Droplets of water, clinging to the bottom of each loop of the wire mesh covering it, were catching the morning light and sparkling in the sun.

Near Exmouth, on the estuary of the River Exe, we turned aside and came out on the Channel coast among the red rocks of Dawlish. Some years before, an artist living in Dawlish, Elsa Godfrey, had written me about my books and had invited us to stop and see her if we ever came to Devon. On this first day of April, we were in Devon. We were in Dawlish. We knocked at her door and found a warm welcome and a warm fire burning in the grate of her living room and artist's studio. We to her and she to us, and Dawlish to us, were only names when we arrived. They were definite images and pleasant memories when we left. Here, beside the fire, we had our first English tea and biscuits. As she filled our cups, Mrs. Godfrey explained that the correct way of serving tea is to put the milk or cream in the bottom of the cup and then pour in the hot beverage. Later, we discovered that in tea making, as in all things, there is variety in England. Our morning dish of prunes, for example, sometimes came in a saucer, sometimes on a plate, sometimes in a soup bowl; sometimes hot, sometimes cold; sometimes with a fork, sometimes with a spoon. The popular idea of the correct Englishman, wedded to unvarying habits, we grew to suspect, is largely a product of fiction.

Before we left, we spent some time enjoying Mrs. Godfrey's paintings, her landscapes and ferns, flowers and other details of the Devon countryside. One of her oil paintings, completed after we visited her and which she sent as a present to us in America, now hangs on my study wall. It seems to me to catch more truly than any other picture I have seen the mood of Dartmoor, that vast tableland—the largest expanse of granite in England—toward which we turned from Dawlish.

Each of the three high moors that descend from Somerset to Cornwall like vertebrae in the backbone of the West Country—Exmoor, Dartmoor, and Bodmin Moor—is the eroded stump of a long-ago mountain. The volcanic rock of which the highest part of Dartmoor is composed is at least 300,000,000 years old. A world of uneven ground, of treeless hills and mist-filled hollows, of waterlogged peat and heather-clad slopes, of high tors capped with broken granite, of hut circles and avenues of stones left by ancient peoples, Dartmoor extends over an area of between 200 and 300 square miles. Even today, in the latter half of the twentieth century, it remains a remote fastness, a brooding land, the home of gloomy legends of headless horsemen and black, spectral hounds as large as calves running in the dark. Sheep and ponies still disappear in its treacherous bogs. It was here, where the land extends away in "long green rollers with crests of jagged granite," that Conan Doyle's Hound of the Baskervilles roamed the moor at night.

Roads are few on Dartmoor. Those we followed we had almost entirely to ourselves. Wet, black and shining, they wound along the high crests, swept down into wide valleys, climbed again. A heron, the first we had seen in England, advanced with stately beat over the hills. It grew dim, then clear-cut against the sky as it passed in and out of successive curtains of mist and rain. Sheep, black of face and leg, marked with splotches of red or blue dye, their long wool bedraggled and hanging down their sides like wet mops, wandered in little bands across the moor.

In our first glimpse, as in our last, we saw Dartmoor grayed by veils of falling rain. For the whole of Devon, the average annual rainfall is about forty inches. But in the region of Dartmoor Prison, at Princetown, it is more than twice that figure, exceeding eighty inches. An old name for Dartmoor was Land of Thunder. It was bestowed by bordering villagers who looked up at the growling clouds and watched the storms gathering on the heights. With its rainy climate, its peaty soil, its relatively impervious granite lying close to the surface, the moor is strewn with morasses and little bogs known locally as "feather beds." They are

The cliffs of Land's End

the mothers of streams, where the main rivers of Devon have their source. Of the fourteen originating there, a few flow north. But most follow a southeast or southwest course to reach the English Channel.

It occurred to us that somewhere in that dripping, rain-soaked world around us some isolated depression filled with sphagnum moss could be the home of a plant so rare on Dartmoor it has been seen only twice in eighty-five years. This is the little bog orchid, *Hammarbya paludosa*. All the moor is a region of specialized inhabitants, both floral and faunal. Snails, for instance, are rare. With its granite base, the soil is low in calcium, thus restricting the population of these shell makers. Wherever we went, in momentary lulls in the wind and rain, we heard the irrepressible skylarks. On Dartmoor, the skylark and the meadow pipit are the two commonest breeding birds.

In spite of this chill and dreary day, the sprawling pile of Dartmoor Prison loomed up out of the mist less stark and grim than we had expected. All around it extended an oasis of cultivated fields, reclaimed from the wasteland in a mid-nineteenth-century project for increasing the local food supply of the prisoners. Several times, along the moorland roads, we came upon old stone highway markers, one with the barely discernible date 1817. Close by, grazing in the rain, stood two Dartmoor ponies, one black, the other sorrel. As early as 1012 such ponies—"wild horses on the land at Ashburton"—were mentioned in the will of the Saxon bishop Aefwold of Crediton. Although these animals live unfenced lives, all are owned and branded, and periodically numbers are rounded up for sale. But no longer are they literally buried alive by being sold as pit ponies. A century ago, in a sudden and fearful change, leaving the wind and the moor behind, they were forced to spend the rest of their shortened lives dragging carts loaded with coal through the darkness and impure air of mines.

Gulls of St. Ives

All we encountered were shaggy with their long-haired winter coats. On Dartmoor, the ponies were shaggy, the sheep were shaggy, and we wished we were shaggy, too, whenever we stepped from the car and were struck by the bitter, bone-piercing cold of the upland wind. It seemed to spear completely through us, entering one side and coming out the other. Whenever the moorland ponies breathed, we saw them give forth small clouds of steam. These vaporous exhalations were whirled away by the wind. The wind and the rain and the cold—these are inseparable in memories of Dartmoor. The earliest snow in England falls on these high moors. Even though April had come, we noticed thin coatings of ice on the smaller bogs.

That night the temperature fell below the mid-January average. The mercury was dropping rapidly when, toward dusk, we reached Two Bridges, where the two main roads of Dartmoor meet almost at its center. On the same site now occupied by the rambling, white, wooden Two Bridges Hotel, inns have stood since before 1066. Although It was out of season and we were almost the only guests, we obtained a room for the night. We were glad to come in out of the wind and rain. But, as we discovered, we were not completely coming in out of the cold. Our room was unheated. While Nellie kept warm by the fireplace downstairs, I bundled up in a sweater, a coat, a lined overcoat, and with a cap on my head and a muffler wrapped around my neck, began setting down the notes of that wet, chill day.

Before dinner, we diverted ourselves by looking over bound volumes of *Punch*, running from the first issue in 1841 into the 1920's. They filled the bookshelves on one side of the lounge. No sooner was the meal over than everyone connected with the hotel disappeared. Not a creature was stirring, not even a mouse. The great wooden structure was wrapped in perfect silence. The only concession made to the cold in our room that night was two hot water bottles placed in the bed to warm our feet. One we hastily jerked out when we found it was leaking. We could imagine the charm of this ancient inn, set in the heart of the moor, during summer months. But this was not summer. This was what William Cowper once referred to as "our severest winter commonly called spring."

Mist and rain and wind and the croaking of ravens among the tors—we met them all when we started out next morning. Toward the western edge of the moor, not far from Merrivale Brook, we stopped to follow a pony path out across the boggy ground to two parallel lines of huge gray stones set upright in the earth. This titanic avenue on the open moor is believed to have been used in connection with prehistoric burial rites. Some 3,000 years ago, during the Bronze Age, pastoral settlers built circular stone huts on hillsides sheltered from the north wind. In many places, we encountered "hut circles," the foundations of these ancient homesteads. Of them all, one returns to mind with special clarity. At the base of one of its stones, a tilted slab, grew a small furze bush. Moorland gales had forced it against the face of the rock where it remained spread out, flattened, pressed down like a herbarium specimen displayed on a sheet of granite.

Seven hundred years ago, Dartmoor was one of the richest sources of tin in Europe. The mines have long been closed. Only peat, scmi-carbonized vegetable tissue derived largely from sphagnum mosses, is now dug on the moorland. This fuel, in older days, used to be kept burning continuously on the hearth all winter long. At the Warren House Inn, which we passed later on the road between Princetown and Moretonhampstead, a peat fire is said to have burned continuously for more than 200 years. When the present larger building was erected, this fire was carefully transferred to the new grate.

All around the edges of Dartmoor, that patchwork quilt of hedge-bordered fields, so characteristic of Devon, descends to lower ground. Whenever we turned aside on lane-like roads among these fields, we suddenly found our view restricted to the narrow path ahead, the hedges beside us and the sky above. Several times in these confined quarters, we met and, to our surprise, managed to pass other cars. One morning we were debating what would happen if we met an American-size machine when, lumbering toward us down the narrow way, we saw an immense double-decked bus. We seemed a mouse confronting an elephant. There was no place for either of us to turn out. Our previous surprise turned to amazement when, by both pushing out against the hedges as far as possible, we squeezed by.

Intermittently that day, the weather made feeble attempts at clearing. For short periods the rain slackened. Then the weeping skies wept again. These cold rains of spring seemed endless. We saw them in all their forms—drizzle and downpour and deluge. We were in the midst of an experience—the kind the German philosopher had in mind when he wryly defined experience as "what a person experiences by experience that he would not willingly have experienced." On this Dartmoor day, it rained harder, more exasperatingly, than on the previous day. We could not get out and look at things. We could not photograph. We could not see anything clearly through the mist and plunging rain. Cold rain on the moor, cold rain on everything! Tacking this way and that, wherever we went we splashed through puddles, seeing what we could see, our philosophic acceptance gone, our frustration complete.

In such a mood, toward the end of the day, we came over the high hills and looked down into a moorland hollow, "a dimple on the face of the earth, a cradle under a many-colored quilt of little fields," as Eden Phillpotts once described it. Cupped within this hollow, a dozen or so houses clustered around a church that lifted its square gray tower of stone high above them. Long famed in Devon folklore, this village, with the titanic waves of the moor rolling away on all sides, was Widecombe-in-the-Moor. As we gazed down through the falling rain, we felt the isolated charm of the village reviving our spirits. The long serpentine of the road carried us down to the open space beside the church. In this space, each year, on the second Tuesday in September, throngs gather to attend one of the oldest fairs in England. The Devon folksong, sung for generations, of Tom Pearse's old gray mare and "Uncle Tom Cobleigh and all," has immortalized the village and the fair.

"When the wind whistles cold on the moor of a night, all along, down along, out along lee . . ." Those words from this song of Widecombe Fair described the night that settled down at the end of this day in April. But while the wind whistled, we were snug and warm in an inn at Moretonhampstead, near the northern edge of the moor. After finishing an evening meal with pancakes flavored with lemon juice, we slept in the warmth of a heated room.

Between the native and the traveling stranger there always lies a gulf. It is a gulf dug by the fact the native is earning his living there. Each sees everything in a different light. The native is anchored fast by a thousand ties. But the tourist, if the mood overtakes him, can flit away as free as the bird or butterfly. We recalled this the next morning. We awoke to more wind-flung rain smashing against our windowpanes. We remembered we were the traveling strangers. We remembered we were unfettered. We remembered we were free to trade these cold, rainy moorland heights for other scenes. As soon as breakfast was over, we rode down the northern skirt of the highland and out across the lower land toward the coast.

chapter 5

THE
SWAN'S BELL

When Charles Kingsley visited the United States in 1874, he wrote to his wife in Hampshire that Americans were "English—with a difference." Making the reverse journey, ninety-some years later, we appreciated what he meant. The English, to us, seemed Americans—with a difference. But that difference was no greater than we had encountered in people of various sections in our own country. From the beginning, the people, the place names, the countryside of Britain made us feel at home.

The currency continued to confuse us. The left side remained "the wrong side of the road." When we stepped on scales, we were bewildered by reading our weight in stones instead of pounds. And in a land where Cholmonde-ley, in Cheshire, is "Chumley"; Mayfield, in Sussex, is "Mearvel"; and Woolfardisworthy, in Devon, is "Oozry," we gave up altogether trying to guess the pronunciation of place names from their spelling. But turnouts soon became "laybys," detours "diversions," and traffic circles "rounda-bouts." Even in these earliest days of our travels, our sense of being foreigners in a foreign land was swiftly fading away.

As we drove north from Dartmoor, except for the unfamiliar hedges and the absence of large tracts of woodland, the rolling green farming country we traversed might have been New England. Everywhere we met names—Exeter, Plymouth, Dartmouth, Taunton—that we had known in the New World. If you erase the place names derived from Britain from a map of the eastern United States, large areas will become virtually blank. It may be that we did not travel in the right social circles, but nowhere did we meet the haughty Englishman of fiction. Almost invariably, we encountered courtesy and friendliness and an obvious desire to be of help. Ours, of course, was a trip through rural England, mainly England without its cities, through a world of country lanes and gentle streams and small villages, through what—for the naturalist at least—must always be the best of Britain.

As the plateau of Dartmoor sank on the horizon, the rain slackened to a drizzle, then stopped altogether. The wind remained chill, but it blew under a clearing and then under a sunny sky. Cloud shadows jumped the hedges and slid across the fields, rising and falling with the rolling land. From hilltops we glimpsed a panorama of hedge-bordered fields whose endlessly varied shapes and sizes added variety to repetition. The impression made by the British countryside is one of lived-in beauty, of a land long associated with man.

Its scenery is not overwhelming or awe-inspiring. It holds no Alps, no Sahara, no Grand Canyon. Yet, within the 50,331 square miles of England, there is amazing variety. Compared with the abrupt, spectacular changes in America, such as where the Great Plains meet the wall of the Rockies, it is variety in a minor key. The English countryside is essentially companionable country. A "green and pleasant land" are words that return again and again to the traveler's mind.

Over the rivers Claw and Waldon and Torridge, past Bideford and Appledore, we worked our way northward to Ilfracombe and the coast. We were traveling through a region of ancient farms. Some areas in North Devon are said to have been under continuous cultivation for 2,000 years. Now, in April, a population explosion of lambs, leaping, prancing, nursing, extended across the pasture fields. Swallows—the "swallow" of England, the fork-tailed "barn swallow" of America, one of the most widely distributed of all land birds—swooped and turned and swept low above the hedges.

Nearing Barnstaple, we descried a far greater bird, immense, with slender, outstretched wings, a soaring plane from a nearby airfield, sporting among the updrafts along the coast. The day was Palm Sunday, and we passed family groups, dressed for church, walking beside the country roads and along the village streets. Some carried handfuls of yellow primroses. This most characteristic wildflower of Devon begins blooming here as early as the latter part of February.

Long before sunset, beyond the sea cliffs of Ilfracombe and the Valley of the Rocks, we came to the winding streets of Lynton. So charmed were William and Dorothy Wordsworth with the scenic beauty of the coast near Lynton that at one time they considered settling here instead of in the Lake District. In the dining room that evening, we sat near the only man we were to see in England wearing a monocle. He removed it carefully and put on horn-rimmed spectacles when he read the menu.

The highlands of the most northern of the three great West Country moors—Exmoor—rose before us as we cut inland in the morning. Nearly half of this high wasteland, the dramatic setting of R. D. Blackmore's *Lorna Doone*, rises to an elevation of more than 1,000 feet. One hill lifts above 1,700 feet. Exmoor has long been famed for its stag hunts and for the gamefish of its swift-flowing streams. At times, when pursued by dogs, Exmoor stags take to the water along the coast. Several times they have been seen swimming well out to sea.

Against a cold wind and through intermittent rains and under a darkened sky, we advanced across the grass-and-heather-covered hills. We seemed to be viewing everything in twilight, or, in the words of *Lorna Doone*, "at gray of night, when the sun is gone and no red in the west remains." For a time, we found ourselves among bands of wandering sheep where every ram had one horn painted crimson. We dipped into wonderful moist combes, deep little valleys, mossy and filled with ferns, where rooks called in the tops of dripping trees whose lower trunks were clothed with the glossy leaves of ivy. And all along the way, seemingly goalless little roads branched off and wandered out of sight across the moorland.

A strange mile is a longer mile. Distances tend to appear greater the first time we cover them. Although the intervening miles number no more than twelve, it seemed a long way from Lynton over the moors to Simonsbath. A mile or two beyond, near Honeymead—as we began the swing back through Exford and Cutcombe and Dunster to the coast— our road brought us to the lonely bog by Cloven Rocks. It was here, in the climax of Blackmore's story, that John Ridd and Carver Doone met in battle and Doone sank to his death in the treacherous ooze.

Most of Exmoor is now maintained as a protected wild area, jointly administered by Devon and Somerset. Before we reached Simonsbath, our road crossed the line into Somerset. During the next few days, the course of our travels followed a meandering path through this county of the Mendip Hills, of Wookey Hole and Cheddar Gorge, of the

oldest roads in Britain, of Bath and Wells and Glaston-
bury.

In spite of a particularly chill and backward spring, each
day brought new changes of the season. A fine stippling of
opening leaf buds ran across the trees at Nether Stowey
when we came to the cottage where Coleridge wrote *The
Rime of the Ancient Mariner*. Horse chestnuts were expanding seven-fingered leaves when we drove into Glaston-
bury, with its abbey ruins dating from the Middle Ages, its
legends of King Arthur and the Holy Thorn. And green
was sweeping over the willows along the brown canals of
the low wet land of the Brue Valley to the west.

Across this Flemish landscape, where wet cows grazed in
wet pastures in the misty rain, we followed such canals with
their bordering lines of pollard trees toward Meare and Catcott Burtle. Straight as Roman roads, these drainage waterways drew their rulered lines along the valley floor. Sometimes, for miles, high banks restrained water that flowed
several feet above the level of our road. Beside these waterways we passed, at long intervals, through dripping villages.
How many thousand villages, in highland and lowland, we
were to see in Britain! Each had its own life that we were
strangers to, its own axis of interest. Like a pond or a tide-
pool or an island or an oasis, each village has its own habits,
its own particular mode of existence, its dominant individuals. And here, in this same wet valley, two thousand and
more years ago, other villages, the primitive clusters of the
Lake Dwellers, had occupied the willowy swamps along the
River Brue.

Also in this spongy land ancient men constructed the
oldest roads known in Britain. Crude timber highways,
roughly formed of logs, they have been uncovered deep in
the turf moors between Meare and Catcott Burtle. Some
are believed to have originated in the Neolithic period. A
number of the remnants lay beneath a protecting layer of

black sphagnum peat as much as seven feet deep. On the day of our ride through the Brue Valley, an otter hunt was scheduled for the vicinity of Catcott Burtle. But we saw no sign of the hunters. Perhaps the rain, which bothers no otter, bothered them.

Somerset is shaped roughly like a horseshoe. We had reached the opposite side before we came to the great gray chasm of Cheddar Gorge. Its serpentine length cuts deeply into the flank of the Mendip Hills. Originally an immense cavern, carved out of the limestone by flowing water, it was transformed by the collapse of its roof into the present gorge. As we followed the twisting, ascending road along the bottom of the abyss, sheer cliffs rose at times to a height of more than 600 feet on either hand. These crags of limestone support vines and mosses and flowering plants. In another of the innumerable echoes of our wanderings in America, we were carried back to wild Smuggler's Notch in the Green Mountains of northern Vermont. Among the plants growing on the Cheddar cliffs, one had been recorded there since 1696. This is the Cheddar pink, *Dianthus gratianopolitanus*, blooming in June and July. Its complete range is recorded as: "On limestone cliffs at Cheddar." In the village of Cheddar, famous since the seventeenth century for its cheese, we saw a sign: "Fresh cut lettuce." So far had advanced the spring.

On our way to the cathedral town of Wells, Nellie and I turned aside toward Wookey Hole to see a river, the Axe, pour full-born from the rock of the Mendip Hills. In medieval times, Wookey Hole ranked with Stonehenge as one of the wonders of Britain. The path leading to this dramatic site carried us up a glen rich with ferns and mosses and wildflowers of spring. Lords-and-ladies, those European relatives of our Jack-in-the-pulpit, were coming into bloom. Overhead, among the treetops, the voices of unknown birds rose above the rushing, liquid sound of the newly released river paralleling our path and flowing a dozen feet below us. This sound multiplied into a confused roaring that swallowed up the songs of the birds completely when we drew closer to the limestone cliff and its base where, from the orifice of a natural aqueduct, the tumbling river suddenly burst from darkness into light.

Above the tumult of its foaming water, jackdaws came and went continually. A score or more whirled about in a ferment of excitement. Many carried sticks. Nests were taking shape on the ledges and in the crevices of the limestone cliff. Such sites as these represent the most ancient breeding places of this social species.

And few birds are more social than the daws. Few species come together in more highly organized communities. The extent to which this avian organization has been developed was revealed, some years ago, by the classic studies of Dr. Konrad Z. Lorenz, of Vienna. At the Eighth International Ornithological Congress, held at Oxford in 1934, Dr. Lorenz gave the results of three years of intensive observation at two jackdaw communities. If one member saw another member of the colony being carried away by a predatory animal, he found, it would flutter its wings and utter a grating call. All the other daws within sight and hearing would do the same. Unless the animal was too powerful, the whole flock, regardless of its own danger, would make a concerted attack upon it. If, during the fighting of the breeding season, one jackdaw was beaten by a rival, it invariably flew to its own nest. Then, if the attack continued, it uttered a characteristic cry. On hearing this, its mate and then the other members of the colony rushed to the scene. Usually the aggressor gave way immediately. If it did not, the assembled daws set upon it and drove it off.

Although each pair defends its own nest, all the birds join together to protect the common territory of the nesting area. Outsiders are admitted only in autumn and winter, when the breeding season is over. In the well-developed hierarchy of a jackdaw colony, Dr. Lorenz noted, domination is exercised only between birds of nearly equal status. Those far down the pecking order are unmolested by those at the top. Young females usually rank near the bottom of the scale. But as soon as they mate they assume the rank of the males with which they are paired.

Around Wells Cathedral and the moated Bishop's Palace—forming a city within a city, an ecclesiastical city within the municipality of Wells—other daws were nesting. Daws and cathedrals go together. The spires and towers and masonry ledges provide the birds with man-made cliffs and caverns and niches for their nesting. We saw daws, with sticks in their bills, ascending high up the cathedral walls. We saw them disappearing into holes where rainspouts issued from the masonry. We saw them alighting among the carved figures decorating the edifice. And when we walked out on the level green expanse of meadows that adjoins the Bishop's Palace, jackdaws paraded over us, going and coming in their search for food and nesting material.

Such material, in numerous instances, contains the unexpected. Writing in *British Birds*, in 1961, E. J. M. Buxton, of Malmesbury, Wiltshire, tells of being puzzled one spring by the disappearance of metal labels from the borders of his flower beds. Made of lead, these labels were nearly six inches long and weighed more than half an ounce. Later he noticed two in the grate under a chimney where a pair of daws had built a nest. When this nest was torn down, he discovered it contained sixty-seven of the missing labels, representing a total of more than two pounds of lead.

At Richmond Park, near London, daws have been observed filling their bills with loose hairs from the backs of shedding red deer. Niko Tinbergen reports that, in the Netherlands, these birds obtain similar material for lining their nests from the backs of ponies, donkeys, and bullocks.

In another instance of the kind, half a dozen jackdaws were once seen getting hairs from a cow while it lay chewing its cud. On this very expanse of meadow where we now walked, W. H. Hudson watched seven of the "ecclesiastical daws" of Wells struggling to maintain their places on the back of one cow.

In all likelihood, daws have been associated with the Wells Cathedral and the Bishop's Palace since their construction nearly eight centuries ago. The palace, for more than six centuries, has been an island within an encircling moat, a quadrangular island fortified by high, turreted walls pierced at frequent intervals by narrow slits in the form of crosses through which defending archers could direct the arrows of their longbows. Looking across the brown water of this moat, we seemed face to face with the Middle Ages.

Over the entrance at the end of the drawbridge, now permanently lowered, white doves nested. Beyond, the close-cut grass of the expanse within the walls was dotted with the small white flowers of the English daisy. A white card thumbtacked to one of the weathered oaken doors caught our eye. It held a typewritten list of the trees within the palace grounds together with their dimensions in 1964. One, a black walnut from North America, had been, at that time, seventy-one feet high and eleven feet, four inches in circumference. How and when, under what circumstances, we wondered as we started along the path that circles the outer edge of the moat, had this New World nut tree—as seed or sapling—found its way to this fortified ecclesiastical enclosure in southern England?

Both the water of the moat and the name of the city of Wells are derived from the famous seven springs of St. Andrew's Wells. During the Middle Ages, the flow of these springs was believed to possess curative powers. Advancing slowly, watching the daws, pausing to listen to blackbirds singing on the turreted walls, halting to examine little maidenhair spleenworts rooted among the rocks of the low barrier that separated path and moat, we arrived at last at the rear of the enclosure. There we were met by a novel sight. An espaliered pear tree, outspread like a vine, had been trained up the surface of the wall. Its branches, one above the other, were flattened against the stone until its form resembled an immense candelabra. Now, at this season of the year, all the branches were white with blossoms.

Beside us in the moat, ducks, mostly mallards, went swimming by. We had returned to the front wall again when suddenly all the ducks in sight went skittering and splashing over the water. They were heading in a concerted rush toward the drawbridge and the entrance to the palace grounds. There came to our ears the harsh clanging of a bell. We followed the ducks. They led us to one of the oddest avian adventures we were to encounter in Britain.

Below the open window in the gatehouse of the entrance, a white swan was surrounded by a milling flock of varicolored ducks—mallards, hybrids, white domestic birds, one black duck. At intervals the swan would reach up its long neck and grasp with its orange-and-black bill a bell rope hanging down along the masonry. With a sharp downward and sidewise tug, it produced a metallic clang from the bell above. Each time the bell rang, a woman in the open window tossed out pieces of bread. A brown cocker spaniel, with its forepaws on the window sill, gazed down fascinated by the stately movements of the swan and the hurried, excited rushing of the ducks as they turned and twisted like whirligig beetles to retrieve fragments of the food.

Nowhere in the world has the majestic swan—Aphrodite's and Apollo's bird in mythology, the magic swan in *Lohengrin*—been more esteemed than in Britain. In older times, all swans belonged to the King. No subject could keep one of these long-lived birds—which commonly reach an age of thirty or forty years and are believed, in extreme cases, to attain the century mark—without a license from the crown. Young swans were greatly prized during the Middle Ages as birds for the royal table. King Henry III is said to have ordered 125 cygnets roasted for the Christmas festivities of 1251. Laws in early England provided severe penalties for disturbing the nests of swans, for pulling feathers from their wings, and for owning "hurtful doggs that doth baite any swann or swanns, worrow them or hinder them in breeding time."

A dozen times, the swan beside the gatehouse tugged at the dangling rope, the bell clanged, and more bread came flying down from the open window. We saw only one swan, but others signal here for their meals in a similar way. Both swans and ducks nest along the edges of the moat. The larger birds have learned that tugging on the rope produces meals, and the ducks have come to associate the sound of the bell with bread that descends like manna from above.

Wild creatures are usually quick to link special sounds with particular sources of food. I remember hearing, some years ago, that when grain was dumped at a storage place in Egypt, birds flocked to the spot to feed on the spilled kernels before they could be swept up and salvaged. To prevent this waste, the owners installed strings of bells that set up a harsh jangling to frighten away the birds whenever the grain was dumped. The plan worked admirably, so far as the birds were concerned. But almost immediately it was discovered that as soon as the jangle of the bells commenced, rats came running. The jarring sound had become associated in the minds of these rodents with a feast of grain. Similarly, in wartime, the boom of exploding undersea mines would bring gulls flying from a wide area to feed on the fish and other sea creatures killed by the detonation.

For nearly a quarter of an hour, the intermittent bell

ringing continued. Then the appetite of the swan, if not of the ravenous ducks, was satisfied. It turned away, majestic and serene, moving in stately advance along the moat. The spaniel dropped its paws from the sill. The woman closed the window. For a time, the ducks swam about seeking overlooked crumbs. Then they all fanned out over the water heading for the opposite bank. We, too, turned away. We congratulated ourselves as we left, on rounding the fortification wall just in time to witness this singular event that for at least a century and more has been part of the daily life at this ecclesiastical palace at Wells.

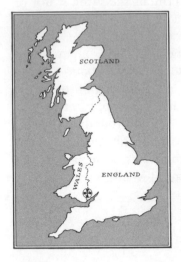

chapter 6

MILES OF DAFFODILS

Between the Severn and the Wye, on the border of southern Wales, the ancient Forest of Dean extends its estimated 20,000,000 trees and 2,000 miles of paths across the hills and valleys of a region shaped like an arrowhead with the tip pointing south. Here prehistoric men dug for iron. Here the Romans constructed roads paved with stone. Here William the Conqueror hunted deer. Here the most ancient law court in the British Isles had its beginning. Verderers, judicial officers in charge of the forest, were originally appointed by Canute the Dane in 1016. Called by the poet Drayton the "Queen of Forests All," this hunting ground of monarchs still remains the property of the crown. No other tract in Britain represents so well the forests of Old England.

In the afternoon of a day of April rain, we reached its venerable oaks and beeches and hollies. Rain and wind and cold were our lot during the time we stayed there. Yet the spell of this misty Old World forest with its wet ferns and mosses, its gnarled limbs and lichen-encrusted trunks, was apparent to us even in the dull lead-gray light under the lowering sky. We could imagine the scene around us in the sunshine of June when large stretches of the floor of the forest are gay with blooming foxgloves.

At what, according to tradition, is the exact center of the original forest, we stopped beside the gray sandstone structure known as the Speech House. With immensely thick walls, it was erected in the time of Charles II to house the court of "The Speech." Traditionally, this verderer's court meets every fortieth day. In recent years the building has become a Trust House hotel, one of the nation-wide chain of ancient inns administered by this organization. The room where the court still meets, with its huge fireplace and high railed-in balcony running the length of one side, forms the dining room where we ate.

Each time we climbed the narrow stairs to reach our room, we examined framed prints that ascended the wall beside us. They were all from John Evelyn's *Sylva, or a Discourse of Forest-Trees*, first published in 1664. Each picture represented a species found in the Forest of Dean. And each was framed in the wood of the tree depicted. Evelyn, called "the father of forests in Britain," published his *Sylva* at a time when English woodlands were being felled to provide fuel for iron furnaces and glass factories, and no effort was being made to repair the damage through new plantings. His book persuaded Charles II to start a nurscry for oaks. It also convinced landowners of the importance of reforestation. This one volume is said to have been responsible for the planting of millions of trees that added their beauty and value to the land.

Looking out into the forest from the two dormer windows of our room, we saw a scene that appeared to be wavering continually. This was partly due to the drift of rain and partly to the imperfections of the ancient glass. As soon as we were settled, we bundled up in our heaviest clothing and, descending past the prints of the trees, started along the forest trails to see the trees themselves. No one else was abroad in the gusty rain. We were alone on the paths of the forest.

Hardly had we started when we found ourselves among some of the largest holly trees in England. We moved from one to another, marveling at the massive trunks and the dense clouds of shining leaves around them. In *Trees, Woods and Man*, H. L. Edlin points out the interesting fact that only the lower leaves of the hollies are always spiny. Higher up, beyond the reach of browsing animals, the spines may be absent. Some of the 3,000 trees in the Forest of Dean's famous Holly Wood are said to have been planted in the reign of Charles II (1660–1685).

Watching the rain drip from the varnished holly leaves, watching it run down the furrows of the great oak trunks, watching it spread in a gleaming coat over the smooth gray bark of the beeches, we breathed deeply the pure, moist air of the ancient woodland. On many of the trunks around us, green lichens—lichens that attain their most beautiful coloring on a rainy day—attested to the purity of that atmosphere. Such growths are unable to survive close to industrial cities. They die in smoke and chemical-laden air. They are indicator plants. They indicate unpolluted air.

In many ways, the old forest lived up to our expectations. But, like all English woodlands, it was more open, less shaggy, more parklike than American forests. In contrast to our tangled Appalachian woodlands, it held comparatively little underbrush. Several times we came upon fallen tree trunks moldering slowly away. They were immense, like stranded whales. Four centuries before us, in the time of England's first Queen Elizabeth, Sir Francis Drake and Sir Walter Raleigh walked here, selecting special oaks for their ships. The famous Newland's Oak, which fell in 1956, measured forty-four feet in circumference at breast height.

We had come to a glade among beech trees when a wild, unfamiliar bird song brought us to a halt. It came from the treetops. We traced it, at last, to a gray-brown bird with heavily spotted breast. As large as our American robin, it was our first mistle, or missel, thrush. For five or ten minutes we followed it as it moved from treetop to treetop. Its ringing song, rich with overtones of a glorious wildness, filled all the open spaces between the dripping trees.

Originally the mistle thrush was the mistletoe thrush, a name derived from its fondness for the berries of this parasitic plant. A footnote in Alexander Hunter's 1825 edition of Evelyn's *Sylva* attributes the propagation of the mistletoe in England mainly to this one bird. The seeds are distributed by its droppings and also when it wipes its bill after feeding. Similarly, in the Anza-Borrego Desert of southern California we had seen the silky flycatcher, *Phainopepla nitens*, spreading mistletoe seeds among ironwood and mesquite.

Coming back by a different path, at the end of our first day in the forest, we entered an area that, for Nellie and me, spread out like an arboreal memory book. Rooted here were trees from many parts of the world. As we wandered among them, we found old friends. A sugar maple recalled the sheets of crimson and gold we had seen filling the valleys and running up the hills of Vermont and New Hampshire in October. And a Port Orford cedar carried us back to an Oregon road beside the Pacific where the incense of this tree rose from fires as workmen burned piles of the branches along the highway. We forgot the rain, we forgot the cold, amid these trees that linked us with other times and places.

But when we started on, we found we were shivering. The chill air, at the end of the day, seemed like that of a night of killing frost. We jogged to set our blood racing. It seemed to us we had never been really warm since we

landed in England. For a few minutes that evening, however, Nellie was, for once, amply warm. At least, inside. At
dinner she ladled onto her potatoes what she thought was
creamed gravy and then discovered it was mustard sauce.

Wind was shaking the treetops and thrushes were singing
in the rain when dawn broke next morning. Over the roads
of the forest, that day, we ranged widely. Several times we
came to overgrown mounds of mine waste. Beneath the
Forest of Dean lies 20,000 acres of coal and iron-bearing
rock. Remembering the wrecked landscapes of Pennsylvania's and West Virginia's coal country, we were amazed to
see how little the centuries of mining, extending back to
before the Roman conquest, had disturbed the beauty of
this English forest.

Somewhere beyond Park End, a small, low-slung animal,
brown in hue and shaped like an elongated frankfurter,
streaked across the road and disappeared. Thus we encountered our first weasel in England. The next animal
we saw was a wet and bedraggled American expatriate—a
familiar gray squirrel in unfamiliar surroundings. Between
1876 and 1929 these squirrels were released in about thirty
areas in England—to the lasting regret of conservationists.
The aggressive animals, since then, have spread over almost
40,000 square miles of Britain. Because it strips bark from
young trees, the gray squirrel was soon classed as a pest. For
many years it headed the list of Forest of Dean vermin. A
bounty of ninepence a tail was paid by the Forestry Commission. Today it is illegal to import a gray squirrel into the
British Isles without a special license from the Ministry of
Agriculture. The experience of England with this "banner-
tail" of American woodlands represents, in reverse, America's experience with the "English" sparrow and the starling.

Other, more welcome visitors from across the sea are now
part of the ancient forest. One is the jewelweed or touch-
me-not of eastern North America, called the orange balsam

in Britain. Famous for its ripe fruits, which explode and hurl out seeds when touched or brushed against, it bears pendant, slipperlike orange-yellow flowers mottled with reddish brown. With that gift for bestowing picturesque flower names that has been demonstrated so often in the past, the English call these alien blossoms "swing-boats."

When we came to one dark forest pond where cattails—the giant reed-mace of Britain—lifted their heads as much as eight feet above the mucky soil, we felt as though we were beside a pond at home. For here we saw a mallard, a moor hen, and a coot—the mallard found virtually around the world, the moor hen identical with the common gallinule of the eastern United States, and the European coot so nearly like the American species that it seems the same bird. As we watched these three, we were suddenly distracted by a fourth bird, tiny in comparison, dusky, with cocked tail and barred plumage—a bird we had last seen among tangles where lumber crews had gone through the great Maine forest. As we watched, it launched into low whirring flight, then perched and gave forth a clear, warbling song that echoed among the trees. In foreign surroundings, we were encountering the winter wren, *Troglodytes troglodytes*. Here it is "the wren," "Jenny Wren" or "Kitty Wren." It ranks with the robin and the swallow as one of the best known and most popular birds of Britain. Yet its origin is American. It was not introduced into Europe by man. As Edward A. Armstrong points out in his monograph on the wren, it represents one of the few instances of a species successfully invading the Old World from the New. It is thought to have reached Britain by way of Siberia rather than by crossing the Atlantic.

Into the midst of these avian reminders of home there dashed, with screeching calls, with a flash of black and white and blue and pinkish-brown, two birds entirely new to us. They were strikingly marked European jays. Hopping from twig to twig, they watched us as keenly as we watched them. When they went screaming away among the trees, their white rump patches seemed to catch and concentrate the feeble light filtering down among the branches.

A new experience of a different kind awaited us next morning. After breakfast in the hall of the verderer's court, warmed temporarily by large chunks of English oak blazing in the great fireplace, we drove farther afield, west of the forest, to follow the windings of the Wye south from Monmouth to Chepstow. Our river road skirted the foot of wooded hills where slopes were carpeted with the white flowers of wood anemone. One sheltered hollow was rimmed with the solid, curiously unfernlike fronds of the hartstongue fern, fronds that reminded us of the leaves of curly dock at home. On the eighth day of January, in 1823, at Usk, no more than a dozen miles to the west of where we stood, there had been born that world-famed scientific rover, Alfred Russel Wallace.

The rain stopped. The skies brightened. Then they darkened. The rain recommenced, then stopped again. In one of the lulls in the sporadic downpours, when lighter patches amid the dark overcast shed an odd pearly light on all the river scene, we reached, in its wild and picturesque valley setting, the ruins of Tintern Abbey.

"Castles and abbeys," William Gilpin wrote in the eighteenth century, "have different situations agreeable to their respective uses. The castle, meant for defense, stands boldly on the hill; the abbey, intended for meditation, is hid in the sequestered vale." For 400 years, in this sequestered vale, occupants of the abbey, Cistercian monks, meditated, studied, copied manuscripts, and carried on the worship of God. Then, following centuries of peace and prosperity, the order fell upon evil times in the reign of an evil man. Henry VIII dissolved the order. Lead was stripped from the abbey roof, the windows became glassless, and the buildings fell into ruins. Today, with its weathered stones, its stark walls, its staring windows, roofless and deserted, the abbey remains, after centuries of decay, more nobly impressive than most of the world's structures that are unmarred and in their prime. This was our first—and our last—impression.

When, in the final years of the eighteenth century, the English painter, J. M. W. Turner, then a young man of about twenty, journeyed down the Wye Valley—traveling twenty-five miles a day on foot and sketching as he went— he produced a delicately beautiful watercolor of Tintern Abbey. It reveals how, at that time, the arches and ledges were encumbered with numerous vines and bushes. Since then, the vegetation has been largely stripped away to provide a better view of the stonework. But smaller plants, ferns and mosses, still find a home on window ledges and where dust collects between the stones. There we saw polypodies and the graceful maidenhair spleenwort. In the wild garden occupying one window ledge, where parachuted seeds had landed, we could see the yellow flowers of dandelions. Some of the plants grew so high on the walls that we could identify them only with the aid of our field glasses.

Along the base of many sections of the walls, we noticed little clumps and tufts of dislodged moss. In places they were scattered densely. We were to see this again and again in our travels, beneath the eaves of city dwellings, beside stone walls along country lanes. At first these discarded bits of moss puzzled us. Then we discovered that starlings and other birds, searching for food among the cracks and crannies and gutters, had ripped up the fragments and tossed them aside.

How many kinds of mosses we saw among the ruins we will never know. Walking there, with the bleating of lambs beyond the river coming to us on the breeze that blew through the open windows, with the voices of house sparrows and the cooing of rock doves—preparing to nest on the upper ledges—echoing around us, with earthworm castings and English daisies scattered over the grass beneath our feet, we debated how long it would take us to become familiar with all the mosses of Tintern Abbey. We could picture ourselves lost in such a project, absorbed and forgetting the world, like the scholars of old who had once meditated here, poring over their ancient manuscripts.

The straight-line distance from the bell-ringing swans of Wells to the upper fringes of the Forest of Dean is nearly fifty miles. We had made this northward run—before swinging across the southern counties—with a special purpose in mind. We hoped to see in their prime those fields of gold, the stands of wild daffodils that run along the topmost verges of the forest.

"The common yellow Daffodilly," Gerard, the herbalist, recorded in the sixteenth century, "groweth almost every where through England." Today, with its range restricted, it is found concentrated locally. To botanists it is *Narcissus pseudonarcissus*, a curiously contradictory scientific name that, as has been pointed out, first says it is and then indicates that it is not. To earlier generations it was the Daffy-Down-Dilly. Another common name, Lent lily, indicates its time of blooming. In the West Country, it begins to flower in early March and continues into April. Best of all is Shakespeare's description in *The Winter's Tale*: "Daffodils that come before the Swallow dares, and take the winds of March with beauty." We once heard a woman at an adjoining table in a restaurant tell of seeing daffodils standing up like soldiers in the snow.

Damp meadows and open woodlands are favored by the daffodils. Each of the flower stalks, from six to fourteen inches tall, supports a single blossom. The appeal of the golden daffodil is to the eye, for it is a flower without perfume. But where the blooms are massed across a lowland field, they provide one of the great dramatic sights of the English spring. It was this we hoped to witness in the country north of the Forest of Dean.

Again the weather seemed to be wringing the sponges of the clouds, without ever wringing them dry, on the morning we set out in search of the daffodils. This time we traveled north instead of south along the Wye, winding with the river from Monmouth to Ross-on-the-Wye, then wandering across lower Herefordshire and into topmost Gloucestershire. Along the way, lambs, their new and unworn springs tightly wound, were jumping in the rain.

The red soil of Herefordshire is famed for its pear and apple orchards. In England, apples have been eaten for more than 4,000 years. Seeds found among pottery on Windmill Hill, in Wiltshire, indicate that Neolithic men enjoyed the fruit. Among the orchards of Herefordshire, the loveliest time of the year lay only a few weeks away. Then, mile on mile, the trees would be clouded with the white and pink of blooming time.

As we advanced, we noticed that nearly every apple tree contained clumps of parasitic mistletoe. The dense, rounded masses—some dark olive-hued, some a lighter shade of green—stood out among the bare branches. This mistletoe is more partial to the apple than to any other tree. For the orchardists these plants represent an auxiliary crop. Every year, in December, tons of mistletoe are shipped from Herefordshire to London. Up to comparatively recent times, a sprig of mistletoe used to be kept in country cottages from one Christmas to the next. This was believed to ward off lightning. For, according to Sir James G. Frazer's *The Golden Bough*, primitive men believed it was flashes of lightning that produced the mysterious masses among the branches of trees. Ever since the days when, with golden hooks, the ancient Druids harvested the plant from oaks on the sixth day of the new moon, mistletoe and superstition have been linked together.

Exactly where we encountered our first field of daffodils I cannot say. We were, I should judge, about ten miles north of the center of the forest. I had become confused on side roads and we were wandering over a rolling, soggy landscape, with lush green meadows and here and there a low willow tree. In many parts of southern England, daffodils became casualties of the war. In the battle to produce more food, fields were plowed up and bulbs destroyed. Our expectations were fading minute by minute when our road, glistening in the rain, curved down into a small dip that was threaded by a tiny stream. Suddenly green became gold. Meadows became fields of flowers. Daffodils were everywhere around us. Hedges ran like dark frames around the pictures of these floral displays.

Slightly smaller than the cultivated daffodil, a little lighter yellow than the dandelion, the flowers extended away, rank on rank, acre beyond acre. Waves of wind and rain swept across the fields, setting the flowers nodding. Even in this dull, crepuscular light, the scene was breathtaking. Tens of thousands of daffodils merged together into field after field of clear and radiant color.

Between Dymock and Newent we found ourselves among the greatest concentrations. Along one road we drove for three miles past a succession of patches and fields of gold. One sweep of daffodils covered more than forty acres. Not far away, a small valley seemed paved with the yellow flowers. They descended one slope and ascended the other. In another valley where a stream twisted on a meandering course, its banks appeared plated with floral gold. A gnarled and hoary oak, standing alone in a field, was surrounded by a sea of waving daffodils. Cows grazed between the flowers in the midst of the densest stands. We stopped, drove on, stopped again, a hundred times reveling in the beauty of this spring display.

In Dymock I bought fruit at a florist's shop, pencils in a wool shop, and bakery goods and a small bag of Devonshire clotted cream toffees at a grocery store called the Daffodil. Driving back, we made a lunch of buns and fruit and toffees surrounded by a host of daffodils. A green woodpecker —the bird the country folk call the rain bird because its call resembles "wet-wet-wet"—loped by in the downpour. As we drove on, we glimpsed the fields of daffodils beyond gates and between bars and through gaps in hedges. The golden tide ran across barnyards. The flowers nodded beside old barns. More than once we watched magpies, the glossy black and white of their plumage in striking contrast to their surroundings, coast down and alight among the flower-filled meadows. This was the same black-billed bird, *Pica pica,* which we had seen in so many places in the American west.

Along the margin of our roads, we frequently observed single flowers or small patches of daffodils. Several times we got out to examine them closely. Under these conditions we could see their two-toned yellow, the darker hue of the tubular center, the trumpet or corona or crown, and the lighter yellow of the outer petals. Near one clump we were attracted by another wildflower rising in a striking cluster of white and lavender blooms. From a distance the whole mass of four-petaled flowers looked white. But a nearer inspection revealed that each petal was shaded with pale pink or lilac. This was our first introduction to that member of the mustard family, *Cardamine pratensis,* that plant of charming colloquial names—lady's-smock, milkmaids, and cuckooflower. In contrast to the extremely local distribution of the wild daffodil, the lady's-smock is found beside streams and in moist meadows throughout Britain.

Several times, that rainy afternoon, we returned to one

glorious chain of daffodil-filled fields spreading away from a moss-covered gate. The flowers carpeted the valley floor and crowded up the slopes on either side. Almost all the way to Tewkesbury, we continued to encounter scattered patches and whole meadows golden with the massed petals of tens of thousands of daffodils.

chapter 7

A PLATE
OF ELVERS

The sign at the crossroads pointed to Dursley. How curious it was, I thought as we drove on, that in all the history of Dursley, in all the lives that had been lived there, the only thing I knew about this Gloucestershire community was the odd custom of the "Dursley lanterns." On February 10, 1873, Francis Kilvert recorded in his *Diary* that his mother remembered how, when ladies and gentlemen of Dursley went out to dinner on dark nights, "the gentlemen pulled out the tails of their shirts and walked before to show the way and light the ladies." These were called "Dursley lanterns."

We were now on the opposite side of the Severn from the Forest of Dean, descending through the dairyland of the wide and fertile Vale of Berkeley. To us it seemed that the whole subtle range of the color green spread around us. When William Gilpin, that eighteenth-century searcher for the picturesque, looked down from the edge of the Cotswold Hills into this valley, his reaction was: "I know not that I was ever more struck with the singularity and grandeur of any landscape."

Up and down this vale, a century and a half ago, a man on horseback wearing a broad-brimmed hat, polished high boots with silver spurs, and a blue coat with brass buttons was a familiar sight along the hedge-bordered roads. The rider was a magistrate, a physician, a poet, a musician, a naturalist of distinction, the builder of the first hydrogen balloon to rise in western England. He had arranged the scientific specimens brought back from Captain Cook's first voyage and had been offered the post of naturalist on the second voyage. He was the original discoverer of how the young cuckoo ejects the eggs from the nest of its foster parent. He was the second man in the world to mark birds for scientific observation. He was correct about the migration of birds at a time when Gilbert White was uncertain. A century before Charles Darwin, he was groping his way toward a theory of evolution. Yet for none of these things is his name most remembered today. Another achievement overshadows them all. For the rider in the vale was Dr. Edward Jenner, the discoverer of vaccination.

After that historic fourteenth of May, in 1796, when he inoculated John Phipps, the eight-year-old son of a farm laborer, against smallpox, Jenner rejected the opportunity to make a fortune by keeping his discovery secret. He turned down offers of lucrative practice in London. Although he was one of England's greatest scientists and one of the world's great benefactors, he continued the life of a country doctor in the valley where he was born. That valley was then, as it is today, a land of meadows and dairy barns. And if it had been otherwise, he might never have made his great discovery. For it was his study of cowpox, a disease peculiar to dairymaids, that suggested the idea of vaccination. The Vale of Berkeley, in its own way, contributed to his achievement.

Occasionally, as we followed roads where magpies, flying low, dragged their long tails over the hedges, we came to

Maurice Griggs at Hudson's seat on the tor above Zennor

farmhouses of stone, lichened by centuries, houses Jenner must have passed, and perhaps visited, as he jogged on his rounds. Sensitive to all beauty, this country doctor, time after time, rode out of his way to watch the sunset from one particular hill overlooking the River Severn. In later life, when John Phipps fell ill with tuberculosis, Jenner built him a cottage and, each spring, this Fellow of the Royal Society helped him set out his garden. The discoverer of vaccination possessed a keen mind, a warm heart, wide-ranging interests, and an engaging manner. At once humorous and wise, his conversation held so much of interest that, it is related, people he visited sometimes rode part way home with him, even at midnight, to prolong a discussion.

The pioneer Dutch microscopist, Jan Swammerdam, in *The Book of Nature*, published when Jenner was nine years old, observed: "Those who would avoid being imposed upon, should study nature in herself: for so many fallacies and errors have crept into the writings of preceding ages that people cannot but be led astray by them, as often taking things on trust, they neglect to see for themselves." Throughout his life, Jenner saw for himself. Like Gilbert White of Selborne, he went directly to nature. By the time he was eight he had made a large collection of dormouse nests, and in his schooldays he assembled a surprising number of fossils from limestone. Jenner's natural-history collection is still an annual feature of the Berkeley Fair.

One of his notebooks contains the reflection: "The great book of nature is open to all." The attention with which he read that book is evident even in his poems. His "Signs of Rain," for example, weaves together the impressions of a poetic mind with the observations of a keen and scientific eye. Jenner was a naturalist in the old philosophical sense, a seeker of scientific truth who avoided recourse to the supernatural. His final paper, on bird migration, was read before

Spring wildflowers: Water crowfoot, upper left. Ramsons, upper right. Primrose, lower left. Marsh marigold, lower right

the Royal Society only two months before his death on January 24, 1823. Less than a hundred yards from the spot where he carried out the first test of vaccination, he is buried in the chancel of the parish church at Berkeley. His stone cottage stands nearby.

We passed it when we climbed to the hilltop church, with its separate tower isolated from the main building and standing at the opposite side of the ancient burying ground. House martins whirled around the tower and, somewhere among the trees, a great tit repeated its call which sounded to us like "Peeto! Peeto! Peeto!" Here and there, where tombstones had been laid flat over the graves, the inscribed epitaphs stood out in vivid green. Moss traced the letters, rooted in dust collected in the chiseled grooves. Old graveyards in Britain provide a literature of their own and here, in somber light under gathering rain clouds, we came upon a noble example. Engraved centuries ago on the tombstone of a long-time mayor of Berkeley, Thomas Peirce—spelled Peirce on the front of the stone and Pearce on the end— were these words:

> "Here lyeth Thomas peirce whom no man taught
> Yet he in iron, brass and silver wrought
> He Jacks and clocks and watches (with art) made
> And mended too when other worke did fade
> Of Berkeley five tymes mayor the artist was
> And yet this mayor, this artist, was but grass
> When his owne watch was downe on the last day
> He that made watches had not made a key
> To winde it up but useless it must lie
> Until he rise a Gaine no more to die."

Beyond the churchyard wall, under an immense beech tree where little clouds of almost colorless gnats hovered and danced, a high-peaked hut, about fifteen feet long and ten feet wide, lifted its thatched roof above whitewashed walls. It suggested something out of *Robinson Crusoe* or *Swiss Family Robinson*. Twisted limbs of solid oak formed the rustic framework. Standing in what once was Jenner's garden, this is the historic summerhouse where John Phipps was vaccinated.

As we were leaving, we heard a scratching scramble among the branches overhead. Looking up, we saw a sight that never met the eyes of Jenner. It was the leaping form of an animal unknown to the Vale of Berkeley and to all of Britain during the years of this naturalist-physician. A gray squirrel leaped from limb to limb and disappeared.

All along its western edge, from end to end, the Vale of Berkeley is bounded by the brown serpentine of the Severn estuary. The river, originating on a boggy plateau high on Plynlimon, drains half of Wales as it traces a 200-mile semicircle that ends below Gloucester in this muddy, ever-widening flow that is more than five miles from bank to bank where it merges with the Bristol Channel. These last estuarine miles of the Severn's course are famous for two movements, widely different. They both forge upstream against the current—one a movement of water, the other a movement of life. The first is the famed tidal bore of the Severn. The second is the return of elvers in the spring.

Upstream from Berkeley, on another day, I suddenly slowed to a cautious crawl as we came out on a road skirting the very edge of the estuary. The hardtop ahead gleamed with a slippery layer of newly deposited mud and water. Two workmen in black rubber boots and brown raincoats, with long sweeps of large push brooms sent mud and water spattering out over the river. They were clearing the roadway in the wake of a tidal bore. This spectacular event, described as resembling a river riding on another river's back, occurs when tides are highest. The major bore of the year comes at flood-tide during the spring equinox. A somewhat lesser bore occurs during the autumn equinox and still smaller bores occur each month at the full of the moon.

Then, at the mouth of the estuary, the rise of the sea water meets head-on the flow of the river. In the course of ninety minutes, the level of the water at the lower end of the estuary may climb eighteen feet. One record tide here reached a height of thirty-two feet, four inches. Each time, the rapidly gaining bulk of the sea water produces a roaring wave, often seven feet high, which rushes upstream, traveling at times with the speed of a cantering horse. A particularly powerful bore—a name derived from the Scandinavian word *bara*, meaning wave—may reverse the flow of the Severn as far upstream as Tewkesbury Lock, thirteen and a half miles above Gloucester. In its passing the water floods out across the lowland along the way.

We gazed down into the muddy stream. Already the Severn had resumed its normal flow. Behind the brown curtain of the floating sediment, that second upstream movement of the spring, the ascent of the elvers, had daily grown in volume.

No thicker than a shoelace and hardly longer than my little finger, each baby eel was coming to the end of an amazing journey, a sea voyage lasting three years and covering thousands of miles, an oceanic odyssey that had its beginnings in the distant Sargasso Sea. Here in the Severn, at the turn of the tide during hours of darkness, uncounted millions of elvers were hugging the banks, slipping upstream, entering, at last, their second world, the world of fresh water.

Nearly twenty years had passed since another day in the spring of the year when Nellie and I had leaned against the rail of a wooden bridge spanning a small brook in North Carolina. Over the sandy bed of the stream, across patches of dark, decaying leaves, American elvers had wriggled, advancing against the uneven flow of the current. They, too, had journeyed from the seaweed-strewn Sargasso Sea. But they had covered their shorter journey in one year instead of three. On opposite sides of the Atlantic, when the related species of elvers reached fresh water, they are approximately the same size and have reached the same stage of development. Yet one is three times as old as the other.

The origin of eels, how they are produced, where they came from, formed a mystery debated for centuries. Aristotle believed they were spontaneously generated from mud and slime. Pliny the Elder maintained that adult eels rubbed themselves against rocks and detached fragments of skin that became small eels. Leuwenhoek, the Dutch naturalist, mistook parasites for the young of eels and announced that the creatures give birth to living young. Even as late as the seventeenth century, men believed eels could be produced by exposing to the heat of the sun two turfs, covered with May dew and placed with the grassy sides together. In parts of England and Scotland, in comparatively recent times, a recipe for producing more eels was to throw chopped-up horsehair into rivers. These ideas were all misconceptions; but they seem hardly wilder than the almost incredible truth.

It was not until the second decade of the present century that that truth became known. It was revealed by nearly twenty years of scientific detective work by the celebrated Danish oceanographer and biologist, Dr. Johannes Schmidt. His quest was to find creatures smaller than a needle, not in a haystack but in a whole ocean.

In the end, by drawing up in nets smaller and smaller eel larvae, he tracked them back to their source in the Sargasso Sea in the Atlantic between the Azores and the Antilles. There the adult eels breed in the dark depths of the ocean, perhaps as much as 1,000 feet below the surface. Each female releases up to 100,000 eggs. Hatching in astronomical numbers, the laterally compressed larvae, shaped like willow leaves and as transparent as glass, drift northward in the Gulf Stream. The only pigment in their bodies is concentrated in the dark pinpoints of their eyes. As they approach land at journey's end, these larvae alter in shape. They become cylindrical and finned, transforming into elvers such as those that, in these spring days, were streaming in millions up the estuary of the Severn.

If you glance at a map of England, you will notice that the mouth of the Bristol Channel, leading into the Severn estuary, opens on the sea like an immense funnel. From the last of March to May, into this funnel pours the flood of baby eels. Then the elver fishers are abroad. Their equipment is simple: a lantern, a bucket or two, a couple of forked sticks and a net. Of age-old design, the homemade nets are about three by two feet with a depth of twenty inches. Dun-colored cheesecloth is stretched over a willow framework. The handles, or "tailpieces," are from five to nine feet long. In the region of Epney we saw nets of this kind lashed to bicycles and attached to the tops of automobiles.

Arrived at the river bank, the elver fisher thrusts the forked sticks into the ground so they extend outward, supporting the lantern above the water. For half a minute or so, he leaves his net submerged, facing downstream. When he pulls it up, it may contain half a dozen elvers or, if the run is strong, a single dip of the net may fill a bucket. During record runs as many as 100 pounds—each pound containing from 750 to 1,000 elvers—are netted in an hour. On most occasions the main run of the night is over within an hour after the turn of the tide.

Because the largest catches are made near Epney, a commercial elver depot is manned, each year, behind the Anchor Inn. There millions of young eels are packed for shipment to the continent. As we arrived, an immense truck,

specially designed to keep oxygen flowing through the
water, pulled away on a non-stop run to the English Channel ferry at Dover. Its living cargo was on its way to Poland.
Continental streams that flow into the Baltic receive a
smaller supply of young eels than do rivers flowing directly
into the Atlantic. To increase the yield of these valuable
fish, such streams are stocked with elvers imported from the
Severn.

This suggests a riddle which may have no final answer.
To which river will the next generation of these relocated
eels return? To the Severn, where the elvers were caught?
Or to the continental rivers in which they were released
and down which, as adults, they swim on their way to their
oceanic spawning grounds? Tagging experiments in the
American northwest have revealed that salmon, after years
of growth in the sea, return to spawn in the very streams
where their lives began. However, in the case of the eel,
such tagging experiments are impossible. Its life story is the
reverse of that of the salmon. Its growth takes place not in
the ocean but in the stream; it returns for spawning not to
inland waterways but to the vastness of the sea.

The elvers shipped abroad from Epney represent only
part of the annual harvest. The rest is consumed by residents of the region. Sometimes the small eels are served
with bacon; sometimes they are mixed with beaten eggs to
produce elver omelets; sometimes they are jellied. All along
the Severn, elver suppers form a feature of the spring. Yet
only a few miles inland away from the river banks, we were
told, this delicately flavored seasonal food is all but unknown.

About two o'clock in the afternoon, as Nellie and I were
splashing through the potholes of a muddy road near
Epney, we passed a square brick building housing a country
inn. The name caught our eye. Printed in letters of gold on
a sign showing a man eating from a heaped-up plate, it

read: PLATE OF ELVERS. We turned around and stopped. It was late for lunch; but we decided to try our luck. At first, the building seemed deserted. We wandered down a dim hallway, looked into the smoking room, and stepped down into the darkened bar before we were noticed. Elvers for lunch? A quick check of supplies on hand and the answer was "yes." While we waited for the meal, we sat on a bench beneath the dartboard and talked to the innkeeper of people he had known who had gone to America, of the bore, the elvers, and the foxes that live along the estuary.

While we talked, his wife prepared the elvers the way her mother had taught her to cook them. First she fried slices of bacon in the pan. These she replaced with the elvers, cooking them slowly over a low fire. From time to time she added a little beaten egg. When the plates arrived, accompanied by rolls and butter, the cooked elvers appeared silvery, almost white. They suggested, at first glance, the chestnut sprouts used in Chinese dishes. Vinegar was on the table. But we desired no condiment. We wished to savor the natural taste of the elvers. That taste was delicious, at once mild and rich, just as the meal was, at once light and nourishing. For us, new foods were coming fast during those early days in England. We had had steak-and-kidney pie the night before, finnan haddock for breakfast that morning, and now elvers for lunch. And ahead lay such unfamiliar fare as steamed whelks, Dorset knobs—small, hard, crumbly biscuits—and devils on horseback—strips of bacon wrapped around prunes.

Ten miles downstream from Epney, the springtime elvers that ascend the Severn swim past an area of flat, alluvial fields reclaimed from the river. Since 1470 these have been known as the New Grounds. Today no other spot on the face of the earth contains so great a variety of waterfowl. For this area, near Slimbridge, is the home of the Severn Wildfowl Trust, headed by Peter Scott. An old saying has it that the Vale of Berkeley, thinly populated even today, contains a larger population of wild geese than of people. Never was this more true than in the present time of the Severn sanctuary.

In planning our British trip, the Severn Wildfowl Trust was one of our special goals. We pictured ourselves wandering there in the warm sunshine of April. We came in April. But we came on the coldest day of that date in a quarter of a century. We came on a day of intermittent icy rain, of bitter, buffeting winds sweeping over the level ground. Disappointment followed disappointment. Peter Scott was away, in Bermuda. Shivering, we hurried to the research center where Nellie watched the birds outside through the plate-glass observation window while I, with overcoat collar turned up and cap pulled down, hunched up against the wind, struggled along the paths from pond to pond, from enclosure to enclosure, taking shelter in the lee of each large object along the way. The waterfowl, too, huddled behind whatever protection they could find. Under these conditions, almost alone on the paths, I came upon such old friends of American waterways as the wood duck, the ring-necked duck, the little ruddy duck, the canvasback and shoveler, the blue-winged teal, and the Canada goose.

The waterfowl of Slimbridge have been drawn from around the world. Gathered here are Andean geese, Hottentot teal, New Zealand scaup, Nene or Hawaiian geese, Chinese spotbill, Australian shelduck and Chilean pintail. Cries, strange and stirring, cries familiar to the rivers and marshes, the estuaries and lakes of remote regions of the globe, were carried on the wind. But all the voices I heard, that day, were mingled with the booming of the great gusts; all the birds I saw, that day, I saw through eyes streaming from the constant whipping of the wind.

A long, straight road runs down the length of the Vale of Berkeley. The Romans laid it out. Now, connecting Gloucester and Bristol, it is one of the most heavily traveled trunk roads of Britain. We followed it south from Slimbridge to Alveston, once a Stone Age settlement. Our window there, at the end of that cold and windy afternoon, looked out on a nook sheltered by a high hedge, with open fields beyond extending away to distant trees. In this small area of grass and hedge, protected by the outstretched branches of an old ash tree, we encountered three new birds in the course of an hour's time, our first blue tit, our first greenfinch, and our first hedge sparrow, or dunnock.

This latter bird was another link with Edward Jenner. More than a century after his death, his nature notebooks were published by Oxford University Press. They record that, in the Vale of Berkeley in 1787, he tested the reaction of parent hedge sparrows by placing a half-fledged blackbird in a nest with two young dunnocks. The newcomer was so large it almost filled the nest and the small sparrows, at times, had to sit on its back. Yet, he found, the parents fed and successfully reared all three occupants of the nest.

The most active birds in that hedge-sheltered nook were a pair of great tits that had discovered a nesting hole in the trunk of the ash tree. Neither the wind nor the rain nor the chill of that gloomy day had reduced their ardor. Watching only a few feet away on the other side of the glass, we saw the female rip up bits of moss from the ground, shake each fragment violently, then flit upward and disappear in the mouth of the cavity. The male, too, seemed carried away with nesting fever. He ran through a similar sequence. But only the female carried material to the nest. The male plucked moss and shook it with equal energy. But always, he tossed it aside and ripped up another billful which he, in turn, discarded. This feverish activity of the tits went on and on. The light became dim and the distant trees grew indistinct before it ended.

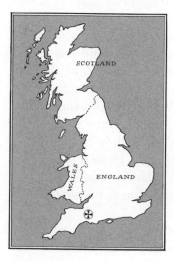

chapter 8

APRIL
BLIZZARD

The next morning, the birds were gone, the distant trees were gone, the scene was blurred and dimmed by scudding snow. Carried on the wind, the flakes streamed past our window in gray-white lines drawn almost parallel with the ground. This was the fourteenth of April. This was the twenty-fifth day of spring. This was the southern part of England. Easter had already come and gone. Yet we seemed in a blizzard on the Great Plains of America. The flakes grew larger. By the time breakfast was over, our car was covered with more than an inch of snow.

On this day we had planned to run sixty miles or more to the south, to the old Saxon hill-town of Shaftesbury, on the other side of the Dorset border. Should we chance it? I found the hotel manager listening to his radio. Snow had been falling most of the night at Plymouth. Already four inches had accumulated. The storm, widespread, was more violent in the south. He thought a long time before he answered my question.

"You should be able to get through. But it may be a bit dodgey at the other end."

With that rather shaky encouragement and with our spirit of adventure strengthened by a good breakfast, Nellie and I reached a unanimous decision. Hastily we packed the car, wiped the plastered snow from the windshield, and headed south. We had no knowledge at that time that before the storm was over snow would have come to thirty-three counties of England and Wales; that, in the coldest mid-April of the century, roads would become impassable, coastal shipping would be disrupted, Britain-bound planes would be diverted to the Continent, farmers would be searching among six-foot drifts for lambs, and helicopters would be rescuing campers overwhelmed by wind-blown snow.

Enclosed as within a swirled white snail shell, we nosed ahead. The storm had come from the Arctic Circle by way of Siberia, Scandinavia, and the North Sea. We had learned long before, in following the four seasons through America, how widely the same season varies from year to year. This, our first spring in Britain, was proving to be one of the coldest, one of the wettest, one of the stormiest in decades. Even the local residents, inured to chill rain and raw weather, were expressing what seemed to us extremely mild discontent. At best, the climate of Britain is only intermittently genial and sparkling. Yet it may well be that the hostility of the weather has played its part in shaping the British character, ingraining the ability to hold on through the storms of weather and the greater storms of history. A few days after this paralyzing storm, we came on a cartoon in a morning paper. It reflected another characteristic of the British, the capacity for retaining a sense of humor under stress. The drawing depicted a ewe and a lamb lying in a pasture swept by rain and snow. The ewe was saying: "Oh, stop saying you wish you'd never been born—you've got to face the summer yet!"

The traffic of Bristol, we had been warned, was "almost

as bad as London's." But on this day few cars were out. We worked our way without difficulty from north to south through the labyrinth of city streets. Somewhere along the way, the air between the buildings suddenly grew rich with a heavy scent, the same strong smell that W. H. Hudson had caught on the day he landed at Southampton. Throughout the rest of his life, it remained in his mind as "the smell of England." It was the aroma of malt from a brewery.

Beyond Bristol, on the road to Bath, the storm increased and decreased. Our anxiety went up and down. When William Gilpin followed this same path, during his excursion through the West Country in 1770, his conclusion was: "The road between Bristol and Bath contains very little worth notice." Whether we would have agreed with him we will never know. For we missed even that "very little." We saw nothing but indefinite gray shapes looming up out of the storm, perhaps woods, perhaps valleys shrouded in the moving clouds of falling snow. What was happening, we wondered, to those miles of daffodils? What were the swans of Wells Cathedral doing now? And what of the ponies of Dartmoor?

It was a little before noon when we groped our way into Bath. Celebrated as a spa from Roman times, when it bore the name Aquae Sulis, it was elaborately rebuilt during the reigns of the four Georges. This was the Bath of Beau Nash, famed as the most beautiful city of England. We saw its winding streets, its colonnades and Roman baths, its statue with "Water is Best" engraved on its side—we saw them all through a wavering screen of descending flakes. Already the snow had accumulated to a depth of half a foot.

Somewhere in Bath we took a wrong turning. But a fortunate misfortune saved us from going far out of our way. On the outskirts of the town we came to a high hill with a steep ascent. Cars and trucks were stalled or, unable to at-

tain the summit, were backing down. Only after we had reversed our course and were back in Bath did we discover
that we had been going west when we thought we were
going east. By now, most of the highway signs were blank
white, plastered with snow, their directions entirely blotted
out. We seemed to be driving in wartime England, with
the roadway markers removed.

The storm grew more violent as we neared the Wiltshire
border. Once we passed a tree filled with the black forms of
rooks huddling together in the gale. Another time we saw
at least a dozen small songbirds clustered densely in one
low bush standing in the lee of a hedge. The next morning
I talked to a man who told of seeing, at the height of the
storm, jackdaws and smaller birds perching within the protection of bus shelters along country roads.

Over the Wiltshire border, at Warminster, we halted on
the main street, sloshed through mushy snow, jumped over
a curbside puddle, and pushed open a restaurant door—a
door with the knob placed in the center instead of at the
side. Hot spring soup of fresh vegetables and the hearty
meal of roast beef and mashed potatoes put warmth into
our bodies and fanned the spark of adventure in our minds.
But even so we were in a quandary. The snow was piling
deeper, drifting in the wind. Should we hole up at Warminster or push on another twenty or more miles to Shaftesbury, where we had made reservations? We studied the
map. We looked out at the falling snow. We gazed up at
the sky. The storm seemed lessening—slightly. The sky
seemed brighter—a trifle. By following a staggering course,
keeping to the main roads, we thought we could get
through. But hardly had we started when clouds more
dense than before closed around us.

We had gone only a few miles when two words on a partially covered sign beside the road caught my eye. They
were "Norton Bavant." Norton Bavant! There flashed on

my mind a memory of William Cobbett of the *Rural Rides*. And this was Norton Bavant, the village where he thought he could be happy all his life!

"If I were compelled to decide where to live," Cobbett wrote during a ride along the Wylye Valley, "I do believe I should fix on some vale in Wiltshire. Water meadows at the bottom, cornland going up toward the hills, those hills being downland, and a farmhouse in a clump of trees, in some little cross-vale between the hills, sheltered on every side except the south. In short, if Mr. Bennett would give me a farm, the house which lies on the right-hand side of the road going from Salisbury to Warminster, in the parish of Norton Bavant, just before you enter the village . . . I would freely give up all the rest of the world."

Somewhere, close at hand, invisible in the storm, lay the very fields, the very house that, to that other man, so long before, had seemed an Eden. I strained to see around me. The roadside hedges rose like higher drifts. The fields beyond were lost in falling snow. From time to time a slight opening and closing of the curtains of the storm afforded us momentary, tantalizing glimpses. The vague bulk of an immense hill rose to our left.

On a later, clearer day, Nellie and I swung back to see all that now was hidden. The great Scratchbury Hill rose up and up from the valley meadows. It towered above the village. It dominated the scene. Straggling upward, hedges enclosed high fields where tiny specks of white revealed sheep grazing. On that day most of the snow had disappeared, but along all the hedges drifts remained unmelted, outlining each green pasture in a frame of white.

Hardly more than a dozen houses, formed of weathered brick or stone, some with thatched roofs, comprised the village. The main road, a new concrete highway of the motor age, drew a straight line between the village and the hill. But an older, wandering road, the one along which Cobbett

had ridden from Salisbury, entered the village from the
east. Here, sheltered by the height of the hill, stood a solid,
venerable farmhouse of stone. This seemed most likely the
house of Cobbett's choice. More than a century and a quarter intervened between his time and ours. We looked
around. The scene, we were forced to admit, held no
greater attraction for us than hundreds of others we had
known. I felt momentary regret at finding I was unmoved
where another had been so profoundly stirred. But for us
something was missing—the magic light, the special mood,
the precise attitude of mind that had made the scene super-
lative for Cobbett.

Down the Wylye Valley, on that day of winter-in-April
blizzard, our road carried us through ever-deepening snow.
It led us through Fisherton de la Mare and past Lamb Down
and to Deptford. Was this, we wondered, where the charming little wildflower, the Deptford pink, received its name?
Here we doubled back on A303 and soon, near the Great
Ridge Wood, began climbing a long ascent. Mounting
slowly, lights on, almost blinded by the storm, I pulled to a
hasty stop when the car in front suddenly halted. Ahead of
us, tilting upward, disappearing into the storm, a long line
of cars and trucks had come to a halt. For some time we
had noticed no traffic was going in the opposite direction.
Somewhere ahead in the blizzard there was a serious tieup.
A police car passed us going up the wrong side of the road.
An ambulance followed. Minute after minute we waited,
sitting there amid the wind-swirled snow, in light heavy and
gray, with all the country around hidden behind the moving curtains of white. Additional trucks and cars piled up
behind us. Half an hour went by. Then the stalled line of
traffic began to move. We inched upward, a car length at a
time.

Eventually we attained the summit and came out on an
open height where drifts, unplowed, had solidified beneath

the wheels of traffic into ruts and icy mounds. For nearly half a mile we slipped and slithered, slewed and floundered, barely able to maintain traction. Then we began descending, and our wheels were on smoother roads. It was our good fortune to be on the side that went through first. Going down the slope, we passed a solid mile of waiting cars lined up on the other side of the road, headed in the opposite direction.

Again it was our good luck at the foot of the long descent, Chilmark Bottom, to be shunted off on a roundabout route to Shaftesbury. For the high road we planned to take, we learned later, remained completely blocked by drifts for more than twenty-four hours. Through Tisbury and Ansty, near Swallowcliffe and Birdbush and White Sheet Hill, always in driving snow, we zigzagged toward Shaftesbury. Wherever gaps in the hedges let gusts sweep through, long tongues of snow extended across the roadway. I remember one place where the scouring action of the wind had exposed a small patch of bare ground. There, even in the midst of the storm, two chaffinches were darting down and snatching up small pieces of grit. During our last miles coming into Shaftesbury, we followed a road where a series of dips extended along the top of snow piled up beside the highway. The wind, scouring through these scallops, drew out a long succession of scimitar-shaped driftlets. They all were curved in unison, all were moving, all luminous with a silvery sheen.

A roadside marker, a mile or so from town, bore the word "SHASTON." This was the ancient name for Shaftesbury, the name Thomas Hardy used in *Jude the Obscure*. As houses drew closer together, we saw children throwing snowballs, children running with sleds, children making snowmen. Splashing through freezing slush, we came to the goal of our travels on that stormy day, the historic Grosvenor, an inn occupying the site where travelers have been coming out of the storm into a succession of hostelries for a thousand years. Warm, snug, safe in port, remembering that line of stalled cars in the blizzard, we added up the sum total of our good fortune and were thankful.

The next morning, as I gazed out over the chimney pots of the lower rooftops, my attention was caught by a starling. It perched where the coal smoke was being whirled away by the wind in the wake of the storm. As I watched, it turned its head, cocked its tail, twisted its body, half opened its wings. It assumed a succession of grotesque postures such as I had seen when birds were "anting." Normally, at such times, birds apply ants with their bills, rubbing them back and forth among their plumage. But, on occasions, various species have been observed using substitutes as widely diverse as moth balls, orange peels, and cigar butts. In Queensland, in northern Australia, red-browed finches were once seen going through the motions of anting in the smoke of a smoldering log. The starling I watched was evidently employing the coal smoke of the Dorset chimney pot as the Queensland finches had used the wood smoke of the burning log.

The lengthy debate, with its many inconclusive answers, over what benefit a bird derives from an application of ants apparently had been decided by the researches of the Russian parasitologist, Dr. Vsevolod B. Dubinin. The three large volumes of his *Feather Mites*—the last appearing in 1956, two years before his death—were based on such exhaustive studies that they included the microscopic examination of the stomach contents of 20,000 of these minute creatures. They show that the mites obtain their principal nourishment from the fat particles adhering to the plumage of birds. In March, 1963, the American ornithological journal *The Wilson Bulletin* published a résumé of Dr. Dubinin's work in connection with anting. He found that feather mites—so small that a magnifying glass is needed to see them—are killed by the application of ants. The formic acid in the ants apparently is lethal to the mites.

On collected Steppe pipits, Dr. Dubinin found, feather mites were in a healthy condition on birds that had not anted recently, while many were dying on those that had. Of 732 mites taken from four Steppe pipits that had just finished anting, ninety were dead and 163 additional ones died within twelve hours; of the 758 taken from four of the pipits that had not been anting, only five died within the same period. If formic acid is thus useful in eliminating feather mites, it seems curious that, over the centuries, birds have not learned to make use of nettles. For the sting of these plants is produced by this same acid.

That day after the blizzard, walking on the rough footing of the frozen slush, we found the market town of Shaftesbury filled with historic interest. We came to the abbey said to have been founded by King Alfred and, at one time, presided over by his daughter. We walked on precipitous, cobblestone-paved Gold Street, so often sketched and painted by artists. We saw outspread below the town the rich Vale of Blackmoor, the patchwork of its fields wavering and indistinct in the snow-mist.

Late in the afternoon, on one of the side streets, I came in out of the cold, stepping down into the basement rooms of a crowded secondhand bookstore. Volumes, mainly dating from before the First World War, ranged in dusty ranks along the shelves or lay in piles on the floor. The proprietor, an elderly man, pale and drawn, huddled beside a small grate where coals were burning. He was bundled in a heavy blue coat such as seamen wear. A woollen blanket was wrapped about his legs and a large vacuum bottle of hot tea stood on a chair beside him. He spoke courteously in a weak, far-away voice, never leaving his seat by the fire. Three small boys, about eight years old, rushed about, helping with the mail and arranging the books.

I wandered down the shelves, gazing at these books of another time, now and then taking down some old, vaguely remembered volume. Here were books by Hall Caine, Marion Crawford, Gilbert Parker, Maurice Hewlett. Here were rows of volumes by H. G. Wells and Rudyard Kipling. Among the authors represented, how many of the great names of the past were almost disregarded now. From Foyle's, in London, to the smallest secondhand bookstall in a remote provincial town, of all the bookstores I encountered in Britain, this is the one that left the most enduring impression. I can see it all vividly now—the elderly man beside the tiny fire amid those thousands and thousands of dusty books.

"I'm afraid," the maid at the Grosvenor told us, "you may find it a bit noisy tonight."

Until long after midnight, we heard the sound of music below. The ballroom of our historic inn was ablaze with light. The blizzard was over. The country roads were open. And "The Young Farmers and Dairy Maids" were holding a dance.

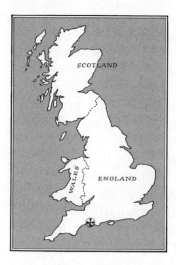

chapter 9

SNAIL CREEP

We followed Puddletown Road to Cuckoo Lane and Cuckoo Lane to Cherry Alley and Cherry Alley to Snail Creep. Beyond this wandering footpath a trail known locally as Black Bottom led away into the Dorset heath. With its back to the heath, a thatched cottage faced flower beds and old apple trees, an abandoned village pump and the half dozen straggling houses of Higher Bockhampton. Beyond, hedge-bordered fields and pastures extended away in rolling farmland. We stopped beside a stone marker. It bore the words: "THOMAS HARDY, O.M., was born in the adjacent cottage 2nd June 1840 and in it wrote 'Under the Greenwood Tree' and 'Far from the Madding Crowd.' This monument is Erected in his Memory by a few of his American Friends."

These were the fields, these were the roads, this was the wasteland of the heath that had colored Hardy's mind and played so large a role in his Wessex novels. Beneath the thatch of this cottage, his first childhood memory was of an immense, shining copper kettle brought home from market

75

day at Dorchester. Somewhere among these fields, as a small boy, he had wondered what it would be like to feed on grass like a sheep and had climbed over a stile into a pasture, got down on his hands and knees, and lowered his head as though grazing. When he looked up, he discovered the sheep in the field had stopped feeding and had gathered in a ring around him and were watching him in apparent amazement. Along these roads, he recalled, he had walked as a schoolboy puzzling over the kind of a world he was going into. And across this countryside he had roamed as a man, thinking and observing, sometimes making notes for his poems and novels on flat stones or on chips left by woodcutters, when no other writing material was at hand.

The pages that resulted contain some of the finest descriptions of nature found in any language. Although it was more than 4,000 miles away and decades ago when I read them first, they remain vividly impressed upon my mind. For who can erase from his memory the arrival of dusk on Egdon Heath once he has known *The Return of the Native?* Who can forget the moonlit hayfield and the sarcastic calling of the nightjar in *The Woodlanders?* Or the wind at midnight on the hill of Norcombe Eweleaze in *Far from the Madding Crowd?* Or the coming of spring to The Vale of the Great Dairies in *Tess of the D'Urbervilles?*

The basis of Hardy's indelible descriptions is the precision of his observant eye. When rain drips from the forest in his pages, it collects and falls according to the varied shapes of the foliage. Wherever we went in the Hardy country of Dorset, we were to observe the scene around us with the illusion of familiarity, a feeling that we had gone this way before. Our attitude was a tribute to Hardy's magic. We saw the scene as we had pictured it, or as he had pictured it for us. His descriptions are as faithful to the original as they are vivid. We see what he describes, and it is as he describes it.

On the morning that we stepped out onto the mossy ground of Snail Creep, more than a century and a quarter had passed since Thomas Hardy's birth. Yet the thatched house at the end of its lanelike road still seemed remote from the world. Under the protection of the National Trust, it is kept as nearly as possible as it was when he was alive. On Wednesday, Thursday, and Sunday afternoons, James and Ruth Skilling, the caretakers and tenants, show visitors through the rooms of the cottage. Of the people we met in England, these two proved particularly congenial. During our time with them, the hours were all too short.

Among the golden pippin and Gascoyne Scarlet apple trees, beyond the flower beds, one gnarled Bockhampton Sweet dates back to Hardy's boyhood. It was at a rectangular deal table at an upstairs window overlooking this stretch of flower gardens and orchard trees that he wrote his earliest books. When we glanced up at the Norfolk reeds that formed the thatching, we noticed several places where those "thatch birds," the house sparrows, had made their nesting tunnels. In some instances, the holes had been enlarged by starlings. The "gossiping" of these birds just overhead sometimes keeps the Skillings awake at night. They have to rap on the walls of their upstairs bedroom to bring it to a halt.

Going from room to room, from the kitchen with its bread oven that was heated for ten hours with furze faggots on baking days; to the dark-beamed, low-ceilinged sitting room which formed the scene of Tranter Dewy's Christmas party in *Under the Greenwood Tree*; to the office room where Hardy's father, a master builder and stonemason, paid his workmen through a small window facing on Snail Creep; to the upstairs bedroom where Thomas Hardy slept as a boy and where he spent his early days as an author, we were seeing things that, to the end, remained close to Hardy's heart. Even when he was a very old man, bent and looking at the ground as he walked, he would come slowly down the road to visit his childhood home.

That afternoon, with James Skilling and Chico, his black border collie cross—the breed of most "working" dogs on Dorset farms—I started out under the old beeches overhanging Snail Creep and along Black Bottom onto Puddletown Heath, a surviving remnant of that "heathy, furzy, briary wilderness" Hardy called Egdon Heath. There was much to see along the way—a small oak gall broken open on one side by a woodpecker's bill; a large black slug that, when contracted, resembled an acorn complete with its cross-hatched cup; and, clean-cut in the trail, the hoofprints of a fallow deer. Deer still come down the path that Thomas Hardy followed as a boy. Sometimes at night they come close to the cottage, even among the flower beds. Such an event, long ago, is celebrated in one of Hardy's poems, "The Fallow Deer at the Lonely House."

As we advanced, the open heath grew more wild. Whole slopes of the uneven ground were brown and shaggy with the dry, dead fronds of bracken stands of the year before. Occasionally, beneath, we glimpsed the bright green of new ferns unrolling. Heather increased, and up and down over the hills ran the yellow of the furze. One reason why this wiry shrub grows in such dense stands is the manner in which it dispenses its seeds. When the pods become ripe, they burst with a popping sound and hurl their seeds for several feet. Thus new furze takes root on all sides. On a hot summer day, an almost continual sound of popping can be heard across a patch of furze where the ripe pods are exploding.

Isolated hawthorns and hollies and spindly birches, widely spaced, rose above this massed lower growth. Several times we passed sinkholes that descended in funnel-like depressions below the level of the ground. The largest, filled with vegetation, resembled the crater of an extinct volcano.

The smallest, we discovered, had been adapted by some burrower as the entrance of its tunnel home. The rank animal smell surrounding the opening suggested the occupant was a fox.

Chico, coursing over the heath, came racing up to investigate. Then he was off in another direction, putting up three pheasants that scaled away down a long slope, low above the furze. All across the wasteland, sheltered nooks held patches of haircap moss, foxglove plants, and tangles of blackberry canes. Interlacing rhododendrons, running wild and seeding themselves, filled the deeper hollows.

"They provide shelter for the deer," Skilling told me.

Once, on an autumn day, he recalled, he found the furze and bracken of the heath clad in silk, shining with streaming gossamer. Countless thousands of tiny spiderlings, ballooning on fine extended threads, distributing their species far and wide, had descended here when the breeze died at the end of their aerial adventure.

Not far from where the line of an old Roman road, now overgrown, cuts in an east-and-west direction across the heath, we skirted an extensive pine plantation set out by the Forestry Commission.

"In earlier times, before such projects began," my companion explained, "the heath was regularly burned over. The process was called swaling."

Now, when flames are a menace to the stand of pines, fire-fighting equipment is distributed at intervals along the path. We came to racks holding clusters of poles, each about eight feet long and ending in a rectangle of laminated canvas, apparently cut from discarded conveyor belting. Using these, a line of men can quickly beat out the advancing flames of a fire spreading across the heath.

When Thomas Hardy was a small boy, it was the habit of his parents to walk this way on Sunday afternoons. Usually, their goal was the three prehistoric tumuli known as the Rainbarrows. From the top of the highest, they would survey the surrounding country through a telescope. Throughout Hardy's life, this ancient, man-made hill remained one of his favorite spots. Its summit formed the stage on which the silhouettes of Eustacia Vye and the furze-faggot bearers appear against the darkening sky in the unforgettable early pages of *The Return of the Native*. On this April afternoon, this highest Rainbarrow was our destination.

When we reached it, we mounted on a bracken-bordered sandy path which—being, according to the lie of the land, the logical ascent—may well have been first trod by the feet of the barrow's prehistoric builders. The hoofs of deer and the padded paws of foxes and the shoes worn by successive generations of human visitors have kept it open. The top of the mound is the highest point on the heath. Standing on its summit, we saw the knolls and hollows of the undulating land spreading away in varying shades of yellows and browns with tinges of green.

As my eyes swept full circle, I observed in reality what I had known only in fiction before. Off to the south, the Frome wound through the fertile Vale of the Great Dairies where Tess met Angel Clare. In the opposite direction lay Blackmoor Vale, the Vale of the Little Dairies. Within half a mile or so of where we stood, near Rushy Pond— now more rushes than pond—Hardy had placed the cottage of Eustacia Vye and her uncle. Skilling pointed to a low roof lifting just above the horizon in another direction. It marked the location of Blooms-End Farm, the home of the mother of the "native," Clym Yeobright. And, off there, on the edge of the Frome Valley, not far from that small body of water marked on detailed maps "Heedless William's Pond," Wildeve kept the Quiet Woman Inn.

I shifted my gaze to the southeast. There, less than five miles away, in a carefully guarded portion of the heath, ultra-modern buildings house the reactors of an atomic research station. Thus, ironically, Hardy's Egdon Heath is playing its part in a further advance in that chain of effort he heralded during the First World War with the lines: "After two thousand years of Mass, We've got as far as poison gas."

We came home that day by a shortcut, following deer trails amid the furze and heather, struggling through rhododendron tangles and coming out, at last, with Chico racing far ahead of us, on the path that led to the cottage. We all had dinner that evening at the King's Arms, in Dorchester. Ruth Skilling brought Nellie two bouquets—one old-fashioned flowers from the garden at the cottage, forget-me-nots and primroses and daffodils; the other wildflowers from the fields around. As we ate, James Skilling recalled that the day before he had heard the first cuckoo of the year along the same path we had followed. For Chico, who was used to being summoned with the call "Chico! Chico!" the cuckoo was not just the first of the year, it was the first of a lifetime. When he heard it, he stopped and looked around, under the impression the "Cuckoo! Cuckoo!" was the voice of someone calling him.

Years ago, in the state of Michigan, the frame house where a friend of mine was born was moved intact to Henry Ford's museum at Dearborn. There it was exhibited as a typical midwestern home of the late nineteenth century. Some years afterwards, when my friend visited the museum, Henry Ford asked him if he would like to spend the night in his old home. The beds were made. Everything was just as he remembered it. So that evening he climbed the old, familiar stairs—now part of the permanent collection of a museum—and slept in the same bed in the same room he had occupied as a child.

Nellie and I experienced somewhat similar emotions during the days we stayed at the King's Arms, on the main street of Dorchester. We seemed to be in a museum of the past, but also where we had been before. The bow windows of our room looked out on the thoroughfare along which we had walked in Hardy's books. Directly below us was the room in which Michael Henchard was depicted as entertaining his friends in *The Mayor of Casterbridge*. Famous as a coaching inn on the great post road from Exeter to London, the King's Arms is the "Casterbridge Inn" of the Wessex novels.

According to reputation, the inhabitants of the region are independent, reticent, and set in their ways. But, so far as I could see, they are not particularly gloomy or melancholy. As I think back on those days, various people of Dorset come to mind—a woman with a dark, gypsy face selling apples at a fruit stall on market day; a countryman shouting to a deaf companion on a street corner:

"Know why the police never catch anybody? I'll tell you why! They won't listen to what you say. That's why!"

But most vividly of all I remember a chance encounter early one morning. On my way to buy a paper before breakfast, I met a woman wheeling a battered baby carriage filled with cauliflowers. Leaving it parked in a nook by the church across from the hotel, she filled her arms and started out to peddle the produce along the street. As she passed, she said in a low, rather sweet voice: "Good morning, Sir." She said it pleasantly but with overtones of deference that disturbed me for a long time. She seemed so subservient, so overwhelmed by life. I had the impression she was treading softly lest she disturb the vicious dogs of Fate. For a moment, I thought of buying a cauliflower, but I couldn't think what to do with it. Probably forty, thin, worn, once rather pretty, she seemed to have stepped from a Hardy novel.

At the top of the main street—which changes from High East Street to High West Street near the local museum

that houses such mementos of Hardy as the only watch he
ever owned—we found his statue. It shows him sitting in a
reflective mood. The bronze of which it is cast, perhaps by
intent, is a dark hue, almost black. Hardy's black moods,
his pessimistic outlook, have often been emphasized. But
another trait, underlying all others, was his immense compassion, compassion for all life. A violent revulsion to
cruelty runs through his writings.

In the margin beside his biographical entry in *Who's
Who*, he wrote in ink—as a facet of his life of special importance—his interest in the prevention of cruelty to animals. Throughout his life he remembered how he once re-
monstrated with a carter who was mercilessly beating his
mare and received the reply: "But she b'aint no Christian."
At the end of one of his most moving poems, "Afterwards,"
Hardy, thinking of such fellow dwellers on earth as hedgehog and moth, reflects that, when he is gone, someone may
say: "He strove that such innocent creatures should come
to no harm, but he could do little for them; and now he is
gone."

Sunday arrived—our last day in Dorset before moving on
to the New Forest. The sun shone warm; the sky was brilliant blue; the air was filled with the scents of spring. But
for Nellie it was a lost day. She spent it in bed fighting a
heavy cold. A little after mid-morning, I drove to Snail
Creep once more and joined the Skillings on their way to
services in the old stone church at the village of Stinsford,
the "Mellstock" of the Hardy novels.

As we came down the shaded path among storm-weath-
ered gravestones, the three bells of St. Michael's, the treble
dating back to 1461, pealed above us. All across the roof of
the church, where moss had gained a foothold in collected
dust, lines of green separated the old slates. Fruit trees, a
short way off beyond the surrounding hedge, rose in clouds
of pink and white. Their perfume enveloped us. In the peri-

odic, momentary silences of the bells, there carried from the hedge the small, sweet song of some unknown bird.

Inside, above our heads where we started down the aisle, a small balcony once projected. There musicians, including Thomas Hardy's father, played their instruments. A pervading chill, a residue of winter cold, clung to the interior of the stone structure. The warmth of one small electric heater extended but a few feet. The organist, an elderly man with a mane of white hair, played with a winter overcoat on and with the collar turned up around his ears. I envied him, for the cold seemed to rise from the stone floor. It seemed to descend from the stone walls. I crossed my arms, wiggled my toes, hugged myself, changed position. This was my introduction to a High Church service. With its frequent standing up and sitting down, it provided, on this day, comfort for the body as well as the spirit. It occurred to me that, perhaps, the universal chill inhabiting old stone churches and cathedrals for a large part of the year, especially in early times, had played a part in the evolution of the service.

On our right the spring sunshine flooded through the stained glass of a memorial window. It brought into the interior glowing, tinted light. Paid for by popular subscription, the window carries the words: "To the Glory of God and in Memory of Thomas Hardy." High on the opposite side of the church, a marble slab commemorates some family of importance in the 1700's. One name carved in the stone caught my eye. It was Angel Grey. How many times had Hardy's gaze wandered over that white memorial? How many times had it come to rest on this name, in all probability the source of Angel Clare in *Tess of the D'Urbervilles*?

Outside the church, after the service, beside the gravelled path, beneath the twilight-at-noontime shade of a wide-spreading yew, we stopped where the graves of the Hardy family are ranged side by side. Cut deeply into the front of one coffinlike horizontal tombstone is the sentence: "Here Lies the Heart of Thomas Hardy." Accompanied by a spadeful of Dorset earth, his ashes are buried in Westminster Abbey. But his heart lies amid these surroundings with which his whole life was connected. Fate, which often seemed so malign in Hardy's eyes, had placed him, by the accident of birth, in this spot where his unique powers had ample play, where he could record not only the tangled lives of human beings but the changes in a vast, brooding physical background—"the seasons in their moods, morning and evening, night and noon; winds in their different tempers, trees, waters and mists; shades and silences and the voices of inanimate things."

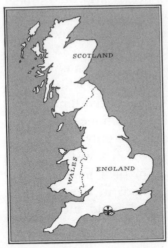

chapter 10

SPRING
IN THE
NEW FOREST

The New Forest, which has been "new" for nearly nine centuries, since the time of William the Conqueror, extends across a hundred square miles of lower Hampshire, occupying the land between Southampton Water and the Avon that flows down from Wiltshire. It is one of the five forests named in the Domesday Book and, long before the Normans, it formed the hunting ground of Saxon kings. Originally the term "forest" applied to any unenclosed tract where the hunting and game were reserved for the king, not necessarily to an area densely covered with trees. In medieval times, royal interest in woodland was confined largely to two things, venison and vert—in other words, to deer and wood.

It was on an afternoon of April sunshine that Nellie and I came down the long, straight Roman road that leads south through the forest to Lyndhurst, the "Linhest" of the Domesday Book. From this central town, the so-called capital of the New Forest, we radiated out, on subsequent days, through a region of picturesque place-names—Broomy

Stone avenue left by prehistoric men on Dartmoor

Walk, Holly Hatch, Marrowbones Hill, Red Shoot Wood, Withybed Bottom. It was also a region of venerable trees, immense beeches and ancient oaks. Some of the latter had stood fast against the wind for centuries before Shakespeare was born or the Pilgrims sailed from England or Wellington won at Waterloo.

Following the forest roads, among these noble trees, we contrasted the open expanses with the dense woodlands of home, with the dark, coniferous forests of northern Maine, the tangled mountain woods of the southern Appalachians, the moss-filled rain forests of the Olympic Peninsula, the still world of the titanic redwoods. We reviewed in our minds the varied and beautiful trees we had met in America—Monterey cypresses, wind-sculptured, clinging to the Pacific headlands, smoke trees in the desert washes, sycamores leaning out over midwestern creeks, the white pines and the sugar maples of the New England hills. Now, in a foreign spring, we were adding to that gallery of arboreal memories. Sometimes, as we traveled mile after mile among the largest of the ancient oaks and beeches, we felt as though we were in some remote time, like the knights of old that "rode all day endlong and overthwart a great forest."

There is, in the heart of the New Forest, an open glade through which a small stream wanders. We returned there often. Sunshine splashed the opening and streaked the smooth, gray trunks of the beeches, spotlighted the cushions of moss among the twisted roots, sparkled across the ripples of water and spangled with a glitter of lines and points the varnished leaves of the hollies. The air was warm and laden with the smell of forest mold. Along the moist brook edge, unrolling ferns lifted their fiddleheads like a maze of shepherds' crooks. Everywhere the trees rang with the singing of birds.

Around us, new leaves enveloped the beeches in clouds

Rookery, above. Swans at Piltdown, below

of palest green. And all along the fallen tree trunk on which we sat, the bark was warm in the rays of the sun. Sitting there, our gaze wandering down the forest aisles or ascending amid the airy green of the new beech leaves, warmed by the sun, surrounded by the voices of singing birds, we lost sight of the earlier weeks of rain and cold. We forgot the piercing wind of Dartmoor, the snowdrifts of the April blizzard. For around us now, in all its charm, spread the warm English spring.

It held, for us, the old and the new commingled. In general, this was the spring we had always known. The stage was familiar. But the cast was largely new. Blackbirds had replaced the American robins. A different nuthatch uttered the quick "whit-whit-whit" of its spring song. The bird that fluttered upward through the maze of treetop twigs was the wood pigeon, not our familiar mourning dove. A sulphur-hued butterfly drifted past, but it was not the sulphur butterfly we knew at home. Actors vary in the pageant of spring, but, no matter which side of the Atlantic they are on, they all respond in similar ways to the increasing light and warmth of the advancing season.

Twin bands of swampy lowland followed the edges of the brook. They were dense with the lush greenness of sap-filled growth. We gazed at them for several minutes, vaguely sensing that something was missing. Then we realized what it was. Nowhere did we see the broad leaves of the skunk cabbage, *Symplocarpus foetidus,* that prominent feature of every spring in eastern North America.

But it was mainly the birds we watched as, relaxed and warm, we rested on the fallen tree trunk. With sudden, explosive alarm notes, so like those of our robin, blackbirds dashed among the trees or flung themselves headlong into holly tangles. Over and over again, from its perch on the massive, ferny lower limb of an oak, a song thrush filled the glade with the clear repetitions of its carrying notes. Tits, those relatives of our little chickadee, flitted from twig to twig, hung upside down, cocked their heads and peered intently in their search for food. In one small, brownish bird, hitching itself up a tree trunk, we recognized an old friend, one we had seen in many a winter woods at home. To us it is the brown creeper; in England it is the tree creeper. But on both sides of the ocean its scientific name is the same, *Certhia familiaris*.

Sweeping our glasses from tree to tree, we added three new birds to our life lists in almost as many minutes. The first, a warbler, the blackcap, flitted about the top of a streamside willow—small, grayish brown, with a crown of shining black. Among the four kinds of tits that worked their way with sudden starts and stops among the branches around us—the blue tit, the coal tit, the great tit and the long-tailed tit—two we had never seen before. They were the coal, the smallest of the British tits, with a patch of white shining out on the back of its coal-black head, and the long-tailed, with a white head stripe and a pinkish flush on its flanks and belly. We hoped to see, but never did, the oval nest made by this latter bird. A work of art, formed usually of wool, moss, cobwebs, and lichens, it takes as long as a fortnight to complete. To form the soft lining of their nest, long-tailed tits may collect as many as 2,000 small and downy feathers.

Starting in the region of the New Forest in the 1940's, an epidemic of ripping paper and opening milk bottles by tits eventually extended through Britain as far north as Aberdeen, Scotland. I remember seeing a photograph, taken by Eric Hosking in 1950, that showed a great tit tearing up a telephone directory. On one occasion, twenty blue tits, entering through open windows, invaded the chapel at Winchester College and shredded papers and open books. Similarly, the birds rip open the metal-foil tops on milk bottles to drink the cream. On the main street of a Hampshire village we were puzzled by flat pieces of gray rock lying on each cottage doorstep. Then we saw the milkman making his rounds. Each time he left a bottle at a cottage door, he placed a flat rock on top of it. This prevented the paper-tearing tits from reaching the cream. Another time, in Kent, I saw several bottles with the tops torn and part of the cream gone on an open truck that had been left unattended for only a short time. Usually the bird punctures the cap by hammering with its bill, and then tears away strips of the foil. Three species of tits, the great, the blue, and the coal, are chiefly responsible.

In innumerable other instances, where food is not involved, these birds have been observed tearing paper. On more than 1,500 occasions tits have entered houses and torn off pieces of wallpaper. One blue tit hung upside down to rip away strips of the ceiling paper. Sometimes stamps have been removed from letters, seed packets shredded in greenhouses, notices ripped up on church porches. Newspapers and magazines, the dust jackets on books, and even ten-shilling notes have been torn up by the birds.

Why do they do it? The movements that tits make in tearing off paper are similar to those used in ripping away pieces of bark during their normal food-hunting activity. Yet the birds do not appear to be searching for food. In many instances they tear paper and ignore food nearby. Fully 80 per cent of those who reported tits invading houses and tearing paper said that they fed birds. In Britain, as in America, back-yard feeding trays have increased tremendously since the Second World War. It is R.S.R. Fitter's estimate that during the abnormally severe winter of 1962–1963, the lives of a million birds may have been saved by food put out by the housewives of Britain. In a curious way this increase in the feeding of birds and the tearing of paper by tits may be related.

For the tits find concentrated at feeders food they normally would have to hunt all day to discover. In consequence, the birds are left with surplus energy. They are like wound-up springs that have to unwind. The extra energy is being used up in activity similar to that of turning over and tearing off bark in the usual search for food. In a report to the British Trust for Ornithology, R. A. Hinde, of the Ornithological Field Station of the Department of Zoology at Cambridge University, points out that when food is superabundant, tits have been seen carrying off particles, dropping them, and returning for more. They continue their food hunting when they are no longer hungry. Their eating drive is satisfied, but their hunting drive is not. The paper-tearing of the tits, Dr. Hinde concludes, may provide a long-term advantage for the species in the continuation of hunting behavior after the bird is satiated. The abundant food-sources at feeding trays may be temporary, they may give out at any time and, in Dr. Hinde's words, "unless a general search is maintained in times of plenty, there will be a hiatus between exhausting one source and discovering the next."

Not infrequently in wandering through the New Forest we came upon treeless tracts, some of considerable extent. At this time of year they extended away in a golden sea of blooming furze. Among the trees, on several occasions our eyes followed upward the sinuous coils of wild grapevines. Were they descendants, we wondered, of those earliest grapes of Hampshire, introduced by the Romans? Lifting above the carpet of last year's leaves between the roots of a gigantic oak, a blue flower caught our attention. We bent to examine it—that first of all the millions of bluebells we were to encounter in subsequent weeks.

Wherever we went through the New Forest, I had the sensation of having been there before. For, in other years and thousands of miles away, I had gazed uncounted times on the fragment of this forest in the spring that forms one of the famous habitat groups at the American Museum of Natural History in New York City. With its birds, beeches, hollies, and bluebells it depicts a scene near Lyndhurst along the path followed by Theodore Roosevelt and Lord Grey during their walk on June 9, 1910. Returning from his African expedition, the year after leaving the White House, Roosevelt spent the day listening to the songs of the British birds. The two men went alone and, as Lord Grey recalls in a chapter in *Fallodon Papers,* "for some twenty hours we were lost to the world." Both agreed that the most beautiful voice they heard, the one with the most spiritual quality, was that of the blackbird. Amid all the spring chorus, Roosevelt recognized but a single voice. This was the thin, high-pitched, lisping song of the goldcrest, then called the golden-crested wren. This bird, *Regulus regulus,* is a close relative of, and very similar to, the golden-crowned kinglet of America.

Among the birds shown in that museum habitat group, the one above all others we longed to see in the open stretches of the New Forest was the elusive Dartford warbler, the "furze fairy" of W. H. Hudson's *Birds and Men,* a bird that is found in small and isolated pockets in the south of England. To see this elusive creature, to be able to say: "But *I* have seen the Dartford warbler"—this surely must rank high on the list of any foreign visitor who has first encountered this shy bird in Hudson's chapter. So it was with us.

In sunshine and mist and rain we sought the Dartford warbler. We searched for it early in the morning, at midday, at dusk. Over how many square miles of open heath, through how many hours of dark heather and yellow gorse we hunted! We knew its habits by heart. We could picture it vividly, skulking amid the furze. In imagination we could see it distinctly, fluttering from clump to clump, appearing and disappearing, cocking its tail, giving its musical chatter, hovering above the furze in the aerial dance of its song flight. But in the end, after days of searching, we knew its habits only from guidebooks, not from personal observation. We saw its actions through the eyes of others, not our own.

However, in this fruitless search, we met other creatures of the heaths. Wild ponies, still shaggy in their winter coats, loomed up suddenly before us in the mist. One we encountered several times was beaver brown with a white star on its forehead. Another, a white mare, nursed a coalblack colt. On all the forest roads, ponies have the right of way. Yet in some years more than 100 are killed in highway accidents. In the whole region, it is estimated, there are about 1,500 wild ponies. They are wild only in the sense that they roam at will through the New Forest. Often they wander down village streets. Numbers congregate on the edges of Lyndhurst. Several times we saw them feeding in yards. Before laws prohibited feeding them, they used to come to halted cars to eat sandwiches and candy offered by tourists. During older times, the ponies were sometimes seen prancing and leaping in secluded places, gamboling with the wild deer.

In the New Forest, as in the Forest of Dean, the introduction of American gray squirrels has upset the balance of nature. Now known as "tree rats," these "bannertails" of American woodlands are charged with the destruction of young trees, fruits, crops, and birds' nests. Since their arrival the lively little native red squirrel, associated with the New Forest for thousands of years, has virtually disappeared. Rabbits of the forest, like the red squirrels, have also nearly vanished, but from a different cause. West of Paris, at Dreux, France, in the spring of 1952, a physician, Dr. Armand Delille, introduced a virulent *myxomatosis* virus to reduce the number of rabbits on his estate. The epidemic that followed wiped out almost all the rabbits of

France and, by the fall of 1963, had crossed the channel into Kent and Sussex and worked its way west into Hampshire. At the time of our visit, the rabbit population was slowly gaining ground in the wake of the plague. We saw but few.

Referring to the rabbits of the New Forest, a writer in the eighteenth century observed: "A young oak, just vegetating from the acorn, is esteemed, by these pernicious inmates, the most delicious food. Thus it may be said, the glory of England may be nipped in the bud by a paltry rabbit." The author of these words was the Vicar of Boldre, the "master of the picturesque," William Gilpin. Another William, William Cobbett, who thought the most productive land the most beautiful, concluded in *Rural Rides:* "A poorer spot than this New Forest there is not in England; nor I believe in the whole world." Yet the more perceptive Vicar of Boldre filled two whole volumes describing the picturesque beauties of the region.

We came to the village of Boldre, on the southern fringe of the forest, when morning mist still clung to the trees that crowded close and imparted an air of woodland solitude to the squat, square church beside which Gilpin is buried. From his fifty-third to his eightieth year he served this church and its extensive parish. It was his habit—until advanced age forced him to ride a New Forest pony—to make his rounds on foot, carrying his lunch and a horn-cup with which to drink from wayside springs. A skilled artist and illustrator, famed as a critic of prints, biographer of religious reformers, once headmaster of the noted Cheam School, Gilpin, through his writings on scenery, molded the national taste and aroused new interest in the beauties of nature.

The scenery he called "picturesque" was the kind that would be "agreeable in a picture." He made the distinction between "such objects as are *beautiful,* and such as are *pic-turesque*—between those which please the eye in their *natural state;* and those which please from some quality capable of being *illustrated in painting.*" When Henry Thoreau was writing *Walden,* he read for the first time Gilpin's book on forest scenery. It was, he confided to his journal, a roomy book, "like a gladed wood." Its smooth-flowing text suggested "some of the cool wind of the copses converted into grammatical and graceful sentences." Oliver Wendell Holmes, comparing Gilpin and Gilbert White, concluded that Gilpin wrote with "a little less observation, but a little more poetry." His books perhaps find few readers today. I remember, some years ago, getting out at the New York Public Library one of his volumes that had been published in 1804. Many of its pages were still uncut. For 160 years it had waited for a first reader. I, who was born nearly a century after it appeared in print, had arrived to peruse it at last. During all those neglected years, it had been waiting —not waiting for me, but rather waiting for *anyone.*

Toward evening, on the final afternoon before we moved on, the weather turned chill. Clouds, pressing down dull and drab, extended their low ceiling over the forest. While Nellie remained snug at Lyndhurst, checking in field guides the identity of wildflowers she had seen, I rode south past Beachern Wood and over Lady Cross Walk to wander on Beaulieu Heath, where Dark Water begins its flow to the Solent. Wild ponies, those path makers of the New Forest, had laid out the serpentine I followed. It wound among dark waves of heather, to which, like a scattering of foam, clung the dry, whitish remnants of last year's blooming time. Wild and lonely—now near, now far—the double-noted call and the clear musical trilling of the curlew carried across the darkening plain. In the distance, like a cluster of small islands, yellow with furze, rounded hillocks lifted ten or fifteen feet above the level of the heather. These were the barrows of ancient men, the Pixie Mounds of Beaulieu Heath.

Pony trails led up their slopes. In sheltered nooks, pale midges danced in swarms. The furze rose in places above my head. Its wiry twigs clawed along my raincoat with a scratching sound abnormally loud in the intense stillness of the dusk. I looked around. Over there to the west, Beaulieu Wood, the setting of Conan Doyle's *The White Company*, stretched its low, black fringe along the horizon. Off to the east, unseen, lay Southampton Water. To the south, a new feature had been added to this ancient countryside. High plumes of flame and slender and lofty chimneys marked the location of the sprawling complex of a huge Esso refinery. The Pixie Mounds, the Roman road that runs by Beaulieu Heath, the twentieth-century refinery—these three bind together diverse ages of civilization embracing thousands of years.

Only the road and the tumuli were here on that June day, at the beginning of the present century, when W. H. Hudson, sitting among these same "mounds of the ancient dead," watched the sun go down and the twilight deepen and the stars come out, overcome by an intense feeling of closeness to those long, long dead, the "men who knew not life in towns, and felt no strangeness in sun and wind and rain." On another continent, under a winter sunset, on a ridge top overlooking sycamore trees and a winding creek in southern Ohio, I had known just such a sense of nearness to a long-ago time. On the summit of that ridge, a primitive race of now-forgotten men, the Mound Builders, had constructed a serpent of earth that extended away for a full quarter of a mile. Standing there in the silence under that flaming winter sky, I recalled the emotion Hudson had felt among these Hampshire tumuli. Now, standing at dusk among these same Old World tumuli, I remembered the sensation I had known beside the New World Serpent Mound. Thus recollection rounded the full circle.

As I walked slowly back along the path, beaten hard by the hoofs of the ponies, fluttering bats, with twists and turns, dives and climbs, gyrated in the dusk around me. The English area said to be richest in bats is this region around Southampton.

Some creatures survive largely through their sense of smell, others through their sense of taste, others through their keenness of sight. But few of all the species of the fauna of the world are more completely dependent on a single sense than earth's only flying mammal, the bat. Deprived of its hearing—which catches the faint echoes of the supersonic squeaks it emits and thus warns it of obstacles and leads it to its prey—the bat is lost and deprived of food. In its life, deafness and death are almost synonymous.

But that hearing upon which this winged mammal so completely depends has a capacity almost beyond our comprehension. The Swedish entomologist, Olaf Ryberg, while on a visit to America once told me of a pet bat he kept in his room as a boy. He remembered seeing a fly resting on a window sill while it cleaned its face with its forelegs. The bat, on the other side of the room, turned its head and pointed its ears, obviously listening. Then, darting directly to the fly, it snapped it up. The conclusion seemed unavoidable that its incredibly keen sense of hearing had caught the tiny, high-pitched squeaking sounds of the insect's legs scratching over its chitin shell. How altered would be our world, what new dimensions would expand around us, if we possessed the hearing of a bat.

The following morning, in one last search for the Dartford warbler, we were out before breakfast. In dense dawn mist, we wandered among the dripping clumps and thickets of gorse. Once we came face to face with a wild pony that materialized suddenly out of the fog. A little farther on, a large woodpecker shot past, appearing and disappearing abruptly within our restricted horizons. It alighted on some invisible tree close by and we heard its strident, flickerlike calling. In the glowing mist, as the sun rose higher, there seemed to be a small singing bird on every clump of furze. But none of them, no sight, no sound we heard, suggested a Dartford warbler.

However, some compensation came to us as we were returning home. A new sound, a longed-for avian voice, reached our ears. Mellow and repeated, it carried through the mist. In a lifetime first, we were hearing the "cooc-oo, cooc-oo, cooc-oo" of the bird so often mentioned in the prose and poetry of England. I happened to glance at my wrist watch. The hands pointed exactly to eight o'clock. For a moment I was uncertain. Were we hearing a real cuckoo or was it a cuckoo clock sounding the hour in some nearby cottage hidden in the mist? I counted the calls. They reached and passed the number eight. We were sure. The bird was real; the sound was authentic. We were encountering, at last, the call that men had listened for for ages before Chaucer, the sound that, each year, is looked forward to as the voice of the English spring.

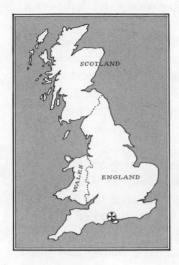

chapter 11

ARCHAE-
OLOGICAL
RABBITS

One late-September day, in the year 1942, a Hampshire farmer named Thomas Porter began digging out a ferret that was "lying up" in a rabbit hole on the edge of the village of Rockbourne. Following the descent of the burrow, he made the dramatic discovery that the rabbits had been unwitting archaeologists. Their tunnel led him downward to a buried Roman villa, more than eighteen centuries old.

In the earth he shoveled out, Porter noticed a number of oyster shells. They puzzled him. What were oyster shells doing so far from the sea? A few days later, when he showed them to A. T. Morley-Hewitt, of nearby Fordingbridge, this archaeologist recognized them at once. They were the shells of a type of oyster the Romans had raised at Poole harbor. At the time of this discovery, in 1942, the Second World War was at its height and, beyond an occasional week-end of digging, excavation was impossible. However, by the summer of 1944, a grid of trial holes, twenty-five feet apart, had revealed the presence of the buried remains of four Roman buildings that extended over a wide area.

Morley-Hewitt purchased the tract and in the mid-fifties began the painstaking work of unearthing his archaeological treasures. This exciting search was still in progress on the morning we drove—across a misty landscape, past a gypsy caravan encamped along a hedge, beside pasture fields strewn with the round knolls of tumuli—from the New Forest to Rockbourne.

If Cobbett could have lived "always" at Norton Bavant, it seemed to us we could have cast anchor in Rockbourne. This picturesque village lies halfway between the New Forest and the cathedral city of Salisbury. Its thatched cottages rise on either side of a clear chalk-country stream in which a multitude of slender-stemmed aquatic plants had burst into white bloom. In front of one of the cottages a boy of six or seven stood staring intently into the flowing water. He was watching, perhaps, some aquatic insect or the flowered plants waving in the current or some small fish stemming the stream. I drew up beside him and asked if he knew about the Roman villa. He did. He was an alert, intelligent boy and enthusiastically related some of the facts of its discovery and gave us simple directions for finding the spot where the work was in progress. We followed the stream-bank out of the village, turned right on a puddle-strewn track among trees and came out beside a low, weathered wooden building. It was the headquarters and museum of the excavation. With mounting excitement we climbed out of the car. Beyond the building we could glimpse piles of earth and the squares and rectangles traced by the remnants of Roman walls.

Once before in our wanderings, beside the valley of the Coln, north of Cirencester, in Gloucestershire, Nellie and I had visited the excavated ruins of a Roman villa. It, too, had been discovered through the burrowing of rabbits. The most famous feature of this Chedworth villa had been the tessellated floor of the main dining room. Its intricate design, depicting the four seasons, was formed of innumerable small blocks of varicolored stone, including purple rock from the Forest of Dean. At Chedworth every foot of the area had long since been excavated. There was a sense of all being completed about the exposed ruin, splendid as it was. But at Rockbourne all was active, nothing was final, the excitement and suspense of discovery still continued.

Here we arrived in the middle of the drama. The villa was taking shape, reappearing, emerging from the earth that had covered it for more than fifty human generations. Every spadeful of earth held the chance of some new discovery. Only the day before, a beautiful bowl, unbroken and unmarred, had come to light. Its design marked it as a product of a Roman pottery that once flourished in the heart of the New Forest. After a thousand years and more of lying unseen, buried in darkness, it had returned to the world of sunshine to be admired once more by men.

We found Morley-Hewitt in his field laboratory examining recent finds, objects of pottery, metal and stone, spread out on a long table. Solid-appearing, with graying hair, he proved courteous and helpful. For many generations, he told us, the area of the find had been used as the village cricket field. Only turf grew there. Thus the relics beneath the surface remained undisturbed by deep-probing roots of trees and bushes. During the early days of digging, portions of one tessellated floor appeared only eighteen inches below the grass.

"The villa," Morley-Hewitt explained," was evidently the mansion of a large farming estate. It was started probably early in the first century and was certainly occupied from the first century until after 500 A.D. Evidence suggests that its owner was a Roman official charged with collecting grain and wool from a wide area for shipment to the army."

In his work, Morley-Hewitt is aided by a band of volunteers who spend their spare time and week ends participating in the continuing adventure of the excavations. Prominent in this group were Mr. and Mrs. William A. Creeth. It was Mrs. Creeth who led us along the paths that thread among the ruins. At the time of our visit, the wall fragments of forty-six rooms—including a bath complex and a central heating system—had been uncovered. Now there are sixty-five, and digging still continues. These rooms are arranged around a courtyard, three sides of which have been excavated.

Just as in the Rockbourne cottages of today, the walls of the villa were formed largely of flintstone. During the intervening centuries, when the structures stood deserted, the walls provided a convenient source of building material and were demolished almost to floor level. Beside one remnant, diggers unearthed an antler pick. It indicated that natives of the region, after the decline of Roman civilization in Britain, reverted to the prehistoric use of deer antlers as picks and that such crude implements were employed in bringing down some of the walls.

Almost the exact time when other walls were destroyed has been established through the evidence of coins. A silver penny of Henry III, minted at Dublin in 1250–1251, was picked up among the remaining fragments of one wall. It is presumed to have been dropped by an Irish priest believed to have visited the spot in search of building material about 1258. In another instance, the archaeologists discovered among the rubble a silver half-penny of Richard II. It was dated 1380.

"What about Roman coins?" I wanted to know.

"We have found more than 500," Mrs. Creeth said. "They represent at least fifty different kinds. The commonest have been those of Constantius II, Constans, and Constantine I and II. We found sixty-seven of Constantius II and sixty-two of Constans. So many coins were scattered over the floor of Room X that we nicknamed it "the Treasury." It may have been used as the office where purchases of grain and wool were transacted."

On a later date, close to one of the walls, diggers unearthed a gray, two-handled pottery jar. It was about a foot high and was solidly packed with coins standing on edge. The hoard contained a total of 7,717 silver, silvered bronze, and bronze coins. They dated from the period 250–290 A.D. Because they provide evidence of dates and are long-enduring, coins are especially prized and valuable in archaeology. In the early 1960's, when a Roman well at the villa was filled in because of the danger of collapse of the old oak walls, a 1964 British penny was left among the timbers. It will provide a lasting record of the time of the present excavations. Who can guess when, under what circumstances, in what kind of a world, that penny will come to light again?

We moved from room to room among the ruins. Mrs. Creeth pointed out where remnants of plaster had revealed the grays and whites and purple-greens, the light blues and Pompeian reds that once decorated the walls. We paused beside a portion of the red-and-white tessellated floor of the main dining room where Romans had banqueted for more than four centuries. In one place, the imprint of a workman's sandals, with stud-marks, are still visible where they were left in the hardening construction material in those far-off days when the Rockbourne villa was new.

With heightened interest, at the far northwestern corner of the villa, we came to the room designated No. XX. It was here that Thomas Porter, on that September day, dug out his ferret. The effects of his shovel are still evident in the disturbed plaster and stones at the eastern edge of the room. This area was part of an elaborate bath complex that included a furnace room, a dressing room, a sun room, and

bathing rooms of various temperatures. Siphonage springs
provided pure water from the chalk downs for these bathing rooms. At one point in this area, a lead drain pipe,
two and a quarter inches in diameter, came to light. In ex-
cavating the site of the furnace room, diggers found a layer
of soot as much as twelve inches deep. Among the carbon-
ized material uncovered at the villa, scientists have identified the remains of oak, ash, hazel, alder, beech, and pine.

Such fuel produced the hot air that—in a remarkably
modern way—flowed in a central heating system beneath
the floors to warm the rooms. More than once Mrs. Creeth
called our attention to parallel rows of short columns or
squared pedestals that had supported the floors while providing open spaces through which the heated air could flow.

While the dwellers in the villa were thus warmed by hot
air beneath their feet, they were protected from wind and
rain above their heads by heavy, diamond-shaped stones
used as tiles to cover the roof. Through a small hole in the
upper point of its diamond shape, each stone was secured
in place by means of a nail. We examined several of these
primitive tiles where they stood propped against a small
shed. They seemed almost as thick and heavy as stones
from a sidewalk. To show visitors how the Roman tiles
were used, Morley-Hewitt anchored a number to the roof
of the shed. They were hastily taken down when it was discovered the building was about to collapse. Because of the
weight of the stones, expecially large and strong beams had
to be used to support the roof of the villa. The weight of
the roof of room III, alone, is estimated to have been eighteen tons.

On a subsequent day, somewhere in the south of England, Nellie and I passed a stone farm building apparently
of great age. The roof was covered with just such diamond-
shaped stones, probably removed from a Roman ruin generations before. When Morley-Hewitt and his helpers exca-

vated the room numbered XIV, they found the skeleton of a man lying on the floor. His back was broken. Stone tiles lay under and over him. Because his height was more than six feet, it is assumed he was not a Roman but rather some later dweller in the region who had been removing stone tiles when the roof collapsed.

A hundred feet beyond the far side of the exposed walls we saw four or five figures clad in raincoats. They were bending down, carefully removing earth, a little at a time, from the site of a fresh discovery where, the day before, the New Forest bowl had been uncovered. Several times they stopped work and huddled together, examining something extracted from the ground. Overhead the sky grew more murky. The wind increased. Then waves of cold rain dashed over the former cricket ground. We hurried to the shelter of the museum-headquarters. But the diggers, water streaming from their coats, worked on.

Within the museum, we were surrounded by the thousands of Roman relics the burrowing of rabbits had revealed. They covered shelves and weighted down tables and filled cases. In the hinges and latches and keys for locks, in plumb bobs of lead, rivets of bronze, clamps and lathe tools forged of iron, in shears and pruning hooks and plane blades, we saw evidence of the high state of Roman technological advance ten centuries before Columbus sailed for America. We examined forged nails of many sizes, all roughly square and some as long as eight inches. Mrs. Creeth handed us a safety pin made of bronze. Although it had lain in the ground through the Dark Ages, we found that its spring, formed of a coil at one end, was still strong. This safety pin of Roman times was as usable now as when it was new.

Surviving through all the events of a long succession of centuries, through the fall of the Roman Empire, the rise of Charlemagne and Napoleon, the settling of America, through two World Wars and the launching of man into space, bridging the gap between spears and atom bombs, the objects within this low wooden building stirred our imagination. In our present age we handled objects intimately connected with the daily life of men and women who had been familiar with these surrounding hills when the Roman Empire was at its height. Here were oil flagons and cooking pots, bone gaming counters, and the shards of drinking vessels broken who knows when? Here were hooks and buttons and buckles of bronze, a whetstone and candlesticks, fragments of leather sandals and a stylus for writing on wax tablets. We examined brooches of silver and earrings of decorated bronze that, long before Richard Cœur de Lion rode away on the Crusades, had adorned the women of Rockbourne. Holding fragments of ancient windowpane up to the light, we noticed the colors ranged from blue-green through white to almost transparent glass. Half a million times the sun had risen and set over Hampshire since those fragments had been part of the windows of the villa.

The kitchen middens of Rockbourne have yielded such remnants of long-ago meals as fishbones and the shells of mussel, whelk, and cockle. When we looked at one oxbone, Mrs. Creeth pointed out marks that have been identified as those produced by human teeth. Bones of farm and household animals, of sheep and goats, oxen, cats and dogs, have been unearthed near the villa. We held in our hands the beak of a raven whose last croaking call fell on Roman ears. At the upper end of the list of bones recovered is the complete skull of a Roman ox. At the lower end is the skull of a mouse. Because both mice and rabbits are burrowers, the bones of these animals found in the ruins are presumed to be modern. Amazingly, even so fragile an object as an eggshell is numbered among the recovered items.

"One feature of the villa that puzzled us at first," Mrs.

Creeth recalled, "was a clay-lined pool. Its purpose was a mystery. Now we have decided it was used for storing live oysters brought inland from Poole harbor."

Among the Romans, these shellfish were a favorite food. As soon as the legions were established in Britain, oyster beds were set out along the Channel coast. The most famous of these, at Whitstable, where the East Swale River joins the Thames estuary in Kent, has been under continuous cultivation for at least 2,000 years.

Oyster shells predominate among the relics retrieved from the kitchen middens at Rockbourne. During the excavations they were unearthed in large numbers. Before we left, Mrs. Creeth presented us with one of these long-buried links with Roman days. It lies on my desk beside me, here on another continent, as I bring this chapter to a close. With white layers weathered and edges crumbling, it meets my eyes on a day in February as, on a day in September, other shells, amid excavated earth, had met the eyes of Thomas Porter at the place of his archaeological discovery.

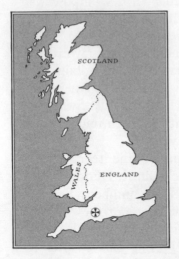

chapter 12

SKYLARKS AT STONEHENGE

Three rivers of the chalk country, the Nadder, the Bourne, and the Wiltshire Avon, meet among the water meadows of Salisbury. Above the meadows, above the rivers, above the city rises the soaring spire of Salisbury Cathedral. We saw it far in the distance as we came north from Rockbourne. We saw it lifting almost directly above us, foreshortened against the sky, as we walked in the cathedral close. We saw it in sunshine beneath drifting clouds, as Constable painted it on one of his most famous landscapes. And we saw it black and two-dimensional, in silhouette against the stars, at night. The immense structure beneath it, at once graceful and imposing, beautiful in form and setting, remains in our minds as the most impressive of all the many cathedrals we saw.

Daisies—always the daisies—bloomed in a scattering across the lawn. Daws—always the daws—rode the tumbling shift of air currents along the stonework of the walls and spire. Blackbirds and song thrushes sang in the trees, just as other blackbirds and song thrushes had sung in the spring through all the years while the oldest clock in England, now housed within the cathedral and still in working order—a clock constructed nearly 600 years ago in medieval days—had ticked an estimated 500,000,000 times. So, too, blackbirds and thrushes had sung while the great block of granite at the entrance door had been hollowed out by the shuffling feet of centuries.

Several times that night, we looked out of our window at the dark spire lifting more than 400 feet into the air, with a tiny red aircraft warning light at its tip. After weeks of shrouded nights, the sky was ablaze with stars. We saw old, familiar constellations. But we saw them shifted, displaced in the heavens. The Great Wain of Europe, the Big Dipper of America, was riding high toward the zenith instead of circling low near the horizon. Such changes in the night sky recorded our more northerly position on the globe.

The red warning light was out and the cathedral spire was tipped with sunshine, next morning, when we walked along the ancient streets of Salisbury. Once it was a Roman town with the Roman name of Sarum. By nine, we were following the Avon upstream onto the vast Salisbury Plain, "the heart of the Wiltshire loneliness." For twenty miles, it stretches west from the Avon, an undulating, open expanse with an average elevation of between 400 and 500 feet above sea level. Large areas, now controlled by the War Department, are devoted to training maneuvers. Few are the streams and few are the villages on this almost treeless plain. John Evelyn, for all his love of trees, found delight in this open land. Writing in the seventeenth century, he described it as: "that goodly plaine or rather Sea of Carpet, which I think for evenesse, extent, verdure, innumerable flocks, to be one of the most delightful prospects in nature."

Like swallows feeding on the wing, we swooped and climbed continually as we rode over the rise and fall of this

billowing land. Under such conditions we reached the brow
of an elevation and there below us, suddenly, unexpectedly,
just as we had seen it in a thousand pictures, lay the gray
circle of Stonehenge. Other visitors in a long procession—
Romans, Danes, Normans—had come across these same
waves of land to marvel at this wonder of ancient Britain.
Ever since its erection, more than fifteen centuries before
the birth of Christ, Stonehenge has stirred the imaginations
of men.

It has also teased and mystified their minds. Many have
been the surmises regarding this production of prehistoric
men. As Henry James put it, Stonehenge "stands as lonely
in history as it does on the great plain." Early writers attributed its construction to Merlin, the wizard of King Arthur's
court. Others suggested it was built by the legendary inhabitants of Lost Atlantis. It has been called a temple of sun
worshippers. Because of the numerous barrows in the region, it has been assumed that it was erected in honor of
dead heroes of the ancient past. Although it antedates the
earliest records of Druids in Britain by more than a thousand years, a widespread belief prevailed for many years that
it was erected by this ancient order to form the spectacular
stage on which human sacrifices were offered up during
pagan rites. Through the centuries, suggestions have been
many, while proof supporting those suggestions has been
slight. Samuel Pepys, who visited the giant stones on June
11, 1668, concluded in an entry in his diary: "God knows
what their use was!"

Recently Gerald S. Hawkins, British-born Professor of
Astronomy at Boston University and Research Associate of
the Harvard College Observatory in America, has presented
a new explanation in key with the scientific outlook of
today. His conclusion, arrived at with the aid of modern
computers, is set forth in *Stonehenge Decoded*, published
in 1965. It has long been known that the axis of Stone-

henge is arranged to point toward the sunrise on the longest day of the year. More than this, Hawkins has discovered, each significant stone in the whole aligns with some other stone or stones to point toward some special position of the sun or moon. The lines of the summer-solstice sunrise and moonset or sunset and moonrise here represent an angle of ninety degrees. This feature occurs on the earth's surface only at the latitude of Stonehenge. To Hawkins the great stone circle on Salisbury Plain, that mysterious handiwork of prehistoric men, represents a primitive but remarkably complex astronomical observatory.

We parked our car in a fold in the green downs and walked toward the titanic circle of the Sarsen stones. Shadows of drifting clouds came sliding toward us, tilting this way and that over the uneven ground. They briefly enveloped us in shade, then moved deliberately on. The rays of the midday sun fell almost vertically down the length of the upright stones, bringing out in sharp detail the texture of the sandstone, the patches of lichen, black and sulphur-yellow, even the marks left by the hammers of the prehistoric workmen who, more than thirty centuries before, had shaped and smoothed the stones from immense blocks of Sarsen sandstone—Eocene sand cemented by silica—found on the Marlborough Downs, twenty miles to the north.

Without wheels, without beasts of burden, without ropes except rawhide, the men of the Bronze Age had transported thirty such stones, each weighing twenty-five tons or more, across those miles of rising and falling plain and had erected them in an upright position in exact relation to each other on this Wiltshire hilltop. Fifteen hundred men, it is estimated, took ten years to accomplish this formidable task with sledges and rollers and with as many as 100 men at a time pulling on rawhide cables. Among the stones enclosed within the Sarsen ring there was originally a second ring of blue stones, sixty in number and each weighing be-

tween 11,000 and 14,000 pounds. They have been traced to
the Prescelly Hills of Wales, 140 miles to the west. It
was not necessary to cut and shape these blue stones. Nature had split them into blocks on the high, bare peak
called Carn Meini. But the clearing of roads among the
mountains, the building of sledges and the construction of
rafts, and the transporting of the seven-ton blocks by land
and water over a distance of perhaps 200 miles must have
required the combined effort of thousands of men over a
long period of time. Thinking of the enormous labors of
those Neolithic years, we looked off to the north, toward
Marlborough Downs; away to the west, toward Carn Meini.

And what of the stones, dolerite and sandstone, brought
with so great an effort to this lonely spot—what of them
today? Of the thirty original members of the Sarsen Circle,
only sixteen remain upright; and of the original thirty seven-ton lintels capping these vertical stones, but six are still
in place. Some of the Sarsen stones were thrown down as a
result of edicts of the early Church ordering the destruction
of heathen monuments. Others fell in consequence of extensive digging around their bases in the Middle Ages when
it was believed treasure was buried there. In this chalkland
where hard rock is at a premium, Stonehenge was considered to be a kind of quarry. Many of the bluestones were
broken up and used in road building long ago. In more recent years, the stones were chipped and marred by visitors.
At one time, shops in Amesbury rented hammers to those
who wished to knock off fragments to take home as keep-
sakes. Such destruction is now a thing of the past. The
stones of Stonehenge are carefully protected under the ju-
risdiction of the National Trust.

When Charles Darwin was conducting his experiments
with earthworms, he became interested in the part played
by those lowly creatures in the slow sinking into the ground
of the prostrate Sarsen stones. Investigation showed that

their burrowing weakened the supporting material beneath these heavy stones while their castings gradually raised the level of the ground around them. On this spring day, beside the same fallen stones, now almost a century older, we saw a new installment of those castings left on recent nights by earthworms. These contemporaries of prehistoric men were continuing the same slow, deliberate changes they had wrought during all the centuries since Stonehenge came into being.

In *English Hours*, Henry James comments, in recalling Stonehenge: "I can fancy sitting all a summer's day watching its shadows shorten and lengthen again." And so one could. But not on a chill April day like ours. The wind, like the wind of Dartmoor, swept unimpeded across the downs under the polished sky. It seemed to pierce us with its cold through and through. In this abnormally moist and chill English spring, there were many times when we felt the cold as keenly as we had during most of our coast-to-coast journey through the American winter. Here at Stonehenge we were reminded of the particularly bone-piercing quality of the gusts that swept across the Staked Plains of the Texas Panhandle. We walked rapidly to keep our blood in circulation or rested behind the upreared stones where the sunshine fell warm on sheltered places. Far above us, an almost invisible plane droned across the sky, the sound of its jet engines coming down to us like the voice of a new age. Another voice, older and nearer, reached us from the top of the Sarsen stones. There house sparrows—those commonplace but surprising birds that possess twice as many neckbones as a giraffe and that, according to Edward A. Armstrong's *Bird Life*, in emergencies have been known to transport their young from place to place in their bills— chirped continually as they searched for nesting sites in crevices under the lintels.

On the 28th of November, in the year 1768, Gilbert

White was writing to his friend, Thomas Pennant, on the habits of jackdaws. "Another very unlikely spot is made use of by daws to breed in," he reported, "and that is Stonehenge. These birds deposit their nests in the interstices between the upright and the impost stones of that amazing work of antiquity: which circumstance alone speaks the prodigious height of the upright stones, that they should be tall enough to secure those nests from the annoyance of shepherd-boys, who are always idling round that place." Almost two centuries later, we saw jackdaws circling and flying low over Stonehenge. Only a few years before, the nesting daws had become so numerous and troublesome that, for a time, all the crevices they frequented were blocked with fine wire mesh.

It is another bird, however, or more particularly the voice of another bird, that predominates in our memories of Stonehenge. On all sides of us, everywhere above the rich green of the luxuriant turf, hundreds of skylarks filled the air with their music. Wherever we looked, the larks were rising and descending or hanging on quivering wings against the vast backdrop of blue sky and drifting clouds. We followed one bird with our eyes while its diminishing form contracted until, in the end, it seemed no larger than a bumblebee. Each lark hovered above its own territory. When it alighted, it usually vanished, its striped plumage well camouflaging it on the ground. How many thousands of larks, undeterred by the chill of the wind, were singing that day above the length and breadth of the Salisbury Plain?

In older times, these singing larks were highly esteemed as a table delicacy. Thomas Fuller—friend of Izaak Walton and once Prebendary of Salisbury Cathedral, author of *Good Thoughts in Bad Times* and *Good Thoughts in Worse Times*, as well as that classic, *The Worthies of England*—reflects the outlook of the seventeenth century when he writes concerning the skylark: "A harmless bird whilst living, not trespassing on grain, and wholsome when dead, then filling the stomach with meat, as formerly the ear with music." Even today, the larks are shot for food in some European countries. In the south of France, for example, mirrors on whirling arms are sometimes employed to catch the attention of the hovering birds and lure them close to waiting gunners.

As early as January, the singing of skylarks begins in England. It reaches its peak during the latter months of spring but continues, off and on, throughout the year. Even in the short days of December, these birds may burst briefly into song. In the music of the skylark there is something of the same bright exuberance found in the singing of bobolinks over New England meadows. But the voice of the bobolink is more metallic, like the jingling of coins; that of the skylark more bubbling and liquid. Tolstoy, writing in *War and Peace*, describes skylarks springing up one after the other "like bubbles rising to the surface of water."

Wherever we walked at Stonehenge—along the encircling bank and ditch or by the so-called Aubrey holes or beside the upright, tilting heelstone—the joyous sound of larks poured down around us. This was our skylark spring. We were never beyond their voices even after we returned along the path to the parking field and rode away across the open miles of the plain toward the north. Only when the day had ended, after we reached the Great West Road that crosses Wiltshire far to the north of Stonehenge, did the singing of the larks diminish in volume. I remembered the old Dorset poet, William Barnes, and his line describing birds of the night "going abroad when the lark goes home." At times, during the nesting season, however, larks continue singing far into the hours of darkness and often they are on the wing as much as two hours before the break of dawn.

Along the Great West Road, next day, Nellie and I found ourselves among other relics of the ancient past. We crossed the Ridgeway, the prehistoric "green road" followed by the feet of Neolithic men. We came to remnants of the Wansdyke, a defensive wall of earth that, in Saxon times, extended sixty miles east and west. And turning aside to Avebury, we arrived at another ring of giant stones, older than Stonehenge.

As we walked about in the sunshine among its irregularly shaped "gray wethers" or chunks of Sarsen sandstone such as still lie scattered on Marlborough Downs, now only a couple of miles to the northeast, black-and-white cows grazed on the grass around us. They fed in prehistoric pastures. The very rocks they rubbed against had been raised and anchored in place by men of the New Stone Age. The great ring of Avebury, a ring so large it encloses most of the village of that name, originally consisted of more than 100 stones. No effort was made to shape or dress the rocks as was done at Stonehenge. This circle, about twenty miles north of Stonehenge, was the product of a ruder civilization. It formed, it is believed, a primitive outdoor temple that was known throughout Britain long before the first word of written history had been set down in Europe. By tracing to their sources the various rocks represented in stone axes unearthed at the site, archaeologists have deduced that those who attended the ancient ceremonies included pilgrims from Wales and Cornwall and even from the north of England almost as far as the Scottish border.

Even more remote in time were the men who shaped three giant concentric rings of earth on Windmill Hill, that dome of chalk which rises 115 feet above the surrounding plain a mile and a half north of Avebury. These Windmill Hill People formed the earliest known community of the Neolithic farmers who colonized southern England from the continent about 2,400 years before the birth of Christ.

The earthwork enclosures are thought to have been used as cattle pounds into which prehistoric herds were rounded up in autumn.

The side road that led us toward Windmill Hill soon became, as a sign succinctly put it: "Unsuitable for Motor Vehicles." On foot we reached the summit. Far prospects of the Wiltshire downs spread away in the sunshine. We could see the red-brick cluster of buildings within the circle at Avebury. We could see Lilliputian automobiles creeping down the Great West Road. We could see a field of vast extent, newly harrowed, where shadings in the soil mimicked a landscape dappled with sunshine and cloud-shadow. Pollen samplings from the earth at Windmill Hill have convinced scientists that in the days of its primitive occupants the downs were less open, more wooded, largely with a growth of hazel.

Among the curving ditches and embankments where we walked, earthworks produced so long ago with the aid of deer-horn picks and shovels made from the shoulder blades of cattle, innumerable relics of the Stone Age have been unearthed. Among such knives and saws and axes and spearheads of flint, archaeologists have found curious objects of chalk bearing cryptic markings and abstract designs. They are thought to be amulets for warding off evil, part of the ritual and magic that surrounded the lives of ancient men. More than forty centuries ago, the eyes of such men looked away from Windmill Hill. They saw the same rolling land stretching to the horizon. But for them it was filled with invisible forms, with omens and portents based on beliefs now lost to memory.

In a famous paragraph in *The Golden Bough*, Sir James G. Frazer emphasizes the chasm that divides us from the outlook of primitive man. "In attempting to track his devious thought through the jungle of crass ignorance and blind fear," he writes, "we must always remember that we are treading enchanted ground, and must beware of taking for solid realities the cloudy shapes that cross our path or hover and gibber at us through the gloom. We can never completely replace ourselves at the standpoint of primitive man, see things with his eyes, and feel our hearts beat with the emotions that stirred his. All our theories concerning him and his ways must therefore fall short of certainty; the utmost we can aspire to in such matters is a reasonable degree of probability."

Like the earthworms still tunneling through the soil at Stonehenge, a contemporary of the Windmill Hill People was still burrowing through the earth all across the green dome of this great knoll of chalk. Even on the embankments and in the ditches, the working of moles was evident. Unlike our American burrowers, these animals produce no shallow, wandering tunnels that push up the surface of the ground. The only evidence we saw of their presence was numerous mounds of earth. Most of the molehills we examined were about a foot across. The range of this European burrower, the *Talpa europaea* of Linnaeus, with its subspecies, extends from Finland to Italy and from Britain to Siberia. The restricted individual range of the average mole is confined to an area having a diameter of only from thirty to 150 feet.

We stood among these small mounds on the greater mound of Windmill Hill, considering the strange existence of their makers—a life with a span of about three years, lived almost entirely in darkness, aided by a sense of smell so feeble that it is useful only at distances of an inch or two; by a voice limited to a weak twitter and a small squeak; by a rudimentary sense of sight, but by a sense of touch so abnormally keen that it detects the slightest vibration of the ground. As is the case with all such animals— moving forward and backward in their tunnels—its thick fur will lie flat in either direction. At one time, the soft,

Furze on the Dorset heath

black, velvety pelt of the mole was prized for making coats.

In thousands of fields along our route, we observed the mounds produced by these burrowers. Once we rode between two wide pastures, one strewn from end to end with molehills; the other, separated only by the width of the road, containing no more than a dozen. Sometimes we saw whole meadows bumpy with old mounds of the rich, upthrust earth, now densely covered with grass. A century ago it was a common custom to collect soil brought up by moles and add it to flower gardens. In his journal, John Clare, the peasant-poet of Northamptonshire, recorded on Tuesday, January 11, 1825: "Began to fetch maiden earth from molehills for my flower beds."

In spite of the fact that moles thus bring fresh earth to the surface, that they drain and plow and aerate the soil, and consume enormous numbers of injurious insect larvae, they undoubtedly cause great damage in farming and dairy country. For centuries, professional mole catchers were a familiar feature of rural life in England. Gone today is this ancient profession. As we passed one Wiltshire fence, on a later day, we saw dangling from the topmost wire a long row of dead moles. Just so, we had seen jackrabbits and coyotes suspended on barbed-wire fences in the range country of New Mexico and Texas. Hanging up moles apparently is an ancient custom in many parts of England. George Eliot describes how these animals were nailed to the walls of *The Mill on the Floss*.

The small mole-made mounds at our feet on Windmill Hill are separated from the largest man-made mound in Europe by a straight-line distance of hardly two miles. We passed the latter—Silbury Hill—on our way back to Calne, where we spent our nights in an old coaching inn that dated from Shakespeare's time and that had a longbow, such as was used at Agincourt, hanging in its lower hall. Silbury Hill we saw again next morning when we returned

New Forest pony, above. Thomas Hardy's birthplace, below

along the Great West Road on our way to Savernake Forest. Visitors, climbing this artificial hill of chalk, 135 feet high and 522 feet across its base, were silhouetted against the sky. Gulls soared in the updrafts above it, and skylarks rose from the grass all up its long ascent. The line of the Roman road, which the modern highway follows, makes a sharp jog around the hill. For the mound was old when the Romans came. It is believed to be as ancient as Stonehenge. In its creation, how vast was the expenditure of human energy! Year after year, its Neolithic builders, digging out rubble with crude tools, transporting it little by little up the steep slope in primitive baskets, had shaped this enduring monument to their tenacity. Still uncertain is the precise purpose of all those titanic labors.

When we came to the outskirts of Savernake Forest, south of Marlborough—once the private hunting ground of Henry II—we entered a different Wiltshire. Woodland aisles replaced the open downs. Undulating fields gave way to damp, secluded glades, noted for their fungi. We wandered in the same mossy realm of ancient oaks and beeches that W. H. Hudson had roamed in another springtime, "forgetting the world and myself in its endless woods."

Around us, as around him, spread all the fresh beauty of the awakening season. I remember especially the edge of one open space in the forest. It was golden with the flowers of coltsfoot blooming at the top of scaly stems rising from perennial creeping roots. Later, with their white, woolly undersides, the large leaves unroll. Flowers first, leaves later— this reversal of the coltsfoot is a regular feature of its spring. In another opening among the trees we encountered an old botanical friend. We had seen it last, the previous autumn, shedding the silvery fluff of its parachuted seeds beside Sandy Stream, near Slidedown Mountain, in the forest of far-northern Maine. This was the willow-herb. Because of its rapid growth in burned-over areas, it is also known as fireweed.

Savernake Forest, on that day, had numerous other things to show us. And the one who saw them first was usually Nellie. This was her day. Almost invariably she looked in the right direction at the right time to see the new. It was she who noticed a nuthatch varying its usual procedure by hopping over the ground searching for food among the mossy roots of the beech trees. And when we stopped along Grand Avenue, that ruler-straight Roman road that roughly bisects the 4,000 acres of the forest, it was she who caught sight of our first great spotted woodpecker. It was hitching itself up a barkless branch in a dead treetop almost directly over our heads. A striking black-and-white bird, it is about the size of America's hairy woodpecker. It bounded off through the air, and we glimpsed the two distinctive fieldmarks revealed in flight, prominent white patches on its wings and crimson beneath its tail.

The days were noticeably lengthening now. Toward sundown we looked back from the Great West Road as we were going home. Mist caught among the branches imparted a curious layered appearance to portions of the forest. Low above the trees, the last of our Savernake birds flapped on its deliberate way—a heron, buoyant on three-foot wings, flying toward some secluded pool or woodland stream or lowland swamp to engage in its evening fishing.

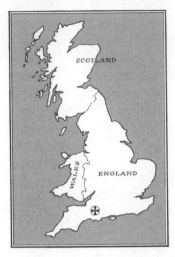

chapter 13

WHITE HORSE HILLS

In 1883 more than half the acreage of England and Wales was owned by 4,217 people. Did any of these wealthy and powerful possessors of so many millions of acres ever know, during any moment of all their lives, that intense emotional response to the land that was the lifelong passion of the Wiltshire farmer's son who, poor and ill, in that same year, 1883, penned the incomparable pages of "The Pageant of Summer"?

"I had no desire to make money or excel in anything," Richard Jefferies once recalled. "All I cared for and desired was the fields, the hills, the sea, the coast." Again he declared: "It is enough to be on the grass in the shadow of green boughs, to listen to the songs of summer, to drink in the sunlight, the air, the flowers, the sky, the beauty of all, or among the hilltops to watch the white clouds rising over the curved hill-lines, their shadows descending the slope, or on the beach to listen to the sweet sigh as the smooth sea runs and recedes." And again: "I do not want change; I want the same old and loved things."

Richard Jefferies—christened John Richard Jefferies—
was born on November 6, 1848, at Coate Farm, near Swindon, in Wiltshire. He died on August 14, 1887, at Goring,
on the Sussex coast. Like John Keats and Henry Thoreau
—whose lives also were short but intensely lived—he succumbed to tuberculosis. The thirty-eight years of his span
on earth were less than half those allotted to Gilbert White
or Izaak Walton. Many have speculated on what he might
have accomplished if he had been given the health and leisure and length of life of these happier men. In one of his
last notebooks, Jefferies wrote that three giants had been
ranged against him—disease, despair, and poverty.

Yet he left behind, as the harvest of his less than four
decades of life, enduring volumes: *The Story of My Heart,
Bevis, Wild Life in a Southern County* and especially such
collections of his highly individual nature essays as *The Life
of the Fields, Nature Near London, Field and Hedgerow,*
and *The Open Air.* Under the pressure of a life precariously
supported by his pen, he sometimes wrote in headlong
haste, with no opportunity for careful revision. There are,
moreover, pages that seem part of an inventory of the out-
of-doors, a running catalogue of its various sights and
sounds. But at his best—in such essays as "The Pageant of
Summer," "Outside London," "The July Grass," and
"Hours of Spring"—his paragraphs become a pure distillation of the freshness of nature. The sunshine and the rain,
the perfume and song of long-gone days live on in them.

"A July fly went sidewise over the long grass. His wings
made a burr about him like a net, beating so fast they
wrapped him round with a cloud." Those beginning words
of "The July Grass" were the first of Jefferies' I ever read. I
encountered them far from Wiltshire and many years ago.
They, like most that he wrote, held a mirror up to nature.
To the end of his life, Jefferies kept growing. His mind ripened into its finest fruit during those last bitter years when

his only sight of nature was through an invalid's window, when its richness and sweetness was lost to all but memory. "The hours when the mind is absorbed by beauty," he wrote in his illness, "are the only hours when we really live, so that the longer we can stay among these things, so much the more is snatched from inevitable Time. This is the real life, and all else is illusion, or mere endurance." Of Richard Jefferies, as a writer, the critic George Saintsbury once expressed the opinion that his importance for posterity would dwindle. Possibly so. But not, it seems to me, unless in some future time the appeal of all nature writing dwindles in a dominantly urban world.

When we came north from the Great West Road and reached the little village of Coate, we found that Swindon —which has more than doubled its size in intervening years —had thrust a long tentacle, bordered on either side by red-brick houses set close together, almost to the village and the farm where Jefferies was born. Coate Water, the lake of *Bevis*, is now a public bathing place. The passing of "inevitable Time" had also left its mark on the white stone road marker in the village. We bent close, unable to make out the number of miles to London, once cut deeply into the stone, now all but weathered away.

Ditches and lines of pollard trees and scraggly hedges running along the boundary lines of farms cut across the flat land of the fields around. They lay in a wide valley bounded by the steep lift of rolling hills. To us the scene held no more of interest or charm than countless other views in rural England. Yet this commonplace spot had nurtured a Richard Jefferies. It was here that he had "mooned about" over these fields and hills, lonely, misunderstood, out of step with his time and his farmer father, who was wont to point with disgust to "our Dick poking about among them hedges." Rather than beauty of the surrounding scene, it was inner sensitiveness that accounted for Jefferies' emotional response to nature. In fact, he seems to have had only a slight attachment for this countryside of his youth. He left it soon after his marriage to a neighboring farmer's daughter, at the age of twenty-seven, and returned but twice for short visits during the rest of his life. However, it was here, on this foothold of earth among the Wiltshire hills, that the inner fire that still warms his pages was first ignited.

During most of his earlier years, Richard Jefferies was a devotee of blood sports. But as time went on he became less the killer and more the observer of wildlife. "The watching," as he put it in one of his later essays, "so often stayed the shot that at last it grew to be a habit: the mere simple pleasure of seeing birds and animals, when they were quite unconscious that they were observed, being too great to be spoiled by the discharge."

It was in Jefferies' "Haunts of the Lapwing," the open country of Wiltshire, that we first became intimately acquainted with this striking and beautiful plover. Our initial close-up view came on a morning after a night of rain. The bird, about the size of our killdeer, stood beside a puddle in a muddy side lane. We saw it in a double view. For its snowy underparts, its black breast, its slender, flowing crest all were reflected in the mirror of the water. Seen under overcast skies, a lapwing appears black and white. In brilliant sunshine, however, blendings of metallic green shot with purple sweep across the dark plumage of its back and sides.

The lapwing is a bird that—like the black vulture of the southern United States—can be recognized as far as it can be seen by its individual manner of flight. Its wings are bluntly rounded, at times appearing almost rectangular. A curious veering, flapping, butterfly-like flight characterizes its advance over the spring downs.

"It might be called a flapwing," Nellie observed.

However, it is from a sound rather than from a movement that the bird derives its name. During the violent twists and turns of the spring display flights, the wings of the male give off a loud throbbing or "lapping" sound, somewhat similar to that of a small flag fluttering in the wind. In the exuberance of mating time, males have been known to perform somersaults and fly on their backs while calling.

Now, in the springtime of the year, wherever we went in open country we were thrilled by the aerial displays of the lapwings. I remember once we passed a football match being played in a corner of a pasture on the edge of a country village. Not far from the players a flock of sheep lay on the grass like closely packed spectators, while behind them the sharply contrasting dark-and-light form of a lapwing gyrated in the aerobatics of its mating time. We were also to see the erratic shifts and sudden wing-overs and sheer plunges of lapwings harrying marauding rooks all the way up through the Midlands, among the Norfolk broads, in the Lake District, and far north among the mountain meadows of Scotland. Lapwings nest only in open country, only where the vegetation is short enough for them to see over it and detect the approach of intruders before they can be seen. Throughout Britain, since 1926, when the passage of the Lapwing Protection Bill made it illegal to collect the eggs for market, these wild and beautiful birds have increased in number.

Tacking this way and that over the Wiltshire map, always in lapwing country, we moved through a population explosion of lambs. They filled miles of pastures with their bleating. One morning we paused beside a harrowed field stippled with white clods of chalk. Across it were scattered more than 1,000 wood pigeons feeding on newly sprouted grain. On another day, we walked for a time in a small West Country churchyard among old gravestones, gray with lichens, green with moss, slowly wasting away. Among them might have been the original tombstone of Walter De la Mare's poem, marking the grave of "the most beautiful lady that ever was in the West Country." In this small Wiltshire burying ground, the final lines came back: "But beauty vanishes . . . however rare, rare it be; and when I crumble who shall remember that lady of the West Country?" In former years, in how many places in America had those same words been brought to mind by varied fleeting forms of loveliness, by the changing clouds of a summer sky, the shimmer of light on a dragonfly's wing, sunset tintings on the winter snow. They, too, had swiftly come and gone. And now—like De la Mare's epitaph—my mind alone preserved the memory of their beauty, vanished long ago.

Through Wiltshire, and in neighboring Berkshire, white horse hills form a dramatic feature of the chalk-country landscape. The immense silhouettes of the animals, visible miles away, occupy steep green slopes, usually within the curve of an amphitheater among the downs. Some are the work of ancient men. Others are of more recent origin. All have been produced by stripping away the vegetation and exposing the glaring white chalk beneath. The first of the hill horses we encountered was near Cherhill, not far from Silbury Hill on the Great West Road. It dates back to 1780. Another, near Westbury in Wiltshire, was originally produced by unknown men, but in 1741 it was remodeled and modernized.

The oldest and most famous of all these chalk horses is the Uffington figure, in Berkshire, a dozen miles or so, airline, east of Jefferies' Coate. This crude, stylized animal, the product of nameless men of the ancient past, suggests a primitive cave painting. Its immense form, 374 feet long from head to tail and 120 feet high from heel to ear, covers more than an acre of ground. It extends across the upper slope of 856-foot-high White Horse Hill. A winding, one-way road carried us up the steep ascent. From the top we looked over a country rich in history and legend.

Directly below us we saw a wide and wooded valley. Since the twelfth century it has been known as the Vale of White Horse. Nestled there is the village of Uffington, from which the hill figure derives its name. It was in this village that Thomas Hughes, the author of *Tom Brown's School Days*, spent his childhood. A few miles to the east, the valley leads to Wantage, birthplace of King Alfred. According to legend, the great chalk horse celebrates Alfred's victory over the Danes in 871. But modern archaeological studies have shown it far antedates that event.

Along the north flank of the hill we could glimpse a gully that cuts into the slope, a ribbed dry valley known for centuries as the Manger. Beyond, to the west rose the bold, flat-topped mound of Dragon's Hill, so called because an ancient legend has it that here St. George met and slew the dragon. Behind us, across the topmost reaches of the hill, extended the ruins of Uffington Castle, a maze of earthworks of unknown origin. One theory is that the white horse represents the totem animal of the early men who occupied the hilltop and constructed the earthworks. Here, as always where white horses were created, the finest setting in the region had been selected. Since 1736 local residents have engaged in a periodic festival known as the "Scouring of the White Horse." Encroaching vegetation is carefully removed and the titanic figure of chalk is restored to the immaculate whiteness in which it was left when the original ancient artists completed their work.

As we stood there, under a heavy sky, all the still, gray land around us seemed enveloped in a brooding sense of great antiquity. This emotion is part of life, part of the everyday existence of succeeding generations here. But it is something rarely met with in America. Where had we known it? Perhaps among the ageless sequoias of the California mountains, perhaps in the presence of the cliff dwellings of the Southwest, perhaps amid the earthworks of the ancient mound-builders beside the Ohio.

One of these, the sequoias or big trees—the Wellingtonias of Great Britain—we saw again, a few days later in northern Berkshire, when we came to the Duke of Wellington's estate. In a towering double row, the trees curved away along the entrance drive, rising high above the lofty pedestal supporting the statue of the Iron Duke. Although few Americans realize it, the California big tree was named *Wellingtonia* before it was named *Sequoia*.

On the day in June, 1815, when Wellington defeated Napoleon at Waterloo, these mighty trees were unknown to science. Nearly forty years went by before, in the spring of 1852, a miner in California, pursuing a grizzly bear among the Sierra Nevada mountains, found himself among the largest trees he had ever seen. Specimens of the leaves, branches and cones not long afterwards reached the pioneer California botanist, Dr. Albert Kellogg. Occupied with other work, he let time go by without publishing a description of the dramatic find. Months later he was still delaying publication when he showed the specimens of the unnamed tree to William Lobb, a visiting plant collector for a British nursery. That enterprising individual hurried to the mountains, collected his own specimens, and sailed for England. There, in December 1853, the British botanist John Lindley published a scientific description, naming the tree *Wellingtonia gigantea.*

Understandable was the anguish of American botanists. However, it was later determined that the mountain big tree and the coastal redwood were closely related. As the redwood had been described in a German botanical publication six years before Lindley had described the *Wellingtonia,* and had been given the name *Sequoia sempervirens, Sequoia* took precedence as the generic name of the tree. It is derived from Sequoyah, the famous Indian chief of the Cherokees, who, among other accomplishments, invented an alphabet and taught his people to read. A later revision, in the subsequent years, has given *Sequoia-Wellingtonia* still another scientific name. It now appears on taxonomic lists as *Sequoiadendron giganteum.*

Other trees, modest trees, trees long familiar to England, shaded the windings of the River Loddon when, not many miles from the avenue of Wellingtonias, we rode into Swallowfield. For us the name had special meaning. In Swallowfield Mary Russell Mitford, the "Miss Mitford" of *Our Village,* spent her last years and here she is buried. The village of her book, however, is neighboring Three Miles Cross. There we found all had changed. A wide ribbon of concrete now slices the village in two. All day long and far into the night, the race of motor cars and the thunder of lorries fill the air with noise and fumes. Far away, gone forever, are the tranquil earlier days that provide such chapters as "Nutting," "Violeting," "The Rat Catcher," and "The Cowslip Ball." A kind of permanent winter grime seemed settled on all the surroundings. Where was the charming Berkshire village Miss Mitford knew? The answer: In her book.

Across from a run-down garage and used-car yard, the house where she lived and wrote, and where a bronze plaque commemorates her memory, stands stained and weathered and set in dismal surroundings. Various signs, all faded, with peeling paint, record the different uses to which the structure has been put. One reads: "County Library," another "The Mitford Mission." On the largest of all we made out the words: "THE MITFORD." This dates from the period when the building formed a temperance hotel. Like the house in which she lived, Miss Mitford's life was filled with vicissitudes. At the age of ten she won a lottery prize of £20,000—then the equivalent of $100,000. She saw it all disappear while she was reduced to privation through the extravagances of her charming but spendthrift father. Throughout her life, however, her good spirits and her delight in the out-of-doors sustained her. In a letter, largely about robins and sparrows, written only three days before her death on January 10, 1855, she listed as one of the things for which she most thanked God: "My enjoyment of little things."

I remember that during the rest of that day we traced a rambling track up to Reading, where, in the thirteenth century, the hand of some unknown monk set down the immortal lines: "Sumer is icumen in, Lhude sing cuccu!"; across the upper tip of Hampshire, where children flew red and white kites and watercress grew in vivid green rectangles; through Farnham, where William Cobbett was born at the Jolly Farmer Inn; and down the western edge of Surrey to the village of Churt. There, close to where the River Wey follows its winding course with Surrey on one bank and Hampshire on the other, we slept in a room high among the chimney pots at the country inn, the Pride of the Valley.

The dawn chorus was all around us when we awoke. I climbed, that morning, up through woods to the high, bare observation point of Stony Jump. Stretching away in waves of green, green fields and green woods, threaded by fine roads and dotted with clumps of tiny farm buildings, extended the vast panorama of the Surrey and Hampshire countryside. On our first full day in England, on that day of rain when, after an hour's instruction, I was turned loose in an unfamiliar car on unfamiliar roads, Nellie and I had immediately headed inland. First of all in England we wanted to see Gilbert White's Hampshire village of Selborne. We never did find it. After the same country bridge reappeared three times in succession, we realized we were going around in circles and were hopelessly lost. We were glad to find our way back to Southampton. Now, after so

many varied miles on so many varied roads, we were close
to that initial goal. Tomorrow, at last, we would see Selborne!

And tomorrow, at last, we would see May. April, that abnormally cold and stormy April, was coming to its end. Few
are those who can be entirely philosophic about the
weather, and I am not numbered among them. As the sunless days, the days of chill and rain, went on and on, I de-
spaired of it ever becoming warm. In reply to Charles
Kingsley's bitter complaints of the cold in New England,
during his American tour, his wife assured him that he
could not be any colder there than she was in Hampshire.
For weeks Nellie had been engaged in a continuing battle,
fighting a chest cold. A day of sun and moderating weather
and she improved. Then days of wind and weeping skies,
compounded by open windows that sent frigid gales rushing
down hotel corridors and through hotel bathrooms, increased her coughing. Medicine prescribed by doctors gave
only partial relief. But her spirit was unbowed. She wanted
to go everywhere, to see everything. Now we had May to
look forward to. It was in the warm sunshine of Italy that
Robert Browning penned that endlessly quoted line: "Oh,
to be in England now that April's there." On this final day,
at the end of this abnormally severe month, Nellie spoke
for us both as we looked ahead:

"Oh, to be in England now that April's *gone!*"

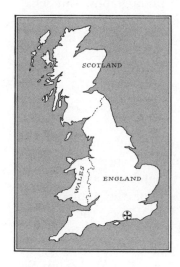

chapter 14

THE SELBORNE NIGHTINGALE

One hundred and seventy-seven years had passed since the publication of *The Natural History of Selborne*. One hundred and seventy-three years had elapsed since the death of Gilbert White. Yet, when we emerged from one of the sunken roads or "hollow lanes" along which White had botanized, and came to the village of Selborne that May morning, we found that it still consisted, as it had in his day, of "one straggling street." Although hardly fifty miles from London, the third largest city in the world, it impressed us—as it had impressed so many others before us —as remote, secluded, part of a simpler, more tranquil past. Television antennas rose from most of the cottage roofs and, a mile or so away, the steel spiderweb of a high-tension line ran uphill and downhill across the countryside. But these recent intrusions appeared to disturb not at all the ancient calm of Selborne.

Ranged along a shelf opposite the fireplace in my study at home, sixteen editions of White's *Natural History* stand side by side. Some are illustrated with woodcuts, others with steel engravings, others with photographs. But whatever the form of the art, its goal is the same—to depict the very scenes we now saw around us. We were arriving at the end of a long procession of pilgrims who—on foot, on bicycles, in horse-drawn vehicles, in automobiles and buses—had journeyed in this Hampshire village that Gilbert White, in the beautiful simplicity of his style, had made famous.

We came to Selborne in the green beauty of the English spring. Sunshine flooded the fields, the new-leaved trees, the sleek, silvery pelts of the old thatched roofs. Soon we were installed in an upstairs room of the annex of the Queen's Hotel, almost opposite The Wakes, the rambling house where Gilbert White had lived. For the next three days and nights, our address might have been given: "Under a thatched roof, Across from The Wakes, in Selborne."

The small leaded panes of our windows looked down on the same street where the old hunting mare that ran loose on the common had died after it had been taken ill and came "down into the village, as it were, to implore the help of men." Near our building, three of the four lime trees White planted in 1756 to screen a butcher's shop and the slaughtering yard behind it, still clung to life. Although they were now mere maimed and hollow stubs of great trees, they were responding with green sprouts to the sunshine and warmth of yet another spring.

Nothing we had ever heard or read, no picture we had seen, quite prepared us for the size of the ancient yew that stands just outside the Church of Saint Mary where White conducted services. Even on the brightest days, a continual twilight lies in the shade of its dense foliage. This yew is believed to have been a well-grown tree, perhaps a century old, when King Alfred was alive. Its age is estimated at more than twelve centuries. When Nellie and I examined its gigantic trunk, nearly twenty-eight feet in circumference, we noticed a roughened vertical strip, perhaps eighteen or twenty inches high and five inches wide. It appeared scarred by the claws of some animal. Turning away, we saw a large yellow-and-white cat watching us from the top of a neighboring gravestone. In the ancient yew, no doubt, it was making use of one of the oldest scratching posts in Britain.

As from the entrance of a cave on a summer day, cool air flowed from the open door of the church. Within the dim interior of the building we stood beside the massive font formed of three blocks of white stone and dating back to Saxon times. Here the children of Selborne had been baptized for nearly 800 years. Still in evidence are the remains of locks that, in long-gone days, secured a heavy cover over the font to prevent theft of consecrated baptismal water for use in sorcery. At one time, an official who bore the title of "Wiper of Doges" and was equipped with a whip and long tongs for grasping animals, was charged with the ejection of dogs during services. Wherever we looked, in this Hampshire village, we saw reflected the long span of history, the continuity of village life, the antiquity of customs.

One feature of the church that had special interest for us was of more modern origin. This was the Gilbert White memorial window. It depicts, in stained glass, St. Francis of Assisi surrounded by many of the birds mentioned in the writings of the Selborne naturalist. Outside, in our search for the modest headstone that marks White's grave, we observed what seemed to be rows of nail heads running between the masonry layers of the stone tower. Each "nail head" was a bit of dark, iron-filled rock that had been pushed into the wet mortar. We saw this same form of decoration, known as "garnetting," on several of the houses of the village. They seemed, as White expressed it, "studded with ten-penny nails." Nowhere else did we notice such architectural decoration. It appeared confined to this small portion of England along the Hampshire-Surrey border.

The only inscription appearing on the low white stone marking the naturalist's grave is "G.W. 26th June, 1793." And so small is that stone that its face is covered by even so brief an epitaph. As we stood motionless beside it, a song thrush, an earthworm folded over in its bill, alighted in the sunshine on another marker even older, a tombstone silvery with weathered age and golden with lichens. Among some of these very graves, two centuries before, Gilbert White had paused to enjoy such sights as these.

In the vicinity of Selborne public footpaths abound. One, open to all walkers, cuts from the Plestor, or "play-place"—the village green—directly through the graveyard to a swinging stile that emerges on one of White's favorite walks, the path that leads to the Short Lythe and the Long Lythe. "Lythe," derived from a Saxon word meaning valley, is pronounced to rhyme with "myth." On springy turf Nellie and I followed the path down a long slope, past stumps of immense oaks in the shade of which the naturalist may well have rested during summer walks, to the clear, narrow flow of Oakhanger Stream. The water was only a long step or a short jump across. Looking down, we saw cases of caddis flies waving in the riffles. Held within a curve of the stream, one muddy stretch lay like a half moon, shining with the yellow of the massed flowers of the marsh marigold.

On the hillside beyond, in a place it had occupied for generations, a rookery filled the treetops. Through some condition resulting on that May afternoon from the wind, the topography, or the thermal currents, powerful updrafts ascended from the valley. Half a dozen rooks, sporting in the sky, circled continually, riding upward on this elevator of air. The upsurge carried them far above us. At the summit of their climb, they appeared no larger than sparrows.

Now in the open, where swallows—spreading and closing their forked tails—skimmed above the tilted pastures of valley slopes; now in darkening beech woods with twisted roots around us, we progressed along the trail Gilbert White had so often followed. It extended before us—a path of wildflowers. We stopped, walked a few steps, stopped again as some new, unfamiliar bloom of spring caught our eye.

For weeks now the barren strawberry had been in flower. This cinquefoil, so closely resembling in leaf and flower the wild strawberry that a careful examination is needed to distinguish between the two, is one of the earliest wildflowers to appear in Britain. White, four-petaled blooms of a different kind rose in loose clusters above the broad, heart-shaped, garlic-scented leaves of Jack-by-the-hedge, also known as garlic-mustard and sauce-alone. Here, too, we found the bitter vetch, bearing flowers that fade from bright reddish-purple to blue or greenish-brown.

With delight we paused beside other Selborne blooms. We bent to examine the striking cowled flowers of the yellow archangel—sometimes called by country people the weasel-snout. At the top of squared stems, they bloomed in whorls, their three-lobed lower lips streaked with red. Along the more deeply shaded portions of the Long Lythe trail, we came upon that lover of the leaf mold beneath beech trees, the woodruff. Ivory white, the tiny funnel-shaped blooms clustered at the top of stems encircled by slender leaves that radiated outward like the spokes of a wheel. In older times, this perennial plant was gathered and dried and placed among folded linens to impart a pleasant perfume reminiscent of new-mown hay.

For yards at a time, ramsons, *Allium ursinum*, spread in dense green carpets beside our path, their loose, ball-like clusters of white flowers supported by triangular stems. A member of the lily family, this wildflower overwinters as a bulb. Its leaves, like those of the Jack-by-the-hedge, give off an oniony odor when crushed. The ramsons is, in fact, a wild relative of the onion. The leek, chive, garlic, and onion —originating in Europe and northern Asia—are all cultivated species of *Allium*.

Somewhere on the Long Lythe path, where the fiddleheads of young ferns were unrolling, we were surprised by the curious unflowerlike flowers of the wood spurge. At the top of fleshy stems, the blooms, which do not appear on these perennials until the second year, suggest small greenish cups. Another odd feature of this plant is its milky and poisonous juice.

The sun disappeared behind the horizon as we were returning to the village and, in impressive sequence, we saw our first sunset, our first twilight, our first star-filled night at Selborne. In the dusk swifts flew over the cottages. In the thirty-ninth letter of his book Gilbert White notes that each year the same number of swifts—eight pairs, about four nesting in the church and the rest in cottages—returned to the village. During the intervening years, at least four counts, the latest by James Fisher, have been made of the Selborne swifts. Each time the number remained the same that White reported in 1778.

When John Burroughs came to Selborne eighty-four years before us, he arrived late in June. He was in the midst of that prolonged and fruitless search that resulted in one of the most appealing chapters of *Fresh Fields*—"A Hunt for the Nightingale." Burroughs arrived too late, when the time of singing was virtually over. We, too, had come to Selborne hoping to hear the nightingale. But we were early. Singing had hardly begun. That evening, and on the succeeding evening, we drove for hours along dark, deserted country roads, pausing often, listening intently, then driving on again.

We listened beside woods, above valleys, along pasture

edges. We circled the extensive Selborne Common, drove toward Wolmer Forest, now largely gone, passed into the deeper darkness of the hollow lanes, formed, as White says, "by the traffic of ages and the fretting of water," their banks rising on either side as much as sixteen or eighteen feet above the level of the road. Clinging to these almost vertical ascents, stitchwort, herb Robert, cow parsley, and lords-and-ladies bloomed. Today, as in White's time, the hollow lanes "delight the naturalist with varied botany."

In our search, we turned toward Blackmoor, the setting of the first bird story related in *The Natural History of Selborne*, White's memorable account of the Raven Tree. In fewer than 100 words, in a classic example of vivid and succinct narration, he records the felling of the great oak while one of the birds was nesting:

"The saw was applied to the butt, the wedges were inserted into the opening, the woods echoed to the heavy blows of the beetle or mallet, the tree nodded to its fall; but still the dam sat on. At last, when it gave way, the bird was flung from her nest; and, though her parental affection deserved a better fate, was whipped down by the twigs, which brought her dead to the ground."

I remember a pasture field where cattle were feeding in the dark while a bat, silhouetted against the sky, veered and twisted above them. Once we looked down on a lower road and saw a lighted portion of the landscape moving across a valley floor, illuminated by the headlights of an invisible car. The moon, almost full, rose, filling the misty, sleepy meadows with glowing light. Tiny windows gleamed in faraway houses. But only once did we hear the barking of a dog. Ours was the silent night. We heard no hooting of an owl, no croaking of a frog.

This latter fact surprised us most of all. Again and again we halted by marshy tracts. Each time they were wrapped in profound silence. Where were the frogs of England?

From Land's End to the top of Scotland, in all our travels through the British spring, we heard not a single batrachian voice. Conservationists, at that time, were becoming increasingly alarmed over the scarcity of frogs. Near Selborne one school biology class found frogs had completely disappeared from a pond where it had been customary to collect eggs each spring. As part of a continuing study of the effect of pesticides on wildlife, the Nature Conservancy launched a nationwide frog census. In fact, so much attention was attracted by the decline in British frogs that, that fall, *The New York Times* published a feature article on the subject.

However, the vast chorus characteristic of the American spring apparently has never been a feature of the season in England. Writing home to his friend Myron Benton, the poet, in 1882, John Burroughs reported: "I have not heard the voice of a frog or toad since I landed in these islands. The nights in the country are as silent as the grave." In our experience, history was thus repeating itself. And when, each night, we returned to the darkened village with our quest for the nightingale unsatisfied, we seemed part of a second return to that earlier time. Were we to repeat, eight decades later, John Burroughs' experience in reverse—arriving too soon where he had arrived too late?

More than once, during those nights, we looked from our window over the slumbering village lying silent in the moonlight. Across the street the rays glinted from the chimneys of various shapes and sizes, shone from the steeply pitched, diverging roofs that crowned the dark bulk of The Wakes. It was there—only a few hundred feet from the site of the old Selborne Vicarage where he was born on July 18, 1720—that Gilbert White had died on June 26, 1793. It was there he wrote his Selborne letters to the wealthy Welsh natural-scientist and author of *The British Zoology*, Thomas Pennant, and the lawyer-naturalist, the Recorder of Bristol, Daines Barrington. It was there he produced an English classic without realizing he was even writing a book.

It was Daines Barrington who first suggested that he publish his letters. The year of the French Revolution, 1789, saw the appearance of the first edition of that evergreen volume, *The Natural History of Selborne*. Today, no series of English classics is complete without it. Not only has it never been out of print since its first appearance, but between 205 and 210 new editions—an average of more than one a year—have been issued during the intervening time.

"What make ye of Parson White of Selborne?" asked Thomas Carlyle. Why, as John Burroughs shaped the question, has "this cockle-shell of a book ridden so safely and buoyantly upon the waves beneath which so many learned and elaborate treatises have sunk?" Burroughs' answer is: "He did not seek to read his own thoughts into nature but submitted his mind to her with absolute frankness and ingenuousness." And Carlyle adds: "He copied a little sentence or two *faithfully* from the inspired volume of nature."

The contributions to science made by Gilbert White are considerable. He was the first to describe Britain's largest bat, the noctule bat, and Britain's smallest rodent, the harvest mouse. He was the first to differentiate between the wood warbler, the willow warbler, and the chiffchaff. The grasshopper warbler was largely unknown when he described and studied it. He anticipated, as James Fisher has pointed out, modern theories about the importance of territory in the life of birds. Twenty years ago, when David Lack began his intensive study of the swift, he found the fullest account of its habits was still that written by White in 1774. It was facts he encountered in the writings of this modest village curate that led Charles Darwin to his study of earthworms.

In an age when speculation—without checking the truth

of the speculation by studies in the field—often held sway, White's outlook was essentially modern. His goal was complete accuracy through personal observation. His great source book was the Book of Nature. It was the living creature in its surroundings that interested him most. It was life in its environment, all aspects of that environment, that engrossed him. "Faunists, as you observe," he wrote to Pennant in his letter of August 1, 1771, "are too apt to acquiesce in bare descriptions, and a few synonyms: the reason is plain; because all that may be done at home in a man's study, but the investigation of the life and conversation of animals is a concern of much more trouble and difficulty, and it is not to be attained but by the active and inquisitive, and by those that reside much in the country." Perhaps White's greatest contribution of all to science was leading subsequent naturalists away from the closet into the out-of-doors. While carrying on his correspondence with Pennant and Barrington, he was, unknowingly, writing his letters to generations unborn.

But there is far more to *The Natural History of Selborne* than its contributions to science. Even a reader who is not particularly interested in nature finds pleasure in it. No other book I know reflects so strongly the sweet and simple life of the country village. White's brother, Thomas, attributed the attraction of the volume to the fact it "counteracts the allurements of the metropolis." Like his life, the naturalist's writings exhibit the charm of the simple. His is a style for all ages. There is no strain, no ornate flourishes in his sentences. They flow like the limpid water of a country brook. And they bring a sense of calm and repose to any fevered time. White was, as has been said, one of the most restful figures in a restless and artificial eighteenth century. When, only four years after his book appeared, his placid, seemingly uneventful life ended in the house now lying in shadows and moonlight, this single book of his lifetime endured. It has continued on in the minds and memories of successive generations of men, bringing to Gilbert White, father of field naturalists, a quiet but enduring fame.

The Wakes, in which he lived and died—so called from the original owners, a family named Wake—is now a national shrine. In 1955 it became a museum housing mementos of the Selborne naturalist. This was made possible by a gift from the Oates family, to which belonged "that gallant gentleman" of Scott's ill-fated South Polar expedition, Titus Oates, who, when too ill to travel, walked out into a blizzard hoping, by the sacrifice of his life, to help his companions. This museum attracts visitors in thousands each year. As we wandered among its rooms, we saw White's barometer, the chairs he used, his desk with "G.W.1755" cut in the front, a letter written to Pennant in the curate's beautiful hand, a first edition of the *Natural History*, and a small child's garment labeled "Gilbert White's first linen suit."

When the naturalist occupied The Wakes, it consisted of eight rooms. Subsequent owners added to it, expanding it into a twenty-room dwelling. However, the middle portion still remains substantially as it was in White's time. The house is set close to the street in front. Behind it extends the wide lawn and spacious gardens where the old Sussex tortoise plodded down the paths in summer and hibernated when each autumn came. The shell of this famous reptile, which outlived its master by one year, is now part of the natural history collection of the British Museum, in London.

Where the garden joins grazing land, a ha-ha, or sunken fence, a specially constructed trench—which the tortoise was careful to avoid—forms a barrier that keeps out livestock without obstructing the view. Beside this barrier, we reached Gilbert White's sundial. It was green with the patina of age. When, a few years ago, a bypass road was pro-

posed that would run through the grounds of The Wakes,
it was greeted with such a storm of protest that the plan
was soon abandoned. Looking across the ha-ha and over the
grazing land beyond, we saw, rising high above us, the most
remarkable feature of the Selborne countryside, the Hanger.
Here the steep drop at the edge of a 300-foot hill or plateau
of chalk is clothed with trees. This hill and hanging wood,
half a mile long, shelters the village from westerly gales.
The Hanger is now under the protection of the National
Trust.

At the foot of this escarpment, only a field away from the
garden at The Wakes, we found three paths. One ran along
the foot of the Hanger; another, the Bostal, angled upward
among the hanging trees; the third, the famous Zigzag laid
out by Gilbert White and his brother, mounts straight up
in a steep stitchwork ascent comprising more than a score
of switchbacks. We turned down the first path. It, like the
Long Lythe trail, was a pathway of flowers. Again we met
the green blooms of the wood spurge. Dog violets and
lesser celandine and wood oxalis and, now and then, a scattering of bluebells ran beside us. The golden disk of one
dandelion measured an inch and a half across. The English
cowslip, sometimes called St. Peter's keys, rose at the edge
of the meadow, the yellow flowers all on one side of the upright stems.

Here we came upon a new bird, one of the 120 on
White's Selborne list. With blue-gray back, black cap and
tail, white rump, and rose-red breast, it was that striking
songbird, the bullfinch. Because of its destruction of fruit
blooms, this colorful bird—said to mate for life—is legally
trapped and shot in the orchard and berry-raising regions of
England. Among the roots of the clinging beech trees, a little farther on, we heard a dry rustling among the fallen
leaves. As we came close, we discovered the source. A black-

bird, tossing leaves with its yellow bill, was searching for food.

Among other beech trees, where a multitude of new leaves—some as delicately tinted as flowers—were unfolding on the branches, we climbed the gentle ascent of the angling Bostal. Above us, up the slope clouded with the pale green of emerging foliage, we heard the ringing "Peeto! Peeto! Peeto!" or the monotonous, metallic "tink —tink—tink" of the great tit. As we ascended, the rasping clamor of rooks rose about us. Half a dozen years before, a number of these birds had moved from the main rookery by Oakhanger Stream and had established their nests in a group of trees not far from The Wakes.

We had climbed over a fallen beech and had stopped to examine another wildflower with greenish blooms, that relative of the wood spurge, the dog's mercury—a plant that flourishes in beech woods and blooms as early as in February and once was employed in medicine—when we came to a muddy spot in the trail. Its soft earth recorded the passing of previous travelers. Imprinted in the mud we saw the tracks of a horse, a dog, a man, and a deer. In the Selborne region roe deer have been increasing in recent times. More rare, but occasionally seen, are fallow deer.

Along the upper portions of the trail, gaps among the treetops revealed glimpses of the village. What we had so often pictured in our imaginations lay outspread below us. The scene remains much the same as White described it. The village, even now, is five miles from the nearest railroad station. It still contains a blacksmith shop. Since the middle of the thirteenth century, there has always been an ironworker in Selborne. Aside from the unpleasant impression made by a few mutilated trees, warped to man's caprice, this Hampshire community epitomizes in our minds the charm of the English village at its best. Here Gilbert

White's life had been cast in pleasant paths and amid pleasant surroundings. Almost his only cause for regret was the lack of any companion in all the region to share his interest in natural history.

At the end of our 300-foot ascent, we came out among great beeches—those dominant trees of the chalk country —on the edge of the Selborne Common. This expanse extended away for upwards of a mile with a width, at its greatest point, of about three-fourths of a mile. Wood pigeons had congregated among the treetops and all around us and in the distance we heard the hoarse, hollow sound of their calling. At times, it suggested the barking of far-away dogs; at other times, the hooting of distant owls. I remembered reading that to some these birds seem saying: "Take *two* cows, David."

During the Second World War, when I wrote to inquire how Selborne had fared, L. Sunderland, then the vicar, reported that, during the early days of hostilities, fire bombs had fallen among the beech trees at the top of the Hanger. Otherwise the village had escaped damage. The effect of the incendiary bombs had been slight. Evidence of their fall had long since disappeared.

Nellie and I decided to save the Zigzag path for the following day, our last in Selborne. But when that day dawned, it came with cold and misty rain. Hour after hour, it splashed on the street, flowed down the windowpanes, streamed from the thatching of our roof. Gloomily we stared out at the deluge. This was our final day in the village. This was the night of the full May moon. This was our last chance to hear a nightingale at Selborne. The Curator at The Wakes, Cyril Reginald Nortcliffe, had told us that a friend had reported hearing the song on Selborne Common not far from the top of the Zigzag. But in pouring rain, the chalk soil of the switchbacks would be as slippery as though covered with lard. Climbing a greased pole would be almost as easy as attaining the top of the ascent.

Not everyone, I found, appreciates the voice of the nightingale. There are those, in fact, to whom the singing of birds in general has little appeal. I was assured by one inhabitant of Selborne that the nightingale's song is "really an awful noise." Students sometimes complain that it prevents them from studying. Near Ringmer, in Sussex, at the very place where Gilbert White had acquired his tortoise, a later occupant, coming from London, had all the nightingales killed because they disturbed his sleep.

As that rain-lashed day dragged on, our chances of hearing the nightingale seemed to diminish and disappear. The fate of American naturalists—early and late—appeared to be to miss the bird at Selborne. But sometime after five the rain slackened. Then it ceased. Rifts extended in channels of blue sky between the clouds. The sun came out; the sun went in; but the rain was over.

I wandered about taking pictures in the unusual lighting that streamed from the west and flooded the dripping village. Nellie, her cough grown worse on this day of chill and rain, went early to bed. About nine, I decided to check on the slipperiness of the Zigzag. Alone in the dark, a slip and fall on the upper part of the 300-foot precipitous ascent might be a serious matter. Yet—if I could get up and down again, there was still a chance of hearing a Selborne nightingale.

When I started out, the sky, all along the western horizon, was filled with a fading greenish glow. Even here, in southern England, I was in the longer twilight of the north. As I passed the inn, light from one of the windows shone on an elderly gentleman just outside taking, between thumb and forefinger, a pinch of snuff from a snuffbox and carefully applying it to each nostril in turn. Surrounded by darkness, standing out in the lighted space, the scene resembled a tableau, a fragment of the eighteenth century displaced in time. Between darkened fields, I followed a footpath to the base of the looming black shape of the Hanger. In lighter lines, the staggering switchbacks of the Zigzag ascended above me. I tried the lowest one. Wet leaves added to its slipperiness. My feet slid back at every step. But always they were snubbed by pebbles scattered through the clay.

Slowly, steadily, sweeping the wet path ahead with the beam of a flashlight, walking flat-footed, carefully placing my feet, taking no chances, I mounted switchback by switchback up the slippery ascent. From trunk to limbs to tipmost twigs, I worked my way upward among the black silhouettes of trees imprinted against the sky. The lights of the village sank away. Ending the evening chorus, the voices of a few blackbirds and song thrushes carried through the increasing darkness. From time to time, an intermittent wind shook the trees, scattering drops of water on my path.

About two-thirds of the way to the top, I came to a small, level spot, a miniature plateau. There, in the eighteenth century, Gilbert White had built a modest hermitage where he often sat and where he used to entertain his friends. I lost count of the switchbacks, but the number was nearing thirty when I reached the summit of the staggered ascent. Here I found another memento of the naturalist, the famous wishing stone he and his brothers transported from Farringdon, nearly two miles away, and erected at the top of the Zigzag. Around the Sarsen stone the ground is hard-packed, perhaps from the feet of those who have engaged in an old superstition, circling it three times backward and then making a wish.

From the top of the Hanger I looked down the steep climb of the switchbacks and then gazed out over the darkened scene spreading away below. Automobiles were pushing stubby paths of illumination before them along country roads. Clusters of glimmering pinpoints of light marked the position of distant villages. Below the Hanger, in a double line, lighted windows of cottages followed the main street of Selborne. The same glass, in some instances, that now transmitted the brilliance of electric lamps had, in White's time, glowed with the softer illumination of candles. Like Concord, in Massachusetts, in the New World, Selborne, in Hampshire, in the Old, represents one of the places of the earth that, for us, holds a special fascination.

After the rain, the smell of wet, decaying leaves was strong in the darkness. My footfalls were silent on the yielding forest mold. Around me as I advanced among the ancient beeches, the beam of my electric torch encountered shaggy masses of ivy; the shine of holly leaves, the darker mats of moss, the twisted roots and the immense, smooth-barked columns of the trees. So widespread are some of the lower limbs that their tips sweep the ground. Several times, above me, I heard wood pigeons fluttering, blundering among the treetop twigs, as they changed position in the dark.

The wind had died down completely. No breeze stirred the branches. The intense silence seemed to be pressing on my eardrums. This was the quiet Selborne night, the night that had seemed friendly to Gilbert White and now seemed friendly to me. I listened intently, straining to catch some fragment of the hoped-for song. Pausing thus at frequent intervals, I advanced among the trees and glades of the common. Pale forest moths fluttered by, in and out of the beam of my flashlight.

When I reached the eastern edge of the common, I looked away between the massive boles of trees out over a far-spread stretch of lower land. To the southeast loomed the black bulk of Noar Hill, where White had experimented with echoes, employing Latin phrases to insure that he was not being hoaxed. To the left of the hill, orange and immense, the full moon had lifted free of the black horizon line. For a time, it remained entangled in low-lying clouds, its light transforming the edges of the floating vapor into glowing, wavy margins. Then it gained the clear sky, lost its fiery orange hue, diffused a silver and magical light over the outspread land below. Somewhere there, I heard the faint, far-away bawling of a cow. Closer at hand, a cock pheasant uttered its sudden, rasping call among the moonlit fields. Then, for a long time, no sound broke the silence. This was the full May moon—the nightingale moon. But where was the singer and where was its song?

Perhaps half an hour more had gone by and I had worked farther along the edge of the common when my ear caught the voice of a distant bird. It grew louder as I advanced. Creeping close in the deep shade of a beech tree, I sat on a mossy log and listened to a song my ears had never heard before. With its deep bubbling notes, its rushing crescendos, it was—at last—the song of a nightingale.

The bird, hidden in a tangle of low shrubbery, was invisible. But its voice filled all the shadows and moonlit spaces around. Where many thrushes sing over and over the same melodious notes, the nightingale seemed musing, improvising, filling its song with phrases and runs and repeated notes infinitely varied. In general form, the song resembles somewhat that of the mockingbird of our Southern states. But it held more marvelously varied pitch and tone, more beautiful liquid notes and running passages, greater intensity and passion. The impression was inescapable that here was a virtuoso accomplishing the difficult with ease.

The song ranged from a low, bubbling "chook-chook" or "jug-jug" to liquid warbles, soaring trills, and bursting crescendos of sound. There were sudden dramatic silences. Some notes were almost guttural. Others were rich and mellow, wild and pure. Edward Thomas, in *The South Country*, well describes these swift, repeated notes "as

Beeches in Savernake Forest

rounded and full of sweetness as a grape." From the time of
Aristophanes, four centuries before the birth of Christ, men
have been trying, with little success, to translate into sylla-
bles the song of the nightingale. Cold words are powerless
to capture the fire of the singer, the richness of the notes,
the purity of the tones, the variety of the phrasing, the
rapid repetition of one clear note, the sudden end, suc-
ceeded by intense silence and then the song beginning
again.

In the first chapter of *The Compleat Angler*, Izaak Walton writes of the nightingale as breathing "such sweet lowd
musick out of her little instrumental throat, that it might
make mankind to think Miracles are not ceased." The
human response to this music depends largely upon the individual hearer. John Keats, best of all, has immortalized
the effect of the song on the sensitive listener.

As I sat there motionless, the nightingale ascended from
the depths of the tangle, where it had been singing, to an
upper branch of one of the bushes. Here it perched, facing
the moon across the valley. I saw it silhouetted against the
luminous sky, its head lifted, its body quivering with the intensity of its song. In shape and size, the nightingale brings
to mind our hermit thrush. Its breast is plain, while the
breast of the hermit thrush is spotted; but its tail, like the
tail of the American bird, has a reddish cast. This I saw
clearly on a later day, at the edge of a wood on the Sussex
border of Kent, when I watched a nightingale fly up in brilliant sunshine. Although these birds often sing by day as
well as by night, the one I saw in Kent remained mute. The
south of England comprises most of the range of the species in Britain. Kent, Sussex, Surrey, and Hampshire are especially famed for their nightingales.

I have no idea how long I listened to the song, surrounded by the moonlit night. There was a dreamlike
quality about the passing minutes. It became increasingly

Oyster shell left by the Romans at Rockbourne

difficult to grasp the reality that I was actually here, in Gilbert White's Selborne, under the full May moon, listening to the singing of the nightingale. I had come so far for such an hour as this! The only gall in the honey of that moment was the knowledge that Nellie was missing what she so greatly desired to hear. But Sussex and Kent, with their nightingales, still lay before us.

When I finally stood up, I discovered what, in my preoccupation, I had been unaware of before. Like a wick, my clothes had been absorbing moisture all the time I sat on the moldering rain-soaked log. Several times I started away only to return and listen again. When I reached the top of the Zigzag, the Sarsen stone gleamed wanly in the moonlight and The Wakes, in shadows, lay sleeping below. My elation at my great good fortune went with me as I slowly descended the still slippery Zigzag. It remained with me for a long time as I lay in bed, too moved to sleep, reliving all I had seen and heard.

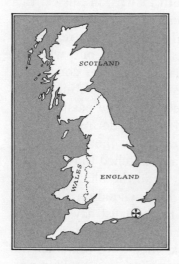

chapter 15

GREEN
DOWNS

As silent as the sunshine, as invisible as the wind, seeing without being seen, the observer unobserved—this is the ideal of the traveling naturalist. Thoreau once noted that the way to get the most from a journey is to travel inconspicuously as a common man. Then you cause no commotion, provide no distraction. Nobody knows you are there. And you see things and people as they normally are.

A year or so after our predecessor, John Burroughs, had traveled south through Scotland and England, in the early 1880's, a traveler asked the landlord of a Scottish inn where the naturalist had stayed what manner of man he was. His reply was: "No verra big, an' no verra wee—joost a plain, ordinar' kin' o' mon, an' no like a writer ava'." I was delighted, when I heard that story, to learn that Burroughs had traveled so inconspicuously.

John O' London's Weekly, some thirty years ago, published an article by a man who made a hobby of tracking down the farmhouses and inns where W. H. Hudson stayed while gathering material for his books. In the course of his travels, he came to the South Downs, in Sussex, the locale of one of the most eloquent of Hudson's volumes, *Nature in Downland*. Although he combed the region of Lewes and Kingston Hill, he could find no one who remembered Hudson or recalled that he had ever come that way. This is as it should be. It was not like a distinguished visitor on a grand tour, but quietly, like the passing of a cloud, that Hudson had wandered over the downs.

On Kingston Hill, on an August day in the year when I was born, he lay in the dry grass and watched thousands of shining flecks of thistledown drifting in the blue sky. They recalled the great thistle years of his boyhood on the pampas of Argentina. The events of that August day occurred before memory began for me. Yet, ever since I read the opening pages of Hudson's book, they have remained in recollection like a vivid experience of my own. This was Hudson's special magic, the ability to make the written record of his own deeply felt contacts with nature come alive in the minds of his readers.

When we approached Kingston Hill, in the valley of the Ouse, we were about fifty miles, airline, east of Selborne. Lush green grass ascended the slopes that had been parched and yellow in the August drought of Hudson's year. Wherever we went across the open downs, we traveled in a world of green. We seemed traversing the swells of a vast seascape, solidified and still, amid the flowing lines of the rising and falling land. This was the "wide, wild, houseless Downes" of the song the shepherds sang for Queen Elizabeth in the latter years of the sixteenth century.

Nowhere in America, not on the Great Plains nor among the southern savannas nor amid the coastal pastures of the Northwest, can I recall a comparable landscape, similar in vast swells of land, bare of trees, green with grass, extending unbroken to the horizon. When William Gilpin came this way in search of the picturesque, the Sussex countryside impressed him as "dreary and tiresome." To us, it was neither. The green sweep of the open downs took on an individual character; it seemed endowed with a particular charm of its own. We were pleased to read, a few weeks after our arrival in England, that the National Parks Commission had designated 380 square miles of the Southern Downs as an area of outstanding beauty to be protected as one of the natural heritages of Britain.

Unnumbered flocks of sheep, through uncounted generations, cropping the short and springy grass, have played their part in creating the velvety appearance of its hills and valleys. Here, where the extinct great bustard once nested, shepherds and sheep dogs worked together long before the Domesday Book. Old volumes tell us that, as late as 1800, shepherds were allowed to bring their dogs to church in Sussex.

When, on a subsequent day, Nellie and I followed the Ouse a dozen miles upstream from Kingston Hill, we dropped down a steep descent and stopped beside a small bridge on the floor of a narrow valley. The river here, flowing swiftly, was only eight or ten feet wide. Not far away, about eighty feet from the edge of the water, a gravel bank had become world-famous half a century before. It was the site where the lawyer and amateur archaeologist Charles Dawson reported picking up parts of the skull and jawbone of what, from the neighboring village of Piltdown, became known as the prehistoric Piltdown Man. Later a missing tooth was discovered nearby.

For more than forty years, as the *Encyclopaedia Britannica* puts it, the bones were "considered by experts to be not less than 10,000,000 years old." During those four decades, the village of Piltdown basked in scientific glory. Its name appeared in textbooks. It was visited by travelers from many lands. It was mentioned in learned university lectures in far parts of the world. Then, overnight, the glory vanished. The name became associated with hoax and fraud. In the 1950's, new techniques revealed that the skull was of relatively modern origin, worthless to science. It had been skillfully treated with bichlorate to produce the appearance of great age. The tooth had come from a rhinoceros and was perhaps forty years old when it was reported found. It, too, had been chemically treated after being ground down to the desired shape.

Who was the hoaxer and why the hoax? Evidence points most strongly to Dawson, who died in 1916, as the author of the deception. What was the motivation? Longing for instant fame? A desire to expose the credulity of men of science? Enmity for authorities who might be humbled? Arrogance of mind? Or a malicious delight in doing mischief? No one will ever know. And what of the after-years? Was praise and honor received with smug complacency or with a hidden dread of sudden exposure? Here on the stage of this small Sussex valley—no more than twenty-five miles from Down House where Charles Darwin had painstakingly assembled his facts, working on the side of light instead of darkness—a human tragedy had been enacted.

We considered it, for a time, beside a rushy pond on the outskirts of the village. Then our attention was diverted to the activity of half a dozen swans and a single coot. Another visitor to the pond was tossing bits of bread to the waterfowl. Each time, there was a swirl and surge as the birds converged on the spot, the swans advancing with deliberate and powerful movements, the coot with a spattering rush. It was white bill against black in the race for the floating food. Except when the bread fell almost within reach of a swan, it was always the coot, moving like a swift destroyer cutting in and out among ponderous battleships, that made off with the prize.

Close to a roadside sign, later that day, we stopped to enjoy other birds—skylarks of the downs, hovering, singing,

making their nearly vertical plunges back to earth. Then I
noticed the sign. It pointed to Crowborough. It was at
Crowborough, I remembered, that Richard Jefferies wrote
the last essay he was able to set down with his own hand—
"Hours of Spring." And it was at Crowborough, with the
short span of his life so near its end, that he listened to the
gay-spirited singing of the skylarks and recorded that each
note "fell into my heart like a knife."

The southernmost edges of the South Downs, where the
chalk country meets the sea, is a region rich in associations
with Jefferies. At Goring, on a short dead-end street now
marked "Jefferies Lane Cul-De-Sac," we came to the cottage where he died in 1887. Then the cottage was called
"Sea View," the lane bore the name of "Bottom of the
Sack" and, at its end, it joined a field-path known as "Cat's
Alley." Today, the dwelling is hedged in by other houses.
In Jefferies' time, it looked away across open country to the
sparkling waters of the Channel. In this same cottage, in
the room where Jefferies died, in the August of a later year,
W. H. Hudson wrote the first pages of *Nature in Down-
land*.

In his admiration for Jefferies, Hudson wished to be buried near him. We found the two graves at Broadwater
Cemetery, in the neighboring town of Worthing. Both are
marked in the same manner with white crosses and marble
curbing. Cut in the edging of Jefferies' grave are the words:
"To the Honoured Memory of the Prose-Poet of England's Fields and Woodlands." Hudson's similarly placed
epitaph reads: "He Loved Birds and Green Places and the
Wind on the Heath and Saw the Brightness of the Skirts of
God." It seemed to me that Jefferies, in the simplicity of
his inscription, had by far the better part. It fitted the
writer of pages rooted so deeply in common things. For you
sink into Jefferies as you sink into summer grass.

Jefferies was the native; Hudson the outsider, the

stranger from a strange land. With his early years spent on the pampas of Argentina and his later years in London, his contact with nature in Britain was, of necessity, that of the visitor, the transient, the vacationist spending a few weeks in the country. This, however, may well have its brighter side, concentrating his attention, heightening his appreciation. The air of nostalgia for something glimpsed and known and left behind colors all of Hudson's writings. By the nature of his contacts, his chapters are filled with sharply focused vignettes rather than with the long continuity of developing events. He preserved nature in fragments. But it is no small thing to make moments live again as Hudson does in his finest pages.

"You don't hear Hudson mentioned so much any more," one English ornithologist told me. "It is hard to place him —in literature or natural history."

Yet few men have been more stirred emotionally by the beauty of nature or have been more devoted to its preservation. When Hudson died, in 1922, he left his entire estate to the Royal Society for the Protection of Birds.

Nellie, still struggling to shed her persistent cough, next day took a "medicinal nap" while I cut in a swing to the east through a land steeped in history, through Pevensey, where William of Normandy came ashore, and inland from Hastings to the battlefield where Harold, the last Saxon king of England, lost his life in one of the decisive conflicts of the world. Later, riding in a Channel wind under drifting Channel clouds, I followed the coast west again. Soaring and dipping and soaring once more, I crossed the seven ridges of chalk that end in the vertical white cliff-faces of the Seven Sisters at Cuckmere Haven. Beyond, where I pulled up beside a dark little pond starred from edge to edge with the white flowers of the floating water crowfoot, the rain began. It pounded down in wavering sheets before me as I turned back. All the streams were rising, rushing down their beds, swirling and muddy, yellow-white with the dissolved chalkland they were bearing to the sea. And everywhere, as I came home, the "short-grass'd green," the "unshrubb'd down" of Shakespeare's *The Tempest* dripped and ran with rain.

In the back of the mind of a traveling naturalist, there almost always beats the same lament: So long in coming; so soon in leaving! We had come so far to stay so short a time. In how many hundred places in Britain we wished to remain for months instead of days. We longed, for example, to see in their seasons those flowers of the chalk—the blue round-headed rampion, *Phyteuma tenerum,* called by some "The Pride of Sussex"; the rare spiked rampion, believed to be the only plant belonging specially to this southern county; and the hound's-tongue, "whose leaves smell like mice." Here, too, grows the yellow stonecrop whose local name so delighted Hudson: "welcome-home-husband-though-never-so-drunk."

But we saw none of these. In truth, in our latter days in Sussex, we looked on the world around us with minds half blinded by growing concern. Nellie's cough, which at first had responded to antibiotics, had become worse in this climate "so wonderful for flowers but so poor for people." She needed days of quiet rest. But we were caught between London and the southern coast. This was spring. Hotel reservations were booked weeks in advance. Whenever the weather improved, cars poured from London like ants from a disturbed nest. Newspapers reported that on one fine Sunday they left the metropolis at the rate of 20,000 an hour. Whenever we found a room for the night it was always reserved for the next day and we must move on. Like gypsies making one-night stands, we advanced across this southern county. Sick in a foreign land: then how dear seems home!

Another doctor we consulted found Nellie's bronchitis was developing into pneumonia. It was imperative that she have day after day of undisturbed rest in bed.

And this is what she found at last, over the border in Kent at the immense Wellington Hotel, in the historic spa town of Tunbridge Wells. I remember we drove there from Crawley New Town, a distance of about thirty miles. I can recall nothing I saw. All I remember is that we traveled through a land both green and pleasant.

At the end of our ride we were installed in a warm, comfortable room looking down from a height on the town. Everywhere along the hotel's corridors and wide stairways we saw statues of Wellington and oil paintings that depicted his victories in battle. One extensive series, in a lower hall, recorded in detail and in sequence the main events at Waterloo. Printed in gold on the door of each room appeared the name of some place or personage relating to the career of the Iron Duke. Our room bore a Spanish name associated with a victory in the 1811 campaign against Napoleon—"Fuentes de Oñoro." Two doors away was "Waterloo." We had the impression of having retreated, in a single giant step, a century and a half in time. Once more, as at Dorchester, we seemed to have taken up quarters in a museum. Under such conditions and in such surroundings, Nellie settled down for her convalescence.

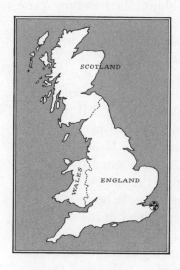

chapter 16

HOP FIELDS
OF KENT

At Tunbridge Wells we took off our traveling shoes. Our wanderings halted. We lived for a time the life de luxe. We rode to the dining room, and to the finest of meals, in a "passenger lift." Warm and snug, day after day, Nellie rested. And, day after day, her condition improved.

During the first of those days, I explored on foot the historic spa town that spread out 440 feet below Mount Ephraim and our hotel. Since early in the seventeenth century, the water of its chalybeate spring, impregnated with salts of iron, has been famed as a curative for "splenetic distempers." The Pantiles, the parade walk paved with special tiles of Dutch or Flemish origin, was laid down the year before the start of the American Revolution. It knew the feet of Samuel Johnson, David Garrick, Beau Nash, and Sir Joshua Reynolds.

One morning of sunshine and showers, I encountered, along one of the main streets of Tunbridge Wells, a minor mystery. In the soil between the bricks of the sidewalk, I noticed numerous small, round, and shallow holes. They

161

suggested the probings of some blunt-billed starling. The puzzle remained for some time before I discovered the simple solution. Passing pedestrians were pressing down the tips of their furled umbrellas as they walked.

Down the slope from the hotel, on another day, I spent an hour of complete mystification watching my first cricket match. Some enlightenment resulted when I fell into conversation with an elderly spectator. He had played cricket on that same green until he was past sixty. What, I wanted to know, is a "sticky wicket"? During a good part of my lifetime, I had been encountering that term applied to situations without being sure of its meaning. When the ground is wet after a rain, my informant explained, it has a yielding surface and the player who bowls the ball can bounce it with a more erratic spin, thus making it more difficult to hit. Remembering baseball in America, I observed that nobody here ever seemed to object to an umpire's decision.

"Oh, no," my companion rejoined. "That would be very bad form in cricket."

Toward the end of the game a diversion occurred. Behind the spectators, where a faucet provided water for drinking, a considerable puddle had formed. A large brown dog stopped to lap up water, then lay down in the puddle. A few minutes later it stood up and shook itself violently, hurling a shower of mud and water over the spectators. Everybody turned around. Everybody glared. But nobody said anything except the owner. He disappeared, hurrying the culprit away and repeating in a loud voice:

"You naughty dog! You naughty, *naughty* dog!"

During subsequent days, while Nellie was gaining strength and losing the last remnants of her cough, I ranged farther afield. I roamed widely over beautiful Kent—Kent, where the Roman conquest of Britain began, where Louis Blériot landed at the end of the first cross-Channel flight, where three-quarters of all the species of wild orchids of Britain are found, where Charles Darwin wrote *The Origin of Species*, where Dungeness forms the greatest expanse of sea shingle in England, where pilgrims journeyed to Canterbury long before Chaucer.

Twenty miles from Tunbridge Wells, a little before ten o'clock in the morning, I pulled into a hilltop layby and studied the map. Across all the rolling fields on either side stretched parallel lines of upright poles. Between them spread a vast brown spiderweb of heavy twine. Extra twine, in balls as large as pumpkins, lay along the edges of many fields, and surplus poles, like immense tepees, were stacked in open spaces. With unnumbered thousands of such poles supporting unnumbered hundreds of miles of twine, the famous hop fields of Kent extended away up and down the hills around me.

Already, the pale green tendrils were ascending the twine, turning always clockwise, from left to right, as they climbed. Many had risen two feet or more above the ground. By the time they come to the end of their growth, such vines are often as long as fifteen or twenty feet. Both stems and leaves are rough with hooked hairs that aid in clinging and climbing. The tendrils I saw represented the first stages in a development that culminates in the massed hops of the late-summer harvest. These conelike pistillate catkins, when dried, have provided for centuries, the bitter flavor in the beers and ales of England.

In Kent perennial hop vines are planted, through cuttings, in the ratio of one male to 200 female plants. Light, dusty pollen, produced by the drooping panicles of the staminate flowers, is borne by the wind to fertilize the cone-shaped pistillate flowers. Just so, for ages before the first hop field, wild vines of the native European hop, *Humulus lupulus*, had fertilized their blooms. This vine ranges over the European continent from Greece to Scandinavia and eastward as far as central Asia. In Belgium, the young vines are eaten like asparagus in spring.

Linked with the life of the hop is the existence of a diminutive but remarkable insect. Its story begins in the fall when eggs are laid on the damson plum. The following spring, the eggs produce winged female hop aphides that fly to the tender vines and leave there the first of innumerable generations of wingless females. All summer long, all the aphides are females. And all the females possess the power of virgin birth. Without mating, they produce a steady stream of living young that, in their turn, are able to produce living young within a few days of their own birth.

In consequence, the population of aphides often becomes astronomical. Occasionally, the wind will lift and transport vast numbers through the sky, depositing them many miles away. Everyone familiar with White's classic will recall the great aphid storm of August 1, 1785, when clouds of the insects, carried from the "hop plantations" of Kent, descended on Selborne. Late in summer, winged males and females appear among the wingless aphides, and eggs once more are laid on damson plums. There they overwinter and begin the cycle of aphid life anew the following spring.

If a man knew enough, he could, no doubt, be set down anywhere in England and, by such things as the design of the country gates, the formation of walls and hedges, the architecture of the houses, could tell where he was. In Kent, he would have oast-houses to help him. These round, red-brick structures with high, conical tops surmounted by white ventilation cowls, pivoted and provided with vanes so the opening is always away from the wind, are distinctive features of the landscape. Oast is an earlier word for kiln. Within the oast-houses, the harvested hops are spread, eight to sixteen inches deep, on finely woven horsehair cloths and dried for nine or ten hours by heated air drawn up around them from a slow fire at the base. Through all the hop-growing regions of Kent, these odd-appearing structures, thirty-five or forty feet high, stand out like bulky windmills in the landscape.

From the hop fields through apple orchards in full bloom to lush green pastures, my way led me toward Canterbury. Blackbirds sang along the way, far more in number than the four and twenty of the nursery rhyme. Once I passed a magpie sitting on the back of a white horse that stood motionless in the sunshine of a meadow where skylarks sang above nests hidden in the pasture grass. The field appeared devoid of landmarks; it seemed to me to stretch away exactly the same uniform shade of green throughout. I remembered Goethe's puzzlement, expressed in one of his conversations with Eckermann, over how skylarks are able to fly through the air and then, without fail, drop down at the precise spot where their nests are located. "They go hither and thither," he said, "as if in invisible leading-strings; but what these really are we do not know." More than 140 years have gone by since Goethe uttered those words. Yet the "leading-strings" of the birds' sense of orientation remain a source of wonder.

A moment ago I spoke of "the same uniform shade of green" extending across the meadow-field. To the eye of the lark, no doubt far keener than mine, a thousand subtle variations in hue may be apparent. Still, even at times when former aids to orientation are suddenly wiped out, when its surroundings alter completely and abruptly, a bird may retain, to an amazing degree, its sense of place identification. An ornithologist in the state of Michigan, some years ago, was studying a killdeer that had made its nest on the level expanse of an unused football field. An unseasonably late fall of snow blanketed the field. All the small markings that might have provided guiding points for the bird were obliterated under an unvarying sheet of white. In spite of this, the scientist found by the evidence of tracks in the snow that the bird had alighted and run only a few steps to arrive at the exact spot where its nest was hidden.

Another similar instance comes to mind. In this case, the bird returned to a place not on the ground but in the air. Alexander Sprunt, Jr., in Arthur Cleveland Bent's *Life Histories of North American Flycatchers, Larks, Swallows and Their Allies,* tells of a martin house in a yard in Houston, Texas, that was taken down, together with the high pole that supported it, for repainting. Before it was replaced, the martins returned from migration. The owner, attracted by a great chattering one morning, found the birds circling and fluttering in the air at the exact place and at the same elevation above the ground where the house had been the previous year.

Probably no other town in Britain, with the exception of London, attracts so many visitors as Canterbury. Few can approach for a first time this ancient cathedral town, so long associated with English history, the goal of pilgrims through so many centuries, without a quickening of the pulse. When I arrived, the narrow, winding streets around the cathedral swarmed with modern pilgrims. They seemed to have come not only "from every shire's ende of Engelond" but from around the world. Streams of pedestrians swelled and flowed and mingled. Human life was at flood stage. I was swept on, around and through the cathedral.

Compared to the spacious setting of Salisbury Cathedral, Canterbury's rises in cramped surroundings. It is within, under the soaring arches, beneath the delicate decorations of the bell tower, in the presence of superb artistry with stained glass and stone, that it takes its place with the most beautiful of the world's religious edifices. Just as it had been the goal toward which Chaucer's Miller and Knight and Monke and Phisicien and Pardoner and Wyf of Bathe had traveled through the pages of *The Canterbury Tales,* so, on this May day of sunshine, it was the goal of all this teeming throng of modern motorized visitors traveling through the twentieth century.

The earliest Roman road in Britain, Watling Street, leads from Canterbury to London. I turned the other way. Paralleling the Thames Estuary, riding through dairyland, I came to the coast near the treacherous Goodwin Sands. Through Deal—where Julius Caesar landed in Kent in his invasion of Britain in 55 B.C.—and on through Dover and Folkstone, all down the shoreline to the south, I ran through the Kentish ports from which, in the desperate spring of 1940, small motorboats had put out to cross the more than forty miles of open water to help rescue the British army at Dunkirk. In something of a modern miracle, I was told, the waters of the Strait of Dover, that day, were like a millpond. On this afternoon waves rolled high. White surf and white chalk met far below me when I looked down from the white cliffs of Dover.

These world-famous cliffs thousands of years ago were part of a larger ridge of chalk connecting England and France. The precipitous shorelines at Dover and Calais, representing opposite ends of the ridge, now are separated by twenty-two miles of salt water. On that July Sunday in 1909, when Louis Blériot, following the line of that long-disappeared ridge, crossed those miles of water in his monoplane, pulled by a three-cylinder, twenty-one-horsepower engine, he landed like an exhausted bird on North Fall Meadow only a few hundred feet from the precipice edge of the English cliffs. Walking down the slope of a small ravine below the dark bulk of Dover Castle, I came to the spot where his machine had rolled to a stop. With dramatic appropriateness, the monument that marks the site is formed of blocks of granite set in the earth and reproducing, even to the propeller, the exact shape and size of Blériot's monoplane.

Bordering this aeroplane-in-granite, English daisies scattered their blooms across the sod. Wood pigeons went arrowing overhead, cleaving the air at a speed as great as Blériot's. On the warm breeze, the perfume—sweet, nostalgic—of some unseen flower reached my nose. It brought to mind the scent of the tiny white blooms of the wild bedstraw mounded up beside forest streams in the great north woods of eastern America.

All the time I remained at this historic spot, I heard the calling of a cuckoo. I walked away wondering why, after mating, a cuckoo should call. Among the species of birds that build nests, the singing of the male serves to announce territories and warn rivals away. But why the insistent calling of the cuckoo? It builds no nest; it has no nesting territory. The answer seems to be that, in its own way, it is maintaining a nesting area, an area of nests to parasitize. It is essential that these birds spread out, avoid concentrating in one area, in order to have sufficient nests to prey upon. So that mellow voice of the spring, the calling of the cuckoo serves as a natural device for spreading out the species. In connection with this sound, R. L. Smith and Eric Hosking, the famous British bird photographer, have reported the remarkable discovery that willow warblers react to an imitation of the cuckoo's call. This seems to imply that these small birds associate the voice of the male cuckoo— which never comes near the nest—with the victimizing activities of the female.

When Blériot steered for the shining cliffs of Dover, heading across the shortest water gap between England and the Continent, he was following the immemorial pathway of returning migrants. All these Kentish shores are a migrant's coast in the spring. Hosts of homecoming birds, some after wintering as far off as central Africa, speed across this water gap by night. Sometimes by day, journeying butterflies, painted ladies that have spanned the Mediterranean, cross the channel and make their landfall on the edge of Kent.

Where a sandy beach ran down to the breaking surf, at
the edge of one resort town, I stopped beside a weather-
grayed wooden stand. It bore the sign: "Crabs. Whelks.
Ready for Eating." For sixpence I bought a plate of hot
boiled whelks. With a dash of vinegar and a bit of pepper,
they were delicious. By now I was far down the coast, almost to the reclaimed land of Romney Marsh and the
southward-jutting triangle that ends in Dungeness. Golden
chain, or Laburnum, trees bloomed in country dooryards as
I turned across the open, level land to Lydd. Bent trees, like
green compass needles, flared away from the sea. Dungeness,
with its vast expanse of shingle and its only breeding colony
of common gulls in England, is now dominated by two
products of present-day technology, an immense nuclear
power station and an ultramodern lighthouse with auto-
matic light and sixty loudspeakers booming a warning in
fog. From the nuclear plant more than twenty million gal-
lons of water an hour pour back into the sea. Ornithologists
have discovered that the disturbed area that results is attracting rare sea birds. Already the little gull, the Mediterranean gull, Sabine's gull, the roseate tern, the gull-billed
tern, and the white-winged black tern have been recorded
here.

Along the roadsides, as I turned inland—north toward
Tunbridge Wells—ran the brown water of drainage canals.
All the thousand dairy fields around had once been part of
that vast, secretive, waterlogged domain, Romney Marsh.
In meadows, at this time of year, the bulbous buttercup
was at its height, the same buttercup that, transplanted to
the New World, blooms in spring beside the pasture path
that slopes away beyond the window of the room in which
I write these words. I lean back, thinking of all the familiar
wildflowers of America, from Queen Anne's Lace to mul-
lein, that have crossed the Atlantic from Britain.

Since it was mainly emigrants from western Europe that,

bringing seed with them, developed North American agriculture, it is natural that a wide variety of weeds should have come with them. The total is more than 1,000 species. In one list of weeds common in the state of New York, published in 1953, more than 40 per cent were common also in England. An account of the important weeds on farms in Canada, issued by the Department of Agriculture, showed that more than 60 per cent were introduced from Europe. As early as 1750 the Swedish traveler Peter Kalm found many of the common plants of Europe already established in New York and New Jersey.

It was Charles Darwin's ingenious idea that, in the past, new species of plants may have been added to Britain's flora from a seemingly unlikely source, the activity of hawks. When birds of prey capture small seed-eating migrants, newly arrived from other lands, he reasoned, some of the undigested seeds—that otherwise would have been consumed in the body of the migrant—would be released by the feeding of the predators.

During the last forty years of his life, while his exploring mind ranged over innumerable aspects of natural science, Darwin lived at Down House, near the village of Downe, in northeastern Kent close to the Surrey border. Writing in October 1846 to Captain Fitzroy, who commanded H.M.S. *Beagle* on its voyage around the world, he declared: "My life goes on like clockwork, and I am fixed on the spot where I shall end it." That spot, still rural and secluded, still deserves Darwin's description: "I think I was never in a more perfectly quiet country," It lay under a silvering of mist on the morning I reached it. I seemed a hundred miles, instead of only twenty, from London.

Today the stolid, three-storied, square brick structure that Darwin described as "a good, very ugly house" is maintained as a public shrine. On this misty day I was the only visitor. I wandered, in high-ceilinged rooms, from case to case among mementos of Darwin's life, his labors, his travels and his achievements. Here were pocket notebooks, with cloth covers and metal clasps, that had accompanied him on the *Beagle*. Here was the printed "Order of Procession at the Funeral of Mr. Darwin at Westminster Abbey, April 26, 1882." Here, among souvenirs of his ventures into wild places, was one labeled a "Life Saver." A variation of a blackjack, it consisted of two metal balls at the end of a plaited cord of leather.

The study, where Darwin wrote all but two of his seventeen books, where he assembled evidence for his theory of evolution and where he set down, at last, *The Origin of Species*, has been restored to the same fascinating clutter of books, pamphlets, skulls, microscopes, chemicals, globes, botanical and zoological specimens that surrounded him in the days of his greatest labors. One well-worn feature of the room is a low swivel stool, with cushions and large wheel-like casters. On it, Darwin could quickly wheel or roll within reach of whatever he needed. High windows, opening on the garden outside, even on this day of misty weather, provided ample light for the room within.

The mist had lessened when I came out. House martins swooped above the rose garden and the old sundial close by. Beyond, growing darker in the thinning of the mist, loomed the strip of woodland around which runs the Sand Walk where Darwin, accompanied by his dog, was in the habit of walking, often several times a day, while pondering on the vast implications of his theory. One feature of the present landscape Darwin never knew lifted silvery-hued in the distance—the staring line of high-tension electric cables that, as near White's Selborne, now cross the countryside not far from Downe.

In the other direction, heading toward home along some narrow, nameless country road that went twisting down through a woods, dank and still, with mossy boles and exposed, intertwining roots, I pulled to a stop in sudden amazement and delight. In this sheltered spot, tens of thousands of bluebells bloomed together. They transformed the whole floor of the woodland into a lake of blue. The moist air was filled with the scent of these wild hyacinths. I was to see this flower of spring, the "Blew English Hare Bell" of old Gerard, in many places. But nowhere else did it bloom in such dramatic profusion as here. The intense stillness, the perfumed air, the waves and pools of color, the solitariness of the scene whose loveliness I alone contemplated, all these impressed the moment on my mind. That vision of sequestered, out-of-the-world beauty remains linked with all my memories of the land where Darwin lived.

During almost all of our travels in Britain, our plans changed from day to day. We rarely knew exactly where we would be two days hence. Nobody in the world knew how to get in touch with us. Nobody knew where to find us. From the time we landed until we left for home, we had only three certain addresses in England. One was the hotel in Southampton where we stayed on our first day in England. The second was the hotel in London which we reached just before our departure. The third was: "Care of Rev. John E. James, Woodstock Rectory, Woodstock, Oxfordshire."

Half a dozen years before, my mail in America had contained a pleasant letter about one of my books from an unknown English clergyman. It was followed by a present of an old and beautifully illustrated edition of Gilbert White's *Selborne*. In subsequent years other editions followed. Although my correspondent knew me only through my books and I knew him only through his letters, a transatlantic friendship developed and Nellie and I were invited to stop at Woodstock when we came to Oxford. We set May 10 for the date of our arrival. May 10 had come. And we were a hundred miles away at Tunbridge Wells. But we met John and Lois James just the same.

On that originally appointed day, they drove over to see us—a round trip of fully 200 miles. It is probably a hazardous thing to meet friends-by-letter who are strangers-in-life. Preconceptions are apt to fall victim to reality. But happy was the conclusion in this instance. From first to last, we were all congenial. In these unseen friends who had materialized we found a remarkable combination of warmth and friendliness and depth and character. The longer we knew them, the more proud I became that such people as these should have been attracted to a book of mine.

To my surprise I discovered that it was the Reverend John E. James who, almost as his first duty as Rector at Woodstock, had conducted, in nearby Bladon churchyard, the burial services of Sir Winston Churchill. We talked on and on that day. Among the accumulation of letters and cablegrams brought from the rectory, many concerned the same subject. Unknown to us, in the fiftieth year of such awards, a Pulitzer Prize had been given to the final, rounding-out volume of my series on the four American seasons, *Wandering Through Winter*. On the morning when this announcement appeared in American newspapers, Nellie and I had been walking along the foot of the Hanger at Selborne. In all the world, at such a moment, in what finer place could we have been? It was long after dinner that night when these English friends of ours began their long drive home. Early the following week, we said, we would be in Woodstock.

By now the days were extending in both directions—into the dawn, into the dusk. They lengthened minute by minute. At Tunbridge Wells, our windows began graying with the dawn light soon after 4:30 A.M. The year was opening its eyes. By now, too, Nellie's cough was gone. Her strength had returned. We were almost ready to journey again.

In our immense hotel, we noticed that people usually stepped aside and waited until we reached a landing on the stairs. We attributed this to English politeness until, one morning, an elderly gentleman smilingly volunteered:

"You know, they say it is unlucky to pass on the stairs."

During the next to the last night of our stay at Tunbridge Wells, we were awakened, toward morning, by the sound of low voices and running feet in the hall. We assumed someone had been taken seriously ill during the night. At breakfast, we heard a different explanation. A gang of thieves had invaded the hotel, tied up the night porter and—from long cabinets outside the dining room directly below us—had stolen a large and valuable collection of silver plate. In telling me of these exciting events, the manager, in the true tradition of the imperturbable Englishman, concluded:

"So I am afraid some shoes may not have been cleaned last night."

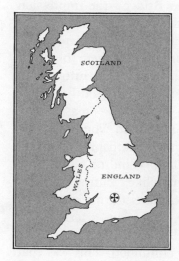

chapter 17

VALLEY
OF THE
WINDRUSH

"Each traveler," Goethe once said, "should know what he has to see and what properly belongs to him on a journey."

What properly belonged to us, we knew, was the outdoor aspect of Britain. As we rode west from Kent through Surrey, the southern fringes of London were no more than a dozen miles away. Yet all around us we observed the face of the countryside we had come to see. Throughout our days in England, a continual source of wonder was the fact that so much of this densely populated land, this most heavily industrialized country in the world, is still so fresh and rural.

Twenty-nine of the fifty states, in America, are each larger than the whole of England. With 3,615,211 square miles inhabited by about 200,000,000 people, the United States has an average of slightly more than fifty persons to the square mile. England, with 45,000,000 people living on 50,331 square miles of land, has a density of population eighteen times as great—900 to the square mile. Yet even close to its largest cities—even, as here, within twenty miles of Trafalgar Square and Waterloo Bridge—the impression of open spaces, of green countryside, predominates.

To Nellie, after her hotel-bound days, spring seemed to have made a sudden leap forward. Everywhere bluebells and buttercups and horse chestnuts had burst into bloom while she rested. Our sweep east through the southernmost counties had ended in Kent. Now we followed an ascending path back to the west, through Surrey and Middlesex and Buckinghamshire and Berkshire into Oxfordshire. Our way carried us past Hampton Court and Windsor Castle and over the River Mole, which, molelike, burrows underground to follow a subterranean channel during part of its course. And beside the Thames, early one afternoon, it brought us to a wide, flower-filled expanse, a riverside meadow we had read about since childhood. This was that field of flowers, Runnymede, where, on a spring day in 1215, in one of the most far-reaching events in history, King John signed the Magna Carta.

Among the daisies and plantain and buttercups and dandelions we walked out on this level field stretching between the river and a wooded ridge. As we advanced among the blooms, we felt something was absent. What was it? At last we found the answer. No hummingbirds! These vibrant, darting winged creatures, displaying such a riot of metallic colors in tropical America and most of the United States, are birds unknown to England.

In the course of our travels on this day, we added to our growing list of picturesque place-names found on the map of England—Nipkins, Littley Green, Sixpenny Handley, Kettlesing and Ryme Intrinsica—two more, Pennypot and Christmas Pie. The day ended remote from meadow flowers, amid brick and glass and asphalt, in heat and dust and noise. At Slough, that teeming center of business activity, we spent the night in a commercial hotel, across from the railroad station, beside a bus-loading area, above a taxi stand and near London Airport. Trains came in. Trains went out. Buses stopped and started. Telephones rang at the taxi stand. Airliners roared overhead. The sleepless hours dragged on. We seemed suddenly set down in a human ant-hill. Frenzied activity, accompanied by noise, continued far into the night. We were overtaken by a problem as old as the prophet Isaiah, who wrote: "Woe unto them that join house to house, that lay field to field, till there be no place that they may be placed alone in the midst of the earth."

Morning dawned at last. We started away listlessly. But only two or three miles to the north we forgot the misadventure of Slough. In the village of Stoke Poges, with the low rays of the early light stretching over dewy grass and lichened gravestones, we walked in the country churchyard immortalized by Thomas Gray's *Elegy*. The scene retained a simple, rural beauty. A remote and ancient air hung about it still. Here the poet is buried. And nearby stands the monument erected in his memory in 1799 by John Penn, grandson of William Penn, the founder of Pennsylvania. On this May morning, Gray's Field, adjoining the churchyard, was carpeted with green and gold, the green of fresh grass, the gold of flowering buttercups. For a time we walked along its edge. When we returned, our shoes were yellow with the pollen of the flowers.

So these days went by, days of spring, days of flowers, days of sunshine. We had crossed the border into Oxfordshire when, one noon, we turned into a hilltop layby to eat our lunch. And there we met with a small adventure.

As I was putting the remains of the meal in one of the trash baskets, my eye was caught by a curious continuous wavering or shimmering movement in the grass beyond. I bent close. Someone had tossed away a partly filled milk bottle. It lay on its side. And swimming in the milk, its claws unable to obtain a grip on the slippery glass, was a reddish mouse. As though bewitched, it appeared running at top speed yet remaining in the same place.

I lifted the bottle and tilted the mouth down. Milk and mouse rushed to the opening. The mouse formed a cork and most of the milk stayed inside. But the animal's tail waved in the opening. I grasped it and yanked. Out came the mouse and a flood of milk. The little animal, apparently unhurt, scurried away into the grass. How long it had been in the bottle I do not know. But, unaided, it would have died in its transparent prison.

Each year, along the roads of Britain, thousands of small animals lose their lives in such thoughtlessly discarded death traps. Wayside tragedies of the kind have been reported from Littlehampton, on the coast of Sussex, to Loch Ness, in northern Scotland; from Croydon, on the edge of London, to Mt. Snowdon, in Wales, where a dead wood mouse was discovered in a bottle 3,000 feet above sea level. Because British milk bottles have smaller mouths than those in America, they present a greater hazard.

A few years ago, *The Countryman* published the results of a nation-wide survey made in Britain. Eighteen hundred animals were found in 850 discarded bottles. The victims included thirteen species of mammals. They ranged from pigmy mice to brown rats. Those most frequently encountered were the bank vole and the common shrew. Usually a bottle contained one, sometimes two, victims. However, in one instance, an empty quart bottle, picked up in Essex, held the remains of twenty-eight small animals.

Why do these creatures push their way into empty bottles? In most cases, in a search for food or out of curiosity. Entering is easy, for the hind feet can grip the ground. But —unless the bottle is tilting steeply downward—the return journey to freedom is impossible. In some of the bottles containing dead animals, flesh flies are also present. These, in turn, would attract other mammals, particularly such insect eaters as bank voles and long-tailed field mice.

Recently British scientists, studying the abundance and distribution of various species of small mammals, have turned to discarded bottles as a special source of information. Using a Land-Rover, zoologists of the University of Durham, in one survey, visited picnic areas and laybys bordered by dense vegetation over a wide area in the north of England. The results, recorded in the July–September 1966 issue of *The Naturalist*, the publication of the Yorkshire Naturalists' Union, showed that, in the order of their abundance, the three most frequently found animals in this region were the common shrew, the bank vole and the long-tailed field mouse. While beer and wine bottles held some mammals, it was milk bottles—quart, pint, and even half-pint sizes—that produced the greatest number of victims.

We were eight miles beyond the many spires of Oxford when we reached Woodstock and a warm welcome from John and Lois James. In the Woodstock Rectory, that afternoon, sitting beside the picture window that looks out on the Grand Bridge of Blenheim Park, we examined the most interesting book we encountered in Britain. A large loose-leaf volume several inches thick, prepared some years before Winston Churchill's death, it was entitled *Operation Hope Not*. Its more than a dozen sections recorded in minute detail—even down to the precise minute when the soldiers of the honor guard were to have their tea—the elaborate plans for the wartime Prime Minister's state funeral. In nearby Bladon churchyard, we visited his grave. From the windows of the room he occupied as a boy during vacations at Blenheim Palace, Churchill could see, through a gap in the trees, the small stone church of Bladon. This gap, according to his wishes, will be maintained permanently.

Both Blenheim Palace and the vast landscaped park around it were presented by Queen Anne to Churchill's ancestor, the Duke of Marlborough, in recognition of his military victories. Beside the Grand Avenue that extends in a straight line from the palace to the towering Victory Column commemorating his defeat of the French on August 13, 1704, near the Austrian village of Blenheim, runs a double line of elms, each elm representing a soldier who fought in that historic battle.

In a way, the grounds of Blenheim Park are also a monument to another man, to the most famous landscape architect of the eighteenth century, "Capability" Brown. Born in the tiny village of Kirkharle, in Northumberland, in 1716, he was christened Lancelot Brown. Neither the day nor the month of his birth is known. His nickname arose from his frequent references to the "capabilities" of the grounds of great estates where he worked. His aim was to pursue the path nature had laid out and to produce scenes like landscape paintings. Blenheim Park was considered one of his masterpieces.

To see the grounds and the palace, as many as 250,000 visitors a year come to Woodstock. Other visitors, a wide variety of aquatic birds, are attracted by the winding lake that Brown produced by damming a small river. A total of thirty-five species of waterfowl have apppeared on this small body of water. It is the main breeding place in Oxfordshire for the great crested grebe and the tufted duck. Here, for a first time, Nellie and I saw a wild male pochard, with its chestnut head and chestnut neck. This duck breeds nowhere else in the county.

At Oxford, the next day, good news awaited us. X-rays showed that all traces of pneumonia had left Nellie's lungs. The road was open again! In celebration, we all set off in John James's red Sunbeam, riding toward the west, toward the beautiful upland of the Cotswold Hills. In many places, beginning in Cornwall, people had spoken to us of the charm of the Cotswolds. Among these rolling hills of oolitic limestone, in former times, there grazed the famed Cotswold sheep, Britain's largest breed.

In the days of Shakespeare's *Richard II*, travel over the fourteenth-century roads of the region was slow and laborious. "These high wild hills and rough uneven ways," the King laments, "draw out our miles and make them wearisome." On the smooth, paved highways of the present day, we skimmed, that morning, up and down the hills, watching the horizons retreat around us as we climbed each higher swell of land. Among the Cotswolds, the average elevation is between 600 and 700 feet. The highest point is Cleeve Hill, 1,130 feet above sea level.

Our circuit of the hills that day carried us onto the land of four counties—Oxfordshire, Warwickshire, Worcestershire, and Gloucestershire. It led us through charming villages, with houses formed of the golden or honey-colored rock of the region. They bore such names as Chipping Norton, Lower Slaughter, Stow-on-the-Wold, Moreton-in-Marsh and Bourton-on-the-Hill. At Lower Slaughter, we walked by an ancient water mill that was still grinding grain. From one height of land we looked down into the fertile orchards of the Vale of Evesham. Our road ran past Stonesfield, the source of slates noted for their ability to attract moss and lichens; by Fairford, with its church window depicting the Devil pitchforking sinners into Hell—all of them women; and near Juniper Hill, the original *Lark Rise* of Flora Thompson's engaging and candid memories of her Cotswold childhood. In her time, it was the custom for children to carry two hot potatoes in their pockets when they set out for school in cold weather. Thus they warmed their hands along the way and were provided with food for lunch at noon.

As we stood on the main street of the village of Stanton,

swifts kept shooting down between the mellowed Cotswold stone of the old cottage walls, streaking again and again just above our heads. Under such circumstances, Nellie and I first heard the "screaming" of the swifts. Far different from the "chittering" or "chippering" of our chimney swift at home, it is a prolonged, piercing screech produced by small groups flying together. We saw a compact flock of half a dozen twisting among the houses and racing down the straightaway of the street, speeding on slim, scythe-shaped wings and filling the air with their shrill din. The sound approached, rocketed by and continued behind us as the birds chased wildly through the air. An old village name for the swift is "devil screamer."

Another name by which these birds are known in Europe is "Thunder Swallow." At times they have been seen storm-soaring below thunderheads, rising higher and higher, riding the violent updrafts amid thunder and lightning, wind and rain. Laboratory studies have shown that swifts, and some other birds that make sudden stops in flight, have thin, single-layered "windows" in their double-layered skulls. Such places, it is suggested, may be capable of expansion, thus reducing the danger from a rush of blood to the head in an abrupt stop.

Have you ever looked closely at the eye of a swift? Once when a chimney swift at home entered a room from a fireplace, I held it in my hand before releasing it outdoors. I have always remembered the liquid beauty of its dark eye. Mine was an exceptional opportunity. For the eye of the swift, like the eye of the toad, is an object of beauty but rarely observed.

The sweeping hills, the far reaches of farmland and pasture, the warm, honey-colored stone of the village buildings —of all the recollections that come back from that day in the Cotswolds, one is predominant. It is the memory of a stream and a valley, both as beautiful in name as in form,

Pollard willows beside a Wiltshire stream

the stream and the valley of the Windrush. The source of this river is only a few miles from the street of the screaming swifts at Stanton. Above Cutsdean a small spring oozes from a hillside. Fed by other springs, the growing river wanders on to reach "The Valley of the Torrent," once the home of mills mentioned in the Domesday Book. During the thirty miles of its serpentine advance, the Windrush, clear, swift, and shallow at its start, spreads out into reedy water meadows, bisects the village of Bourton-on-the-Water, and traverses some of the most picturesque landscape of the hill country.

Between the source of the river, "up in they hills" as they say in the Cotswolds, and its junction with the Thames, we crossed the stream a number of times. We stood on old stone bridges watching the wavering waterweeds anchored to the stream bed. We stopped to smell the perfume of the wayfaring tree, rising, all in white, beside the river. We looked down from hilltops, tracing the stream's course through pasture land by the richer, more luxuriant growth along its banks. We halted to watch moor hens threading their way among the reeds and flowers of water meadows. All down this valley, in a few weeks' time, multitudes of emerging gauzy-winged May flies would rise from the water to dance and mate and rush through the swift cycle of their ephemeral lives. Our last view of the Windrush came as we were turning back toward Woodstock. In dramatic lighting, the shining serpentine of the river lay outstretched, its valley in brilliant sunshine, the sky behind it dark and swollen with the clouds of a local storm.

That evening, at dinner, it was our good fortune to become acquainted with Bruce Campbell and his wife. This naturalist, whose writings were familiar to us in America, was one of those we had hoped to meet in England. After the baked Scotch salmon Lois James had prepared, we sat

Earthwork surrounding Avebury, above. Stones of the prehistoric Great Circle at Avebury, below

back and talk turned to the pets kept by a young girl in a nearby cottage. One was a basset hound, another a donkey that cropped grass among the gravestones in the church- yard. When a difference of opinion arose in the congrega- tion over the propriety of the animal's presence there, it was Rev. James who settled it by pointing out:

"If a donkey was good enough to carry Jesus into Jerusa- lem, it should be good enough to be in a churchyard."

Every hour, on the hour, the chimes of the Woodstock church peal out a tune, religious on Sunday, secular on weekdays. Several of the airs set off the hound and the don- key. As soon as the bells chime out, the basset begins to bay and the donkey joins in a raucous duet. It lasts as long as those particular tunes continue.

During the war, Bruce Campbell recalled, the roar of heavy bombers passing overhead at night seemed to stimu- late the singing of nightingales. These birds respond with melody to even the loudest and harshest of sounds. Oliver G. Pike, one of England's noted wildlife photographers, tells of being in the trenches at the edge of a French wood in 1916. High explosives had ripped apart the undergrowth and shattered many of the trees. Yet a pair of nightingales had returned to nest where they had been in previous years. At the height of an enemy bombardment, with star shells drifting down, shrapnel bursting over the trenches, and the ground trembling from the violence of the artillery fire, the male nightingale, seemingly stimulated by the detonations, sang from its perch in the remnant of a tree. During each momentary lull, its glorious melody carried to the men in the trenches until a shell burst in a direct hit and tree and singer disappeared.

Nellie still longed to hear a nightingale. She had missed it at Selborne. She had been sick in Sussex and Kent. From now on, we would be moving farther north, away from the main concentration of these birds in southern England.

Bruce Campbell volunteered to take us out on the following night in search of the longed-for song.

Our start was late because of the slow waning of the northern twilight. A glow still tinged the sky at 9:30 P.M. Even at ten o'clock, as we followed dusky roads in Campbell's Hillman Minx, the landscape around remained dimly visible. For a long time we roamed over darkening Bladon Heath. There, although we heard no nightingales, our ears caught the voice of a far different singer. Repeated monotonously, like the stridulations of a summer locust, it reached us—the odd, dry little song of a grasshopper warbler.

"Nothing can be more amusing," Gilbert White wrote to Thomas Pennant in 1768, "than the whisper of this little bird, which seems to be close though at a hundred yard's distance; and, when close to your ear, is scarce any louder than when a great way off." Because of the song's resemblance to the sound of a fisherman's reel, the warbler is colloquially called "the reel bird" and its singing is referred to as "reeling." We noticed how the position of the unseen singer seemed to vary as the song continued. In reeling, with its bill wide open and its wings quivering, the warbler turns its head from side to side. This produces a striking ventriloquistic effect. The singer seems now here, now there, among the bushes.

Although its thin song has great carrying power, the voice of the grasshopper warbler is so high-pitched that it is inaudible to some listeners. Another warbler—a summer visitor that, after a lapse of a hundred years, has begun nesting again in Kent—has a somewhat similar song. This is the Savi's warbler. But its trill is lower in pitch. A saying among English bird watchers, Bruce Campbell told us, is that if you begin to lose your hearing and cannot hear the grasshopper warbler but think you can, you are hearing a Savi's.

To the reeling of the former bird, we added, in that gath-

ering night on Bladon Heath, another new bird sound, that
of a "roding" woodcock. Against the sky, from time to
time, we glimpsed the speeding form of this chunky bird.
Unlike the spectacular song flight of the American woodcock, with the climax of its wildly veering, falling-leaf descent and the sweet twittering of its song, the European
bird circles at no great height above the ground. The only
sound we heard was a sibilant, spitting call, a kind of sneez-
ing "tsiwick" as the woodcock sped by.

Later, as we followed the curves and seemingly aimless
wanderings of the country roads, our lights, here and there,
picked up the forms of little hedgehogs disappearing into
the weeds. As Oliver Goldsmith noted in his eighteenth-
century *Natural History*: "Animals of the hedgehog kind
require but little accuracy to distinguish them from all others." Once a young hare, as though demonstrating its dodg-
ing ability, zigzagged in the lights of our slowly moving car.

The chill of the night increased. The wind rose. Chill
and wind are neither to the liking of the nightingale. Both
lessened our chances of hearing the sought-for song. But we
kept on, visiting valleys, stopping by patches of brambles
and undergrowth, turning aside to situations favored by the
birds. For more than thirty miles we drove that night—to
Ot Moor, to Horton-cum-Studley, to all the places where
Campbell was accustomed to find nightingales singing in
the spring. Midnight had almost come before he admitted
defeat. Disappointed, but deeply aware of our indebtedness
to him, we turned reluctantly toward home.

The next morning, bidding our Woodstock friends good-
bye, we turned north to Banbury—Banbury of the Banbury
Cross and the nursery rhyme of the fine lady with rings on
her fingers and bells on her toes. Then, angling upward toward the west, we crossed into Warwickshire. About noon,
we came to Stratford-on-Avon.

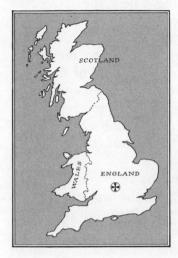

chapter 18

SHAKE-
SPEARE'S
RIVER

Thirteen heifers, black-and-white, stood side by side in the
shade of the willows on the riverbank. They stared silently
at us as we went by, my oars rising and falling and rising
again. Woodstock lay nearly thirty miles to the south. Before us, endlessly winding, the placid Warwickshire Avon,
Shakespeare's river, flowed toward us out of the Vale of Evesham.

A mile or more downstream, behind us, at Stratford-on-
Avon, crowds thronged the sidewalks and swarmed about
stalls displaying varied wares. We had arrived on a market
day. For seven centuries and seven decades, ever since the
Middle Ages, Stratford-on-Avon has been designated a market town. It received the first charter of the kind in Warwickshire. Working our way through the crowds, we had
found a room at the White Swan, where some of the timbers are said to be 500 years old.

As part of the annual parade of more than 200,000 visitors to the town of Shakespeare's birth, Nellie and I
roamed about the historic town. We walked along the nar-

row streets, lingered in the house where the creator of *Hamlet, Macbeth,* and *King Lear* came into the world, drove to Anne Hathaway's cottage, with its garden filled with old-fashioned flowers. Then, leaving the multitudes behind, we followed the serpentine water road of the River Avon. Rowing and floating and now and then halting along one bank or the other, we advanced slowly among willows and lowland meadows. In the rich pastoral scene watered by the river, we saw the heart of Shakespeare's middle England.

Our craft was a shallow boat; my oars were curved at the ends like spoons. Pushing out into the sluggish current below Clopton Bridge, we had passed beneath one of its massive arches as we headed upstream. Built by Hugh Clopton, a native of the town who became a merchant of great wealth, a one-time Lord Mayor of London, the stone span has been a landmark of the region since the reign of Henry VII. This bridge, this river, Shakespeare knew as a boy.

As we emerged from under the span, we saw people looking down. They were watching the swans that floated on the surface of the stream. The Avon, since early times, has been a river of swans. Inns in the town have long borne such names as the Swan, the White Swan, and the Swan's Nest. In the vicinity of the bridge, as I rowed on, we counted more than sixty of these majestic waterfowl. One of them attached itself to us and swam beside us. For a mile and a half or two miles it kept us company.

Once, when I leaned on my oars beneath on overhanging willow, it came alongside and thrust an extended neck over the side of the boat, looking about the interior for food. One of its black legs, the left, I saw, was encircled by a yellow band. In the days of William Shakespeare, nearly 900 distinct swan-marks were recognized by the Royal Swanherd. Like brands on range cattle, these markings on legs, feet, wings, bills, indicated the owners. Today it is estimated there are about 18,000 mute swans in Great Britain.

Overhead, fleecy clouds drifted in the sunshine, their images mirrored on the surface of the stream. As the swan swam in and out of these reflected clouds, it lost and gained in whiteness. The brilliance of its plumage decreased amid the shining images of the floating vapor; grew luminous and immaculate against the dark stream-water. Occasionally the convoying swan wandered off to pick among the sedges of some shallow bay within an arm of the river or to reach up and break off a leafy willow twig from some low-hanging limb. Then, with powerful strokes that sent the water swirling, it would come swimming upstream and overtake us again. All its movements were stately and unhurried. But it swam with surprising speed, keeping ahead of me for long stretches as I rowed.

When Nathaniel Hawthorne came to the Avon on a June day in 1855, he commented in one of his English notebooks: "I do not know an American river so tame." On our day, a month earlier in the season, this peaceful stream meandered through a land of orchards and meadows—orchards now white with blossoms, meadows now golden with buttercups. Thousands of miles away, in America, at this same time, the two commonest buttercups of England were also blooming—the bulbous and the meadow buttercup, *Ranunculus bulbosus* and *Ranunculus acris*. The generic name, *Ranunculus*, incidentally, is derived from *rana*, the Latin word for frog. Apparently it was applied to the plant because it so often favors wet lowland fields where frogs abound. Naturalized from Europe, the buttercup has spread across the eastern United States.

On both sides of the Atlantic, farmers view the beauty of its golden blooms with an unfriendly eye. The plants, of little or no economic value, replace valuable grass. Because of their burning, acrid juice, horses and cattle usually avoid

them and their numbers increase in meadowland. Among
the long list of common names applied to the buttercup,
you find: butter-cress, butter-rose, butter-daisy, goldcups,
kingcups, St. Anthony's turnip, blister-flowers, cuckoo-buds,
horse-gold, and butter-flowers.

Sometime before our accompanying swan deserted us, we
stopped beneath four immense horse chestnuts. Leaning
out over the stream at a bend in the river, all were laden
from top to bottom with the white pyramids of their flower
clusters. About the time of Shakespeare's death, this tree, a
native of the Balkan mountains, first appeared as an introduced species in England. Close by, in a little bay sheltered
by weeping willows, we watched, for five or ten minutes, a
moor hen as it stalked along the edge, feeding with quick
darts of its yellow-tipped red bill. Hardly had I taken up my
oars again when we came upon a dark damsel fly struggling
on the surface of the water. As I turned toward it, there
was a swirl and the insect disappeared, gulped down perhaps by a perch, one of those "tawny-finn'd fishes" Shakespeare watched as a boy swimming among the lily pads by
Clopton Bridge.

Every once in a while, on every trip we make, I have the
feeling I am about to learn something by making a mistake.
So it was, about three o'clock that afternoon, on Shakespeare's river. We pulled up to rest beside one bank and I
noticed among the wildflowers growing in the rich alluvial
soil a clump of stinging nettles. Among Britain's 2,270 native plants, the nettle is both widely distributed and, with
justice, widely known. In a dramatic way, the power and
permanence of its sting was demonstrated during the early
days of the Second World War. When a photographic record was being made of the Linnaean collections, Geoffrey
Grigson recalls in *Wild Flowers in Britain*, the photographer, in arranging the herbarium speciments, was stung by
a nettle Linnaeus had dried 200 years before. On the Avon,

that day, looking at the nettle clump, I remembered the old admonition about grasping a nettle boldly. For the first time in my life—and suspecting I was on the verge of an educating mistake—I put the saying to the test. I reached out in a quick, hard grab. Neither as severe nor as long-lasting as I expected was the pain of the stinging hairs. I surmise this may be due to the thicker skin on the palm of my hand.

It was our impression that the country through which the Avon flows had been left relatively unmarred by the twentieth century's technological progress. Man's hand had touched it lightly. On opposite sides of the Atlantic, a century ago, two men, ahead of their time, set down similar convictions regarding that problem of ever-increasing complexity and urgency—the relation of man to his environment. In England, William Morris was laying down the dictum that the external aspect of the country belongs to the whole public and that whoever wilfully injures it is a public enemy. And across the sea, Henry Thoreau was writing in his *Journal* under the date of September 28, 1857: "If some are prosecuted for abusing children, others deserve to be prosecuted for maltreating the face of nature committed to their care."

Wherever we went in following the Avon, winding with its serpentine course, the swan now left far behind, we found the air filled with the perfume of the hawthorn. Often I paused in my rowing to breathe deeply, enjoying to the full the delicately scented air. Hedges now were snowbanks of white blossoms. It is unlucky, according to an old-time superstition, to pick and bring indoors blooms of the hawthorn, the "whitethorn," the "mayflower," the "May." Close up, the fragrance of the hawthorn is strong, almost overpowering, like the heavy perfume of plum blossoms. But distributed in the air, carried on the breeze, it becomes the sweet characteristic flower scent of the English spring.

At last, I pulled on one oar, swung around, and, with the current, headed home. A flowing river is the escalator of nature, powered by gravity, set to run in one direction. Drifting for long stretches, we passed small islets with their upper ends hidden beneath bleached floodwrack left by the high water of other years. We passed willows pollarded long ago for firewood and fencing material. We passed wide green meadows holding graceful elms—elms once so common they were known as "the weed of Warwickshire." Where the river ran more swiftly on the outer curves of its meandering course, the vertical side of the undercut bank was often armored with exposed and twisted tree roots. Here we saw the holes of water rats, their entrances slick and shiny, smoothed by the wet bodies of the animals entering their burrows.

Frequently, as we floated along, the reflections of passing birds appeared in the mirror of the glassy stream. From treetop to treetop, rooks swung back and forth across the river. With a bill full of food, a starling—the bird that was introduced into America by an admirer of Shakespeare who sought to establish in the New World all the birds mentioned in his plays—crossed the stream and disappeared into an abandoned woodpecker hole high on a dead tree stub. In the water of one tiny baylet where rushes grew, a small, dark sparrow continued bathing as we went by. And everywhere in the sunshine, over the meadows and over the river, swallows swept through the air with graceful swoops and sudden fluttering stops, feeding on the wing. Once nearly a dozen landed in a willow tree, twittering incessantly, agitated by some swallow excitement of spring. In how many lands has the return of the swallow led to a similar reflection! Aristotle set down in Greek the axiom: "One swallow does not make spring"; Cervantes worded it in Spanish: "One swallow does not make summer"; and John Heywood, in the sixteenth century, put it in English: "One swallow maketh not summer."

In the final act of Richard Wagner's opera *Lohengrin,* "Ladies and Men (in great excitement)" cry: "The Swan! The Swan! The Swan! . . . Ah, he comes!" With somewhat less excitement, we greeted our former companion, the swan, when, rounding a turn, we came face to face. The white bird floated near the farther bank. It did not seem, I must report, particularly glad to see us. Evidently it had given us up as a source of food.

Enjoying the prospect of the winding river and the drifting clouds, enjoying the perfume of the hawthorn, sometimes in sunshine, sometimes in shadow, we advanced down this stream along which Shakespeare's boyhood had been spent. In his time, the region had fewer men and more trees. The great Forest of Arden extended then from the Avon to the present site of Birmingham. In these more populous days, when forests have been felled, it is hard for us to conceive the extent of the woodlands that originally occupied so much of Europe. Down to the first century before the birth of Christ, so immense was the forest that extended eastward from the Rhine that its boundaries were unknown. Natives that Julius Caesar questioned told him they had traveled through it for two months without coming to its end. At one time, all of Kent, all of Surrey, all of Sussex were covered by one far-reaching woodland, the vast Forest of Anderida. And so dense was the Forest of Arden that even down to historical times an old saying had it that a squirrel might leap from tree to tree and thus traverse almost the whole length of Warwickshire without touching the ground.

Whenever I think of this forest—the setting for William Shakespeare's *As You Like It*—my mind leaps back through time to a lowered curtain on the stage of an auditorium in a high school in mid-continent America. Woven into the fabric of that curtain was the picture of a glade and a forest stream and these words that had come from Shakespeare's pen in the last year of the sixteenth century:

"tongues in trees, books in the running brooks, sermons in stones and good in every thing." That pictured glade became for me a personal magic place. A hundred times, in schooldays, I drank in the wildness of that forest scene. It lightened the days of a difficult period of life. I wonder if any other of all the thousands of students who, in successive years, faced that depiction of the Forest of Arden found in it the solace it brought me?

After the passage of so many years, its image was vivid in my mind as we continued on down Shakespeare's river. It remained with me as we descended the last windings of the stream, now filled with other boats and echoing with the shouts and laughter of students on holiday. People still leaned over the edge of Clopton Bridge and stared at the swans below. I slipped with the current beneath it, drifted downstream and then, where we had started, pulled to shore and beached the boat.

For a time we stood idly watching the river flowing by. Always we would remember the Avon as we knew it that day—winding amid the white of the hawthorn, wrapped in the fragrance of its perfume. We saw it but once, we knew it in a single season of the year, this perfumed river we probably will never see again. One visit. One recollection. One season's aspect. It lives in memory—like the scene depicted on Keats' Grecian urn—forever fresh, forever unchanged. For us, Shakespeare's river will flow, without ceasing, through an unending English spring.

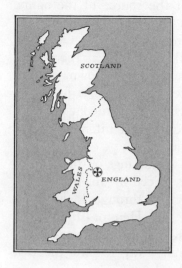

chapter 19

THE BLACK COUNTRY

A cat with a Mona Lisa smile dozed near the old inn door. Above it, rays of early sunshine highlighted the name: THE MARCH HARE. Everywhere we went in England, we found the names of country inns and village pubs derived from birds, from mammals, from fish, from flowers, from trees. The natural history of inn signs, with their paintings of foxes and pheasants, of songbirds and wildflowers, might well form the subject of an entire chapter.

During one day, I remember, we passed the Dog and Badger, the Dusty Miller, the Cock Robin, the Three Pickerels, the Mountain Ash, and the Falcon Inn. On other days there were the Magpie, the Peacock, the Bluebell, the Salmon's Tail, A Bunch of Cherries, the Rat's Castle, the Lion and Lamb, and the Swan Revived. We saw a White Lion, a Black Lion, and a Golden Lion. At various times we came to the Bird in Hand, the Four Swans, the Beehive, the Wild Boar, the Fox and Ducks, the Fox and Barrel, the Dog and Partridge, and, repeated a score of times, the Royal Oak.

When natural history was not the source of the name, occupations of the region often supplied the inspiration: the Hop Vine, in Kent; the Tinner's Arms, in Cornwall; the Jolly Sailors, on the Norfolk coast. Then there were such oddities as the World Turned Upside Down, the Jingling Gate, and the Live and Let Live Inn. As during so many other days, on this day when we turned west from Stratford-on-Avon, a source of continuing interest was the names of inns and pubs along the way.

As I look over the trail of our wanderings on the map of England, I see a rough oval. It is traced by our travels during the next few days. Our way led through lower Warwickshire, across Worcestershire into Herefordshire, north through Shropshire, east again across Staffordshire and south into upper Warwickshire, to trail away toward the east through Leicestershire and Rutland.

Near the beginning, in Herefordshire, amid its red soil, its lush green grass, its rows of apple trees, we were hardly forty miles north of Jenner's Vale of Berkeley; less than that above the Forest of Dean and the lowland fields where we had seen miles of daffodils blooming in the early-April rain. We came to Leominster, and beside an antique shop named the Den of Antiquity I bought a quart of milk for a wayside lunch from a deliveryman wearing a huge leather pouch. It was weighted down with small change, the large and heavy small change of England.

Then we turned north toward Shropshire. Houses with black timbers and white plastering between, the "magpie houses" characteristic of the west Midlands, appeared more frequently along the road. The country changed. In the words of that small volume, with its coat of scuffed tan leather, that rode with us—James Thomson's *The Seasons* —"the broken landscape, by degrees, ascending, roughened into rigid hills." The hills grew higher, partly farmed, partly wild and wooded. And always to our left rose those greater hills, blue-tinted in the hazy distance, the mountains of central Wales.

Half a dozen times, on curves of the twisty road, we saw the crushed bodies of little hedgehogs. To the age-old enemies of these relatively harmless creatures—the badgers, foxes, dogs, polecats, tawny owls, and gypsies—the twentieth century has added another, more deadly than all the others combined, the speeding motor car. From our earliest days to our last, from the beginning in southern England to the end of our northward journey at the top of Scotland, the animal we most often saw killed on side roads and highways was the hedgehog. When danger threatens, this simple-minded creature tends to curl up and lie still. Its outthrust quills protect it from many of its foes. But not from its great steel-and-rubber enemy, the automobile.

When driving at night, we not infrequently caught sight of these nocturnal animals along the edges of roads. Compared to the North American porcupine, which may have a length, from nose to tail tip, of more than three feet and may weigh more than thirty-five pounds, the hedgehog is a midget. It is only twice as long as a house sparrow. Its average weight is but a pound and a half. Its spines, which normally lie flat and number approximately 100 to the square inch, are about three-quarters of an inch long. The manner in which these spines are anchored at the base provides a special protection for the animals. Each quill rises from a hemispherical base which has a narrow, flexible neck above it. The neck prevents the spine from being driven back into the body of the hedgehog if it falls from any height on its back or side. For, in spite of its short legs, the creature is a strong climber, often ascending drain pipes and the sides of rough buildings, particularly where vines are growing.

During the day, the fuzzypig, hedgepig, or urchin, as country people call the hedgehog, is usually found sleeping soundly beneath a heap of leaves or moss in the protection of some thicket or hedgerow. It is said that, at times, it gives away its presence by the small, rhythmical sound of its snoring. Occasionally, after a heavy summer shower, the nocturnal animals are abroad in full daylight searching for slugs and snails. But normally it is dusk when they appear. Frequently, as they search for food, they lift their pointed faces, their noses moist like a dog's, to sniff the air. Although a hedgehog's eyesight is poor, this defect is more than made up by the keenness of its senses of smell and hearing. With little grunts and snorts, it forages, often noisily, among the litter.

About 95 per cent of its food consists of insects. So efficient is it as a destroyer of pests that it is often introduced into gardens and sometimes even into country homes. In spite of the enormous benefits resulting from its destruction of injurious insects, the hedgehog is on the gamekeeper's list of vermin to be killed on sight, because it sometimes stumbles on, and consumes, the eggs of partridges and pheasants. The most surprising item on this creature's bill-of-fare is the venomous adder, to the poison of which it appears to be immune. The strangest untrue belief in connection with its feeding is one widely held in Pliny's time: that it collected grapes and apples to eat by rolling on them and spearing them with its quills.

When winter comes, the little hedgehog retires to some hole, most often in a bank, and there, in a nest of dry leaves, grass and moss, sleeps away the coldest months. May or June sees the arrival of the first litter, consisting of from three to seven young. This is sometimes followed by a second litter, born between July and September. This rapid rate of reproduction has enabled the hedgehog to survive, even in a motor age. The highway mortality of these animals has been put to use by scientists in several ways. A few years ago, an appeal was broadcast for the bodies of killed hedgehogs by a research worker in London who was en-

Selborne seen from the Hanger. Following page: Zigzag path laid out by Gilbert White

gaged in a study of ageing. Again, zoologists have been collecting data on the number of the animals killed on the roads in determining the population density of hedgehogs in different parts of England. It is interesting to note that when the English hedgehog was introduced into New Zealand—where many of its natural enemies were left behind and where motor cars were less numerous—the animals multiplied so swiftly that now the population density there is greater than in Britain.

We slept that night high above a brick-red town, in Shrewsbury's famous old coaching inn, the Lion Hotel—not the Black nor the White nor the Golden Lion, just the Lion. Here Benjamin Disraeli had stayed, and Charles Dickens and Thomas de Quincey and Jenny Lind. Here Nicolò Paganini had played his violin in the Minstrel's Balcony. When we left, the following morning, the sky was a gray waste, the roads ahead were glistening, rain was falling steadily. It dimmed the form of the Wrekin, Shropshire's celebrated mountain, where it rose from open land, its sides banded roughly with woods and strips of open fields, its bulk made up of some of the oldest volcanic rock in England. All along the way we saw farmers working in the rain. Little would get done in the English spring if country folk waited for dry weather. We drove on remembering the old rhyme: "Rain, rain, go away; come again some other day!" It was the second half of this admonition, rather than the first, we concluded, that seemed most certain to come true.

But later that morning, when, beyond Oakengates and Crackleybank, we left the straight east-and-west line of the old Roman road we were following and veered to the north, rifts began appearing in a breaking sky. Blue patches shone among the clouds above the outskirts of Stafford, the town of Izaak Walton's birth, and along Walton's stream, the River Sow, on whose banks he built a cottage at Shallowford. When we left behind this placid rural scene, with its

White's Long Lythe path in the spring. Preceding
page: Selborne after rain, The Wakes at the left

meandering stream winding among willows and through lowland meadows, we turned south toward a land of smoke, toward the heavily industrialized portion of the Midlands, toward the Black Country of England.

At the beginning of *The Old Wives' Tale*, Arnold Bennett writes of Staffordshire: "England can show nothing more beautiful and nothing uglier than the works of nature and the the works of man to be seen within the limits of the county." In the main, northern Staffordshire represents the works of nature; southern Staffordshire the works of man. This latter portion of the county comprises the bulk of the Black Country lying to the west and north of Birmingham. The fact that coal, lime and iron are all present in the area attracted industry and shaped the character of the region.

As we advanced toward this land of polluted air and industrial wealth, the smell of coal smoke grew ever stronger in the atmosphere. High chimneys increased along the horizon. For a time, they were scattered singly or in small clumps. Then, as we neared centers of industry, they drew together, clustering into copses or groves or massing into forests of brick. In long, black, slanting plumes, coal smoke trailed from their summits.

Each town and village we passed through appeared soiled and drab. The fences were stained, the houses were darkened by that universal pigment of the region, the black soot of the burning coal. Piles of industrial waste ran in low, saw-toothed ranges below the chimneys. For me, these sights and smells brought back memories of another midland Black Country, of the steel and railroad town in midland America where I was born and where fences also were stained with soot and the sky also was darkened by coal smoke.

Such smoke hung in a heavy pall over Birmingham, off to the south, as we ran on to Coventry. Somewhere along the way, a vision of sudden, arresting beauty appeared in the heavens. Flying high, a pure white swan passed before us, a luminous, ethereal body moving across the drab expanse of a discolored sky. We came to Coventry across open country where fields were bright with the yellow of blooming mustard. Within those old farmhouses we passed, people must have listened, on that terrible night of November 14, 1940, to the rain of Nazi bombs that shattered and almost leveled the town. New brick buildings, we found, replaced the rubble. The scars were nearly healed.

It was in Coventry, on a winter night in 1889, that Rev. John G. Wood died while on a lecture trip. He is buried there. Few other writers have done more than this Victorian clergyman to arouse popular interest in natural history. One of his many books, a cheap edition of his *Natural History*, fell into my hands when I was a small child in Illinois. The impression it made has never completely faded. The world of interest it opened up remains of interest still. In speaking of Wood's influence in the field of popular nature study, the *Dictionary of National Biography* notes: "To him was due the impulse that, coming at the right moment, turned public attention to the subject. Not a few naturalists of today owe their first inspiration to his writings."

All through the industrial regions of England, the tree trunks, like the fences and houses, have become begrimed and darkened under the canopy of smoke. In nature, nothing alters without altering conditions of life for something else. This shift in the color of the bark on Black Country trees has produced its side effects. The most dramatic, recorded in the lives of certain moths, is known to entomologists as industrial melanism.

The first insect in which this was observed was *Biston betularia*, the peppered moth. For centuries, in rural England, its normally light color and speckled pattern contributed to its inconspicuousness when it rested, in its customary position, with wings outspread, on the lichen-splotched bark of tree trunks. Then, around such industrial centers as Birmingham and Manchester, as the trunks grew darker and lost their lichens, the light-hued moths, instead of being camouflaged, became more and more conspicuous, more apparent to their enemies.

About 1850 a variety of this moth named *carbonaria* was collected at Manchester. Except for a white spot or two at the base of its forewings, this melanistic insect was completely black. On the soot-stained tree bark, it was as well camouflaged as the light-colored "normal" peppered moth had previously been. From then on, a rapid change took place. The dark form of the moth became common where it had been an extreme rarity before. Then it became the dominant form. Science was thus vouchsafed a thrilling glimpse of evolution in action. It was able to see a whole evolutionary change telescoped into the space of half a century.

In the *Transactions of the Cambridge Philosophical Society*, in 1924, J.B.S. Haldane published a paper entitled "A Mathematical Theory of Natural and Artificial Selection." It was his conclusion that the gene-frequency of the *carbonaria* form of the peppered moth was 1 per cent, or even less, in the Manchester area in 1849; while in 1898 it had become 99 per cent, or even more. This fifty-year shift forms the most striking example known of the evolutionary process taking place in any organism. The darker form of the peppered moth has since spread away from the industrial centers and is now found in a majority of the counties of England. But the proportion of light and dark forms varies according to the degree to which the countryside is darkened by industrial pollution.

It is the belief of Dr. H. B. D. Kettlewell, Britain's leading authority on industrial melanism, that not more than 10 per cent of the night-flying moths that are now predominantly dark were dark before the beginning of the Industrial Revolution. The dramatic change from light to dark, he concludes, can spread through a moth population in as short a time as fifty generations.

Precisely how this evolution takes places has long been debated. The most obvious contributing factor, however, is the effect of predation—the elimination of the more easily seen forms and the survival of the more camouflaged forms. Bats, spiders, and birds prey on moths. But bats catch moths on the wing, locating them not by eyesight but by hearing. Thus their activity would play no part in furthering evolution to darker forms through selective predation. Similarly, spiders catch whatever flies into their webs, irrespective of color. From the beginning, most scientists believed that birds are the chief agents in this evolutionary change.

Yet, curiously enough, almost no observations were recorded of birds picking resting moths from tree trunks. It was 1953 before Dr. Kettlewell conducted experiments that provided proof of the long-held assumption. In the Black Country, near Birmingham, he collected 587 of the peppered moths, 171 light, 416 dark. Before releasing them in suitable surroundings, he marked them with small spots of cellulose paint, placed on the underside of each moth where it was invisible when the insect rested with wings outstretched on a tree trunk. Watching through field glasses, during daylight hours, the scientist saw great tits, robins, and hedge sparrows destroy large numbers of the moths. Each time, the insect was snatched from the bark in so swift a movement that an observer, unless he was concentrating on seeing exactly what happened, would have missed the occurrence entirely.

By means of mercury-arc light traps to which his marked moths were attracted at night, Dr. Kettlewell checked on changes in the numbers of light and dark insects, thus indicating which form the birds were most often destroying. His figures confirmed the better survival chances of *carbonaria*. Not only does the adult of this form enjoy greater inconspicuousness on darkened trees, but its larvae seem able to survive better amid soot-stained foliage.

The Black Country was receding behind us and we were traversing a region of wide green fields, of oaks and elms and willows, when, late in the day, we came within sight of the red bricks and the red tiles of another red town of the Midlands—Leicester. Here, where we spent the night, the far-ranging life of Henry W. Bates had begun. Here the eyes that were to see the Amazon first saw the light. For eleven years, along 1,400 miles of untamed river in the dawn of scientific exploration in South America, Bates collected natural-history specimens. Eight thousand of the insects he brought home were new to science. His account of his adventures, *The Naturalist on the Amazons*, has taken its place among the classics of travel literature.

It is no accident that such books so often have been the product of naturalists, particularly in the days of the pioneer scientific explorers. The naturalist travels with a purpose. There is a point to his adventures. There is something of pursuit and attainment binding his pages together. By temperament and training he concerns himself with both the cause and the effect of what he sees. Moreover, a breadth of interest, a concern for fundamental things, distinguish the travel books of such great naturalists of the past as Bates, Alfred Russel Wallace, and Charles Darwin.

Workers were driving into town next morning when we set out. They were coming from homes in the country. In medieval times, laborers lived in the protection of villages or castle grounds and went out into the surrounding fields to work. The men we met were reversing the custom. They were coming to town to work and returning to the country to live. The rural scene in which they dwelt was dappled, that morning, with sunshine and shadow. Perhaps a dozen miles to the east of Leicester, our road crossed Eye Brook just above the Eye Brook Reservoir. Near here, on another day in May, an amateur ornithologist, N. L. Hodson, had stopped to watch swallows swooping down and picking food from the surface of the road. A closer examination showed they were getting tiny, winged adult froghoppers. On a later spring day, at Great Bridge in Staffordshire, another watcher of birds, F. Fincher, observed a female house sparrow feeding its fledglings on immature froghoppers obtained by pecking them out of the frothy masses of cuckoo-spit on the stems of willow-herb. The concealing blanket of froth that shields the soft, moist, defenseless cercopids from the eyes of so many of their enemies had proved unavailing against this perspicacious sparrow.

When we crossed Eye Brook, we crossed the boundary into the Rhode Island of England, the smallest of its counties, Rutland. Measuring only about fifteen by seventeen miles, Rutland is one of the hunting shires. Foxes remain here in spite of all the years that hounds and riders have pursued them over the hedges and over the fields, with great noise and color and excitement. I must admit that my sympathies run with the hunted. The traditional "blood sports" of Britain—or of any other country—leave me hoping the fox will escape and the gun misfire.

A high road carried us into Rutland over the ridgetops. Far vistas of hill country rolled away in the sunshine on either hand. And all across the nearer fields, the wind raced among the slender ribbon leaves of the green new wheat— the growing "corn" of England—now eight or ten inches high. The angle of the sun, the direction of the wind, the line of the road, all combined, for hours that morning, to produce a scene of rare and ever-changing beauty.

Like shining frost, a silvery sheen of reflected light went

sliding this way and that over the moving blades. The fields came alive. The landscape, as though animated by moving, running, crawling, swimming multitudes, was filled with shifting light and shifting movement. A radiance of frosty green ran up and down the slopes. Whole hillsides were swept by successive waves of shimmering light. This was "the hour of splendor in the grass."

One of the most beautiful sights in the out-of-doors is the wind running over the long grass of a hayfield or the bents of the dunes or a field of ripened grain, and here, with the sun and the moving air in partnership, we had the fluid grace of grasses in the wind combined with vibrant light as ethereal as an aurora shimmering in the sky. Close, so close, to the grim, smoke-stained land we had left behind, this vision of running light spread around us, shining and spiritual, symbolic of the incomparable beauty of nature unmarred.

chapter 20

LAND OF THE TWO POETS

Six hundred minutes of our sixty-first day in England had passed when, east of Stamford—at ten o'clock in the morning on the twenty-third of May—we stopped beside a high wall of gray rock flecked with yellow lichens. Behind the wall lay Burghley Park and Burghley House, for nearly four centuries the seat of the Cecil family. It was not the park nor the house that interested us most. It was the wall, or rather one day connected with its history.

In the dark before dawn, on that day so many years before, a boy of thirteen had passed it walking to Stamford. In the sunshine of that morning, he had returned, carrying a precious possession, a small, newly purchased volume. Climbing over the wall, he sat under the trees of the park, reading on and on, lost to the world, hour after hour. Like St. Augustine, he was one of those who could mark a great turning point of a lifetime with the words: "I fell upon a certain book." The boy was John Clare; the book, James Thomson's long poem, *The Seasons*.

Born into poverty, the son of a farm laborer, denied all

but the beginnings of an education, laboring in the fields as a child, John Clare, the ill-starred "peasant-poet of Northamptonshire," was born in the village of Helpston, in the Soke of Peterborough, in 1793, the year that Gilbert White died. At the age of thirteen he was employed at the Blue Bell Inn in that village. There one of the guests loaned him Thomson's poem. His burning desire, in the days that followed, was to own a copy himself. When he heard that a bookseller in Stamford, eight miles away, had one for sale, he could not wait until morning. He set off on foot in the night, arrived at the shop before sunrise, and waited at the door until it opened. In exchange for one shilling and sixpence, Clare carried the book away.

Under its influence he set down his first poem. He called it "The Morning Walk." Thomson's classic released the poetry innate in his nature. "I wrote," he once declared, "because it pleased me in sorrow, and when happy, it made me happier." On another occasion, he described himself as: "A peasant in his daily cares, a poet in his joy." He said of his poems that he "found them in the fields" and "only wrote them down." They record mainly his delight in nature. He wrote on odd scraps. Frequently, when he had no other material, he used grocer's wrapping paper. To sustain himself, while his poems accumulated he worked long hours in the fields. For a time he helped the gardener at Burghley House. He joined the militia. Again he worked as a lime-burner.

By chance, a bookseller named Drury read a poem of his entitled "The Setting Sun." He befriended Clare and introduced him to John Taylor, the London publisher of Keats and Shelley. Fourteen years after that morning under the trees of Burghley Park, when Clare was then twenty-seven, Taylor issued his first volume, *Poems Descriptive of Rural Life and Scenery*, "by John Clare, a Northamptonshire peasant." The success of this volume was immediate and immense. During the first year, four editions were required to meet the demand. Almost overnight, Clare became a celebrity. This was the one short, glorious period of sunshine in a life shadowed by deprivation and tragedy.

A second volume, *The Village Minstrel*, appeared the following year. It sold less well. Two subsequent collections of his poems, *The Shepherd's Calendar* and *The Rural Muse*, passed almost unnoticed. The strain of supporting a wife and six children, of constant financial worries, of heavy labor during ill health, sapped Clare's physical and mental strength. His mind gave way, and in 1837 he was placed under the care of the humane Dr. Matthew Allen, at his institution in Epping Forest, north of London. Four years later he returned home briefly. But after five months of freedom he was confined for the last twenty-two years of his life in the Northampton Asylum.

It was the opinion of the doctor who treated him that, if a small pension could have been obtained for him, relieving him from his most pressing financial cares, the peasant-poet could have lived out his days a sane man. But efforts in that direction failed. So did Clare's many ideas for literary projects. At one time he worked up a draft for a *Natural History of Helpstone*—as he always spelled Helpston—patterned on Gilbert White's *Selborne*. How extensive and exact was his knowledge of Northamptonshire nature is indicated by the fact that there are references to more than 130 species of plants in his writings, at least forty of them identified for the first time as found in Northamptonshire. From his own personal observation Clare wrote of 145 species of birds. Sixty-five of these, James Fisher points out, were first records for the county. It is Fisher's justified conclusion that of all of England's major poets, Clare was "by far the finest naturalist." The life of this observant and sensitive man, who deserved so much better than he received from the hands of fate, ended in 1864. He is buried in the village where he was born.

We were on the same road along which John Clare had trudged homeward carrying *The Seasons* when we came to Helpston. Just before the village, we passed thirteen deformed trees encircling a tumble-down building in a field of growing wheat. They seemed symbolic of the maimed life of the Helpston poet. The village itself, when we entered its one long main street, appeared to be in the throes of a construction boom. Red brick walls of new homes and factories were rising everywhere among the weathered stone of the old buildings.

Beyond, across flat, reclaimed fenland, we ran to Northborough, where Clare once lived. Then, turning south down the length of Huntingdonshire and west across Bedfordshire—through country that reminded us of northern Ohio—we came, in the far upper tip of Buckinghamshire, to Olney, linked with the life of that second tragic figure in the poetry of the out-of-doors, William Cowper. For Clare, fame bloomed early and faded soon. For Cowper, it arrived late but continued constant. He was more than fifty when his first volume of verse appeared and he had only fifteen more years to live when the success of his second volume, including "The Task," placed him among the leading poets of the English language. But his life, like that of Clare, was darkened by periods of insanity.

"Wherever else I am accounted dull," he once wrote a friend, "let me pass for a genius in Olney!" This town, for nearly twenty years, formed the hub of his existence. Today, its unusually wide main street is bordered by pollarded trees and the vertical faces of old stone buildings, all joined together, with rows of television antennas, like scraggly lines of leafless underbrush, running along the rooftops. We gazed about us with double interest as we traversed the length of this street—the interest aroused by its associations with Cowper and the interest connected with a 500-year-old tradition, Olney's pancake race run on this street each year on Shrove Tuesday, the day before the beginning of Lent.

Carrying skillets and flipping pancakes three times during the race, women cover a course of 415 yards. As we looked about us, Nellie and I remembered a dusty Kansas town on the Great Plains close to the Oklahoma border where, on a burning August day, we had seen a sign: "Liberal, Kansas. Pancake Hub of the Universe." Each year, Liberal and Olney compete. The race, which has been run in England since long before Columbus discovered America, is now an international event. At last count, the score stood: ten wins for Olney and nine for Liberal. The fastest time ever recorded for the course, one minute and three seconds, was set at Olney by Janet Bunker in 1967.

If you turn north from Olney, a mile or so outside of town you find yourself on the edge of a wooded tract. This is that special haunt of Cowper's, Yardley Chase. Of all the nations of Europe, England has the smallest percentage of its area devoted to forest. Yet I suspect no other land appreciates its forests more. And who appreciated what other tract of trees in England more intensely than Cowper treasured Yardley Chase? Famed for its magnificent oaks—one named Cowper's Oak—the area is now under the administration of the Forestry Commission.

We pulled up beside a little glade. While we ate a sparse wayside lunch of currant buns and small ripe tomatoes, robins sang and turtle doves, with fluttering wings, alighted in a nearby tree. The sun was warm and the trilling voices of pied wagtails rose around us in that bright bird music that sounded to Edward Thomas "as if the sun itself extracted the song as the hand makes sparks from the fur of a cat." Ahead of us a small tree appeared dripping with gold. It was a golden chain tree. Originally introduced into English gardens during the reign of Elizabeth I, it has since spread widely and in places has become wild. From Dungeness, on the Channel coast of Kent, in May, far into Scotland, in July, we encountered the brilliant yellow of the pendent racemes of this arboreal member of the pea family.

In *Walden*, Henry Thoreau asks: "Could a greater miracle take place than for us to look through each other's eyes for an instant?" For me, this miracle seems most nearly within my grasp when I imagine the world as seen through the eyes of someone who, like William Cowper, felt a passionate attachment for small portions of the earth. In his fifty-sixth year, looking back on the Hertfordshire village of Great Berkhamsted where he was born, and where his mother and father died, and from which he was parted in youth with such infinite regret, Cowper wrote to a friend: "There was neither tree, nor gate, nor stile, in all that country to which I did not feel a relation. I sighed a long adieu to fields and woods, from which I once thought I should never be parted, and was at no time so sensible of their beauties, as just when I left them all behind me, to return no more."

To see this countryside that two and a quarter centuries before had made so deep an impression on another mind, Nellie and I swung fifty miles out of our way the following morning. We rode through a land of open fields and tall elms. Up to the nineteenth century, the hollowed-out trunks of such trees, with a long life underground, formed the water mains in English towns. Great Berkhamsted, when we reached it, reflected the rapid growth of Hertfordshire, where London spills into the country. It is the fastest-growing county in England. In a single decade, between 1951 and 1961, its population increased 36½ per cent. But down every side street of the village we glimpsed the rolling farmland to whose gates and stiles and trees Cowper once felt so close a "relation." Did anyone today, we wondered, experience such an emotion? In a time of increasing alteration, increasing change, of mechanical aids and rapid obsolescence, of apartment dwellers moving from shell to shell like hermit crabs, in a time of increasingly broken continuity, the roots, the attachments, the relations of old were growing rarer year by year.

Coming down the Lea, before cutting in a wide swing north again through East Anglia—Essex, Suffolk, Cambridgeshire, and Norfolk—we found ourselves engulfed in a London-bound tide of buses, trucks, motor cars, scooters, and motorcycles. In air thick with fumes we passed through Hoddesdon and Broxbourne and Cheshunt, names we remembered from Izaak Walton, who often fished along the Lea. Our stopping place that night was in Epping Forest, between the Lea and the Roding, in Essex. When we left Kent, we had been close to London's southern fringe. Now we were even closer to its northern edge. For Epping Forest extends within a dozen miles of Charing Cross.

In a far-seeing provision, in 1882 this tract, once the hunting ground of kings, was set aside to be preserved forever as an open space for the enjoyment of all the people. Originally this woodland tract—where stricken John Clare was confined and where the eighteenth-century highwayman, Dick Turpin, rode by night—was part of the ancient Waltham Forest which, in turn, was part of the Forest of Essex that once covered the greater part of the county. One of its famous oaks, which fell in a storm in 1820, measured forty-five feet in girth. The present remnant of this great woodland is about seven miles long and contains about 5,600 acres.

It was in the midst of this forest that we came upon a new and memorable bird. We encountered it at the edge of an open glade where bracken covered the floor, the brown of last year's ferns intermingling with the bright green of the new spring plants. At one side, close to the surrounding wall of ancient beech trees, rose a slender birch. Above it, over and over again, a small bird, streaked and brownish, ascended on swift-beating wings. Each time it came to the summit of its climb and then, almost on set wings, parachuted down, filling the glade with its song. The music had an explosive quality that reminded us of the chestnut-sided warbler at home.

This singer was a bird we had never seen before, a tree pipit, a species that often nests among bracken. Unlike the pipits of open country, it habitually perches in trees. The wood lark also perches in trees. It also is small and striped. It also makes song flights. However, the two birds, the lark and the pipit, can easily be told apart by the manner of their descent. The lark ends its aerial singing with a plunge to earth, but the pipit—before it alights in a tree—drifts slowly down as though prolonging the ecstasy of its song.

When we remember Epping Forest, we remember the lingering flame of its nine o'clock sunset, the dull glare of London on the night sky to the south, the watery light of a misty dawn. All around us in the vapor of that early morning rose the eerie "golliwog trees," pollard hornbeams, each squat trunk, short and gnarled, crowned by a grotesque mass of radiating branches. They remain from the days of lopping rights when branches were cut for faggots. Of all of Britain's native trees, the hornbeam, *Carpinus betulus*, is the hardest. Its wood has long been used for such things as chopping blocks, buttons, knobs, and chessmen.

We were riding down one forest road, in the slowly breaking dawn, when a cuckoo, strikingly barred, appeared from among the trees and for a hundred feet or more flew beside us, almost within reach of an outstretched arm. This was our closest view of this creature linked with so many odd legends and strange beliefs. At one time it was held that cuckoos were cuckoos only in summer; that in winter

The River Dove flowing through Dovedale

they turned into birds of prey. It was thought that the female laid her eggs on the ground and carried them to nests
in her bill. And it was believed that young cuckoos, as soon
as they were full grown, devoured their foster parents.

In modern times, scientific studies of this famous avian
parasite have revealed features of its life that, at first glance,
seem as incredible as these erroneous beliefs of the past.
Cuckoos, it has been found, parasitize mainly the same species that reared them. That is, the female deposits her eggs
in the nests of the species to which her own foster parents
belonged. Moreover, as Paul Barruel notes in his *Birds of
the World*, these specialized strains of cuckoos tend to lay
eggs that resemble those of the species they parasitize. In
Finland, for example, a preponderance of cuckoos that vic-
timize the redstart lay blue eggs. The redstart lays blue
eggs. Similarly, in Japan, cuckoos that parasitize buntings
lay eggs that are marked with vermiculations almost identical with those on the smaller eggs of their victims.

Pasture fields of the Midlands

chapter 21

SUNKEN CITY

They were cutting the roadside grass between White Notley and Black Notley. The air was redolent with the greengrass scent of the mowing as we came over the Essex hills to the birthplace of the first great naturalist of England.

The seventeenth century had just ended its first quarter when John Ray—"our countryman, the excellent Ray" as Gilbert White referred to him—was born at the smithy at Black Notley on November 29, 1627. By the time of his death, on January 17, 1705, at his country home, Dewlands, close to the village of his birth, Ray had contributed vastly to scientific knowledge. He has been called the father of modern zoology. He has been described as the greatest field naturalist that ever lived. It is generally conceded that John Ray was to the seventeenth century what Thomas Pennant was to the eighteenth.

Whenever possible, it was Ray's custom to set down notes on the lives and habits of the creatures he collected. In a single decade, with the help of his four small daughters, he bred and recorded the life cycles of nearly 300 local

216

lepidoptera. And all of his carefully observed explorations in natural science were made at a time when it was possible for a woman to be hanged, only thirty miles away at Cambridge, for keeping a tame frog. It was sworn to at her trial that she was a witch and the frog was her imp.

Close to the edge of the village of Black Notley, we crossed a small stream with white cow parsley and red campion blooming along its banks. This was Ray's "little brook that runs near my dwelling." In the year 1655 he built his house, now gone, on rising ground beyond. The countryside, that morning, appeared to us little changed by centuries. But Ray's village of Black Notley, like John Clare's village of Helpston, was in a state of upheaval. For the better part of half a mile we rode along the main street with buildings of brick going up on either hand. Only thirty-five miles northeast of London, the village was caught up in a program of expansion—expansion, that is, so far as buildings were concerned, but compression so far as human beings were concerned. For henceforth men would live in Black Notley in greater numbers closer together.

In John Ray's time, a visitor to Dewlands was a boy from Castle Hedingham, another village to the north. His name was Mark Catesby. Thus, from two neighboring Essex villages, less than ten miles apart, came the first great naturalist of England, John Ray, and the first great naturalist of the American colonies, Mark Catesby. More than a hundred years before Audubon published *The Birds of America*, Catesby was painting and studying the avifauna of the southern colonies. With Indians as guides he roamed the frontier wilderness in the early years of the eighteenth century. His *Natural History of Carolina, Florida and the Bahama Islands*, published in London in 1747, stands as the great initial milestone in the scientific study of birds and plants in North America.

I remember one midwinter day, at the Pierpont Morgan

Library in New York, leafing through the two volumes of Catesby's classic work—the very volumes that Thomas Pennant had owned and used when he was writing his *Arctic Zoology*, two centuries before. These were the identical pages he had turned at the time he was corresponding with Gilbert White. On the flyleaf of the first volume he had noted that he had purchased the books from Catesby's nephew, "Catesby, the haberdasher, of Covent Garden, in London."

All along the road to Castle Hedingham, golden chain trees bloomed in the farmyards. Beyond the village, with its crumbling castle walls and brooding air of ancientness about it, we rode beneath many an overarching elm through a countryside that recalled eastern Massachusetts. This resemblance was heightened by the Essex names, Sudbury and Chelmsford and Braintree, that homesick colonists transplanted to New England. But one thing we missed in the scene. There were no rural mail boxes. Here letters are delivered at the door. That night we slept at the mouth of the River Stour, in the harbor town of Harwich, once the home port of the Pilgrims' *Mayflower*.

Not far from Harwich, three centuries ago, a small island was celebrated for a curious reason. It was called Peewit Island. There, each spring, large numbers of peewits, or lapwings, nested in the short grass. In those days when birds had no protection under the law, the young were much sought after as food. "Being young," an old book tells us, "they consist only of bones, feathers and lean flesh, which hath a raw gust of the sea. But poulterers take them then, and feed them with gravel and curds, that is, physic and food; the one to scour, the other to fat them in a fortnight, and their flesh thus recruited is most delicious." In fact, the chief natural commodities of Essex, in Thomas Fuller's seventeenth century, were listed as oysters, hops, and peewits.

A fine drift of mizzling rain was advancing inland from

the sea when we started north next morning. Under its low ceiling of gray clouds, the day was like an echoing room, with occasional sounds carrying far. We were close to Flatford Mill, the locale of some of the most famous of John Constable's landscapes, when we crossed the Valley of the Stour. But where were the wide skies, the white drifting clouds, the sunshine of the artist's canvases? Ours was another kind of day and, as this observant painter once noted: "No two days are alike, nor even two hours; neither was there ever two leaves of a tree alike since the creation of the world."

In the early years of the present century, windmills whirled beside dark drainage ditches all across the coastal lowlands above the Suffolk border. On this day we saw but two. Past a sign: "Narrow Streets with Numerous Turnings," we entered, about mid-morning, that town of gardens, Woodbridge. It was in a garden here, on solitary walks, that Edward FitzGerald repeated aloud the quatrains of his translation as he shaped and perfected *The Rubaiyat of Omar Khayyam*.

Each highway we followed these days was a road we had never seen before, a road we probably would never see again. A-12, which carried us angling north toward Lowestoft, was laid down by the Romans. It runs well inland from the shore. If you examine a map of Suffolk, you will see that no major highway follows the line of the coast. This reflects the unstable character of the land where it meets the sea. It has shifted ceaselessly for centuries. To reach the site of the most dramatic consequence of this altering of the shoreline, Nellie and I turned aside across lowland pastures, rode among hills clothed in bracken and heather and furze, twisted along lane-like sideroads, and stopped at the water's edge.

Where the gray, muttering waste of the North Sea spread before us, there once stood the proud and powerful port city of Dunwich. Within historical times, its houses, its streets, its inns, its shops, its churches of stone vanished beneath the waves. All were swallowed up by the encroaching sea. Today, nothing remains except a village of no more than 150 inhabitants, still clinging to the shore. "Dunwich," Henry James wrote in *English Hours* after a turn-of-the-century visit to the spot, "is not even a ghost of its dead self; almost all you can say of it is that it consists of the mere letters of its old name. There is a presence in what is missing—there is history in there being so little."

The story of this sunken city has its beginnings far back in Anglo-Saxon times. It was known successively, during the Saxon era, as Dommocceaster and Dunwyk. For centuries it was the most important commercial center of the region, and when Sigebert became King of East Anglia, in the early seventh century, he made Dunwich his capital. As early as 630 A.D., according to the Venerable Bede, a bishopric was founded there. The vanished city was known as "the nursery of Christianity in eastern Britain." How great was the wealth and power and importance of this port on the Suffolk coast is indicated by the fact that, during the reign of Edward I (1272–1307), it maintained a fleet of its own. This included eleven ships of war, twenty-four fishing boats and thirty-six vessels used in trading "to the North seas, Iceland and elsewhere."

But neither its wealth nor its power protected it against the ravages of the sea. By the middle of the eleventh century, the coast on which it was situated was already being gnawed away. In the single year of 1347, more than 400 houses disappeared beneath the waves. In 1570, one terrible storm brought such disastrous consequences that an appeal was made to Queen Elizabeth for help. Storm after storm, the heavy seas cut farther and farther into the shoreline until this famed center of trade, this onetime capital of East Anglia, this power on land and sea, disappeared entirely, swallowed up beneath the waves. Even down to the present time, the wearing away of the coast continues. During the First World War, the last ruined tower of an ancient church was undercut where it clung to the edge of a seaside cliff. Crashing down, it added its rubble to the submerged ruins of engulfed Dunwich.

In that battle zone of land and water at the edge of the North Sea, Nellie and I walked for a long time under the wave-worn headlands on a beach of pebbles and stones. The tide was out. A continual muttering ran along the shore. Each retreating wave was accompanied by a prolonged growl, the commingled noise of thousands of rolling stones grating together. No ship was visible on the gray sea. Except for skylarks and lapwings of the salt meadows and black-headed gulls slanting above the tideline, we were alone. Leaning against an overturned boat, with black fish nets spread out to dry around us, we thought of the thronging city, now gone. All that remained of the work of those past generations were drowned streets and the wreckage of submerged buildings lying invisible beneath the sea's rising and falling surface. The finality of the disaster was overwhelming. A community destroyed by earthquake or leveled by hurricane can rise again. But who can repair a city swallowed by the sea?

Drifting moisture, half mist, half rain, became real rain. The pelting drops multiplied into a deluge. Our plans to visit the nearby Minsmere refuge, maintained by the Royal Society for the Protection of Birds, were literally washed away. We thought we could come back on another day. But, as it developed, we never could. So, on every journey, a few of the things we look forward to are missed.

From a modern port on the Suffolk coast, Lowestoft—the easternmost point in Britain, "first to see the sun"—we turned inland on the succeeding day. Scattered over the open country of the Suffolk-Norfolk border, along the River

Waveney, derelict aerodromes, abandoned wartime air-fields, form natural wildlife sanctuaries. They are unused and untended. Nobody bothers to spray them with poison pesticides and herbicides. Wildflowers flourish in the open spaces and birds nest around the rusting hangars.

We turned into one such airfield, abandoned and falling into decay, a few miles south of the river. Ivy wandered up the concrete abutments; moss clung to the old brickwork; sulphur-hued lichen splotched the corrugated metal of the roofs. In and out of broken louvers, house sparrows darted. Their nests filled lamps, now bulbless, that once illumi-nated the hangars. House martins, sweeping back and forth, twittered low among the Quonset huts. Where wartime planes lifted from the runways laden with bombs and bul-lets, skylarks now hung in the sunshine. Where the thunder of engines had shaken the earth, now only the sweet jingle of the hovering birds came down to us.

Wherever we walked across the open spaces, wildflowers of spring were blooming. On all sides extended the purple of vetch, the red of campion, the white of dead nettle and cow parsley, the yellow of mustard and dandelion, black medick and meadow buttercup. Below the lavender-pink petals of herb Robert, the red stems, richly hued, shone out like flowers themselves in these fields of blooms. Among the clumps of taller weeds, the berry tangles and thorn clus-ters, many a small creature was finding shelter. In one mass of weeds I met again the ebony acorn form of the con-tracted slug I had first encountered on my walk to Rainbar-row, on Egdon Heath. A little later, amid hawkweed-like plants, we saw the shining white foam masses of froghop-pers. On the same May day that we came upon the bubble clusters of these insects amid the vegetation of this aban-doned airfield in England, similar masses were clinging to plant stems across millions of acres of American fields. In the tiny froghopper we had encountered an old, familiar friend.

In the nine-hundreth year after the Norman Invasion of England in 1066, we followed on this day a highway numbered 1066. It led us up the Little Ouse, over the Norfolk border, to Thetford. This birthplace of Thomas Paine is situated on the edge of that vast, wild tract of "rabbit warrens, heath and lonely wastes" called the Breckland. Strong winds and scanty rainfall characterize its climate. How many miles we rode through this sparsely settled region, with yellow-hammers and wagtails collecting food along the sun-warmed hardtop, I have no idea. Once, I remember, we looked down into a bowl of land holding Mickle Mere, where prehistoric lake dwellers once lived. Half a dozen miles to the west, between Snake Wood and the Little Ouse, we stopped again in a dry valley about 100 feet above sea level. Around us, over an area of more than thirty acres, extended the remnants of 366 pits dug deep into the chalk. Before fame was recorded in any book, this valley was famous. It formed an armory of the Stone Age men. Thousands of years before the birth of Christ, its pits supplied flint for axes and knives and arrowheads to the tribes of eastern and midland England.

When these pits were first encountered by modern men, they were filled with the debris of centuries. All that met the eye were hundreds of puzzling, roughly circular depressions in the ground. Locally they were known as "Grimmer's Graves." Grim, the Masked One, was one of the names of Woden, the Anglo-Saxon god of victory, death, and magic power. In the course of time, "Grimmer's Graves" was contracted to its present form: Grime's Graves. Now surrounded by the dark conifer plantations of the Forestry Commission, thirty-four acres of the valley have been set aside as an ancient monument under the administration of the Ministry of Public Building and Works.

A Danish encampment, an Iron Age village, a fortified settlement of pre-Roman times—these were some of the surmises put forward to explain the depressions during generations when their origin remained a riddle. It was a clerical archaeologist, a canon named Greenwell, who about 1870 demonstrated by careful excavations that each depression marked the mouth of a Neolithic flint mine. "It was a most impressive sight," Greenwell wrote after reaching the bottom of one such vertical shaft, "to look, after a lapse of, it may well be, 3,000 years, upon a piece of work unfinished, with the tools of the workmen still lying where they had been placed so many centuries ago."

Those tools were primitive implements—picks made from the antlers of red deer, rakes formed from the antlers of roe deer, shovels shaped from the shoulder blades of oxen. For lifting levers the Stone Age miners used the long bones of oxen and, in at least one instance, a human femur. In two excavated pits archaeologists unearthed 250 red-deer antlers. It has been estimated that more than 50,-000 such antlers were employed in digging through the chalk to reach the "floorstone" flint for which Grime's Graves is famous. This layer, running in a dark stratum through the zone of chalk, sometimes more than thirty feet below the surface, extends in a north-and-south direction across the wilds of the Breckland.

Rung by rung, Nellie and I descended a steel ladder into the depths of one of these Stone Age mines. At the top, where sunshine and rain reached them, ferns and moss had found a foothold on the rough-hewn chalk. But as we descended, the pure white of the walls was relieved only by isolated nodules of dark flint. At the bottom, lateral galleries radiated away in all directions. Crawling on hands and knees along these low passages, lighting their way with torches or crude lamps formed of hollowed-out blocks of

chalk holding animal fat, the Neolithic miners had extracted, piece by piece, the prized floorstone flint. Soot
marks still remain where their guttering lamps burned so
long ago. As we walked about on the bottom of the shaft
and stooped to peer into the lateral galleries, we were
keenly aware of the unbridgeable gap that separated us
from these men of another world. Like the far, far ahead,
the long, long ago belongs to other people, not to us.

Mining at Grime's Graves is believed to have ceased about
1900 B.C. Yet, even today, in open spaces near the pits,
you may come upon layers or heaps of small flint fragments, sometimes five feet deep. They represent the work-
places of the flint-knappers. These were the experts who
chipped away excess stone to shape the raw material into
finished tools and weapons. It was with axes thus formed
that the long process of felling the primeval forests of England began. In his *Trees, Woods and Man*, H. L. Edlin at-
tests to the effectiveness of such axes. One day by chance,
on a Surrey down, he picked up one that had lain buried
and forgotten for thousands of years. When he swung it,
merely holding it in his hand without benefit of the customary wooden handle, he found it was sharp enough to
bite into the trunk of a beech tree.

Emerging into the sunlight again, out of the stillness of
the pit, we heard the skylarks singing, the larks that had
sung at Stonehenge, as at Grime's Graves, above all the labors of the ancient men. Beneath their hovering forms,
brownish sand martins skimmed over the grass blades. Another contemporary of the Stone Age miners, it is interesting to note, has recently re-established itself in the pits that
have been cleared of debris. This is the whiskered bat, believed to have been absent from Grime's Graves for nearly
4,000 years.

At Thetford that evening, before our meal of steak-and-
kidney pie, we heard exciting news. Ever since the night of

the full May moon on Selborne Common, we had been in search of a nightingale for Nellie. We had listened at the edges of woods near Tunbridge Wells in Kent and at Haslemere and Box Hill in Surrey. We had strained our ears along the Thames and Avon, in the valley of the Windrush with Bruce Campbell, at Stoke Poges and among the misty glades of Epping Forest. And all our listening had been in vain. The nights had been too chill or the nights had been too windy or the birds had suddenly ceased singing.

Curious folklore beliefs have grown up around these birds as a consequence of the fact that their British range is limited and spotty. In some localities it was once accepted that nightingales are found only where cowslips are common; in others, only where hops are grown. Here in Norfolk we were nearing the upper fringes of their range. Nellie's chances of hearing their song were lessening day by day

Then, on this evening in Thetford, we talked to a man who, a few nights before, had heard the voice we sought beside the River Lark. Another suggested we might find a nightingale in a wood near the Six Day Inn, north of the village of Elveden. With hope revived, we hurried through the evening meal and started out. Before us the western sky streamed with the garish colors of one of the few flaming sunsets we met in Britain. At Barton Mills, ten miles west of Thetford, a side road turned upstream beside the wandering course of the Lark. Every few hundred yards we paused and listened. In the hush of the evening we heard cock pheasants calling from the fields and the voices, near and far, of song thrushes and blackbirds. We may have heard, also, fragments of a nightingale's song. But we were never sure.

At Isleham a pleasant, elderly man, whose face wore the slightly startled expression of one about to sneeze, filled our fuel tank and, at the same time, regaled us with a monologue of misinformation about nightingales.

"They sing for only two weeks—in April. You are too late. Every spring, fifty or sixty nightingales sing in a small grove five miles from here. My wife and I go over to hear them. This is the heart of the nightingale country. There are more here than anywhere else. But they have all stopped singing now."

As we were leaving, he added a final summary:

"It's queer about nightingales!"

The sunset had faded and our headlights were switched on when we approached the strip of woodland near the Six Day Inn. I pulled into a deeply shadowed lane and turned off the motor and lights. Around us rose the dark forms of maples, Scots pines, and English oaks. Ivy vines, climbing and intertwining, clothed the trunks with a dense pelt of leaves, while nettles, in luxurious stands, overran the woodland floor. It is among nettles and similar vegetation that nightingales most often nest. The birds may return year after year to the same weed tangles, nesting on or near the ground. Thickets and overgrown hedges, frequently near streams, are also in accord with their secretive natures. In such damp and shady places they find the beetles, worms, spiders, and insect pupae that form their principal food.

The woodland in which we found ourselves, with open fields beyond, was perhaps a hundred feet across and a quarter of a mile in length. As the dusk deepened, the light of a half moon illuminated the upper limbs of the trees. But it is lower down, in the deeper shadows, usually no more than a dozen feet above the ground, that the nightingale perches when it sings. We opened the doors softly and walked deeper among the trees. There we stood motionless, listening. Rising and falling in a steady surf-like sound, the noise of night traffic on a distant highway reached our ears. It was vacation time, and a rushing stream of cars poured toward the sea from inland towns. But all around us the dark trees remained intensely still.

Ten minutes went by. Then fifteen. We had been standing there for nearly twenty minutes when out of the darkness before us there came a clear, liquid "wheet." Then silence. Minutes passed. Then the woods around us echoed with the song Nellie so long had hoped to hear.

I listened once more to the haunting magic of that song. Here again were the pure tones, the soaring crescendos, the rapidly repeated notes, the rich quality of that musical voice so varied in volume and range. And scattered through it was the bubbling sound, the deep "chook-chook" or "jug-jug" that is diagnostic. Unseen, perched low in some nearby tree, the bird sang on. "All the music of the moon," wrote eighteenth-century William Macgillivray, "sleeps in the plain eggs of the nightingale."

So, at least since the late Ice Age of the Pleistocene, the voice of this bird has echoed through darkening woods. It was the belief of the Persians that the singer, in its passion, pressed a rose thorn against its breast to ease its heart's pain. In many lands and many languages, writers have attested to the profound effect this moving voice has had on human hearers.

This, at last, was Nellie's nightingale. Our search for it, begun near the south coast, had continued almost to the Wash. Its age-old music came now to our ears above the murmur of a new-age sound, the sound of motor traffic. For us, the song ended too soon. We wanted to hear it again and again. We wanted to hear it night after night. We wanted to hear it at its best, when bird competed with bird at the height of the breeding season. But even so, we went home that night richly content.

Of all the nightingales that sang in this English spring, only two were ours. Only two touched our lives. But they touched them in a way we will never forget.

chapter 22

ADVEN-
TURERS
FEN

The Gentlemen Adventurers. So the band was known. Its bold enterprise began in the seventeenth century under the fourth Earl of Bedford in the reign of Charles I. Its enemy was water; its battleground was the Great Fen.

At that time, this watery wilderness extended over an area of nearly 2,500 square miles. From Cambridgeshire in the south into Lincolnshire in the north, it stretched in a morass of rustling reeds, will-o'-the-wisps, and dark meres haunted by waterfowl. The area it occupied originally formed an arm of the North Sea. Today the Wash, that wide and shallow bay that cuts inland above the bulge of Norfolk, is the only surviving remnant of the original larger bay. Ages of slow silting converted it into marshland where, for untold centuries, the decay of lush vegetation added each year to the black richness of the soil.

Over a period of more than twelve hundred years, men sought to drain the water from the Great Fen and transform its humus-laden earth into the most fertile fields of England. The first to make the attempt were the Romans.

Car Dyke, the oldest canal in Britain, remains as a relic of that endeavor. This long catchwater basin stretched down the western side of the fen from Lincoln to Ramsey. For seven centuries after the legions left England, the fen remained undisturbed. Then William the Conqueror's chamberlain, Richard de Rulos, sought unsuccessfully to drain a portion of the great morass. Two centuries more went by before the Bishop of Ely, John Norton, tried and failed anew where others had failed before him. Another century elapsed. Then came a fresh attempt and a fresh failure. Under the leadership of Lord Chief Justice Popham, in the first years of the seventeenth century, a group of wealthy Londoners organized a company whose objective—unfulfilled—was draining the Great Fen.

This was the history of the various projects for reclaiming this water-logged land when, in 1634, the fourteen Gentlemen Adventurers, led by the Earl of Bedford, signed an agreement with Charles I. Through a long succession of political and financial and engineering reverses, through the Civil War and the Great Plague, the band persevered. Its grand design was carried out against the opposition of the fen-dwellers, the "stilt-walkers," who saw their ancient privileges of wildfowling, fishing, and turf-cutting endangered. All of the original Gentlemen Adventurers were gone and generations had passed before the end of the project arrived in sight. It was not until the conclusion of the eighteenth and the beginning of the nineteenth century that the drainage of the fens was finally achieved.

In its early stages, the success of the enterprise was largely due to the Dutch engineer Cornelius Vermuyden, who came from Holland to direct the drainage operations and who was knighted for his achievements. Collecting dark marsh water into drainage ditches, then pumping it with windmills into streams held to their courses with embankments as much as fifteen feet high, Vermuyden and

Coot and swan. Following two pages: Heifers beside the Avon

his successors drained away the stagnant water and transformed the marsh into dry, tillable soil. This area, the largest tract of low-lying land in England, now stretches mile after mile in rich and level fields. So highly prized is it that it sells for as much as £600, or $1,500, an acre.

With the passing of the Great Fen, age-old occupations disappeared from the region. For centuries the fen dwellers had cut the peat that built up at the rate of about one foot every twenty years. They harvested the leaves of the sweet flag which since early times had been used to strew the floors of priories and monasteries. They collected rushes for the manufacture of horse collars, and osiers for use in wicker baskets. They cut reeds and sedge for thatching. Sedge from the Great Fen, outlasting the reeds, sometimes remained along ridgepoles for half a century. Coopers bought bulrushes from the fen to place between barrel staves, where they swelled with liquids and kept the casks watertight.

Fish, fowl, and goosefeathers were other staple products of the drowned land. Domestic geese were plucked two, three, even five times a year for their down. And in the autumn enormous flocks were driven to London to help feed the metropolis. Old records of the fenland monks show that so plentiful were wild waterfowl that ducks sufficient for a full meal could be obtained for half a penny. Eels swarmed in such numbers in the shallow waters that the monks of Ramsey, before the Conquest, received from one fen-country manor 60,000 eels a year. To objections of the alarmed "stilt-walkers" that draining the marshes would eliminate these sources of income, the Gentlemen Adventurers answered: "Is not a fat sheep better than a goose, a stalled ox better than a dish of eels?"

Viewing the prosperous farms and remembering the vast untamed marshes teeming with wildlife, Nellie and I were of two minds. Much has been gained; but much, also, has

The Wiltshire downs

been lost. When I stopped, on a later day, to buy some apples at a small store, I found myself facing crates of fruit from South Africa, from the United States, from New Zealand. England has insufficient farming land to feed its population, and draining the vast expanse of the fen undoubtedly added a rich area to the economy of the country. But it also subtracted forever from that wildness which Thoreau called the preservation of the world. The greatest of all disasters for wildlife is the destruction of its habitat. As an old English writer observed more than 150 years ago: "The fault is great in man or woman who steals a goose from off a common; but what can plead that man's excuse who steals a common from a goose?"

In the face of the demands of an ever-increasing population, the best that can be hoped for, oftentimes, is the preservation of a remnant, a sample, of former wildness—a specimen sanctuary that reveals what the whole was like. So Wicken Fen and, up to recent times, Adventurers Fen, have retained in fragmentary form the character of the wild marshes that once extended across what is now an almost treeless plain of immense fields broken only by long straight roads, isolated farmhouses, and the shining lines and serpentines of dredged canals and embankment-bordered streams.

For the better part of a day, Nellie and I followed the straight, intersecting roads that imprint their grid on this open land. Nowhere did we find what that great walker, William Hazlitt, considered the most interesting feature of the landscape, a curve in a winding road. Highways as straight as a ruler's edge led us to Friday Bridge, Sandy End, The Smeeth, Forty-Foot Bridge, Pincushion Drove. Sugar beets, potatoes, wheat, oats, barley, soy beans flourish in the siltland. Vividly green, the new grain spread for miles across the level fields. Square houses of brick, alone or clustered into tiny villages, appeared forlorn, lost between the immensity of the sky and the monotonous flatness of the land.

For many years in this region an inn carried a sign reading: "No Hurry. Five Miles from Anywhere."

On hot spring days before the crops are up and when the ground is bare, dust devils spin across the level fields. The peaty soil of the former fens is a wasting asset. It dries and shrinks and blows away. To lessen such annual loss, deep plowing is practiced. This mixes the underlying blue clay with the humus-laden topsoil. But even when clay and peat are mixed, in windy springs the whole first sowing of a crop may vanish, the seeds disappearing with the top layer of the soil. Everywhere the hard-surfaced roads we followed were elevated, running several feet above the level of the depressed fields which have been lowered by oxidation and the scouring of the wind.

With their bicycles lying beside the road and their raincoats folded up and placed on the ground near where they worked, men hoed down the long rows of the immense fields. Some bent to their task; others stood upright, wielding hoes with abnormally long handles. In a few fields, women worked by themselves. Two, one young, one old, advanced on hands and knees side by side, weeding down rows that, it seemed to us, extended for half a mile. Nearby two small children, no more than two or three years old, sat between the rows facing each other, playing some game. Signs here and there announced that large tracts of the land were owned by companies with headquarters in London. We rode on, considering the dragging, deadening hours of day laborers caught amid an endless succession of interminable rows running in parallel lines across fields so vast.

The commonest bird we saw among these farms of the reclaimed fen was the house sparrow. Once well down in Cambridgeshire we came upon something I had seen but a single time before—in a small valley in Pennsylvania—the whole side of an old strawstack riddled with the holes of nesting sparrows.

It was an entirely different kind of bird and an entirely

different kind of nest that absorbed our attention, later on, beside one wide canal bordered by lines of brilliant red where field or corn poppies bloomed. Beyond their red flowers and across the brown water of the canal, moor hens were engaged in building a nest. One swam back and forth, transporting crosswise in its red bill long pieces of the dead sword-leaves of the great reed mace or broad-leaved cattail. Each was passed to its mate who wove it into the interlacing mass of the growing nest amid low aquatic vegetation. The birds continued busily at work, paying no attention to us. The bulk of their nest had increased noticeably by the time we moved away.

We rode for more than eighty miles that day and ranged beyond Ely and Chatteris and rose at times on higher ground that once formed islands in the Great Fen, where Anglo-Saxons sought refuge from the Vikings, before we turned southward toward the rolling Gog Magog Hills and the university town of Cambridge.

There we spent the night with W. Gerald Humphrey, of the University, and his wife Peggy, friends of friends of ours in America who soon became valued friends of ours in their own right. They welcomed us warmly and made us feel at home at once. Interested in natural history themselves, they proved a mine of helpful information. As we walked about their garden that evening—one of those beautiful and extensive English gardens filled with birds and flowers—a song thrush sang in the twilight from the ridgepole of the house. We felt we would travel to Britain just to hear the song thrush and the blackbird, as we would travel to the north woods of America just to hear the hermit thrush and the white-throated sparrow.

At their feeding tray among the rose bushes, Peggy Humphrey told us, they have discovered that parings of cheese are irresistible to long-tailed tits. Cheese and cream—how did tits develop a taste for such foods? That seemed as much a puzzle to me as the origin of the house cat's fondness for fish seemed to Gilbert White—when, as he pointed out, of all quadrupeds cats are "the least disposed towards water."

A visitor, one of the people we had looked forward to meeting in England, called that evening. This was Edward A. Armstrong, Vicar at Cambridge and author of numerous books including *Birds of the Grey Wind*. In the single instance of a foreign author being so honored, he received for this book the American award for distinguished nature writing, the Burroughs Medal. It reached him, he told me, during the war, having crossed the Atlantic in a diplomatic mail pouch. At the time he was working in the grim surroundings of the slums of Leeds. All of his substantial list of books, for which he received an honorary M.A. from Cambridge University, have been produced on the margin of his time while carrying on his duties as a clergyman of the Church of England. The evening passed swiftly while our talk ranged along that borderland where the world of nature unites with the world of books.

During the long centuries when the fenland air was rich with the smells of wet peat, damp reeds, and brown water, marshes and mountains were in popular disfavor. They were considered "rude" rather than "romantic." First the mountains and last of all the wetlands came into their own and were appreciated. Wicken Fen, ten miles to the northeast of Cambridge, symbolizes this change in viewpoint. It is probably England's outstanding instance of the preservation of a marshy tract for its natural beauty and historic interest. It was my good fortune to come to this remaining fragment of the Great Fen with Gerald Humphrey as my guide.

Signing the guestbook at the National Trust headquarters, we started on a two-mile circuit of the paths. At Wicken Fen, which now includes part of the old Adventurers Fen, botanists have recorded more than 170 species of flowering plants. One of them played an important part in preserving the area from those vast changes that have overtaken the surrounding country. This is *Cladium mariscus,* the fen sedge. Its keeled leaves, used for centuries for capping the thatching along the ridges of cottages, shade the ground and, interlacing into dense, durable mats, prevent the growth of other plants. Every four years the pure stands of this sedge were harvested at Wicken Fen. The economic value of the leaves weighed heavily in the decision to keep this portion of the great marsh intact.

A second consideration was the value of its spongy soil as a reservoir that would lessen the damage to neighboring fields when floodwaters—known as "The Bailiff of Bedford"—descended from higher land to the west. In places the peat of Wicken Fen has a depth of eighteen feet. Near Drainer's Dyke, large holes remain where bombs that were jettisoned by an aircraft in 1943 were dug with great difficulty from the depths of the soft and oozy earth.

Gerald Humphrey pointed out a small tree with black bark and oval leaves set in "more or less" opposite pairs along the twigs. It was the water-loving alder buckthorn, *Frangula alnus.* Because no other wood provides charcoal with such uniform and even-burning characteristics, it is widely employed in making time fuses. In the early days of the Second World War, when supplies of this charcoal were no longer available from the continent, Wicken Fen and the New Forest became England's main sources of this ingredient essential to the war effort. In no other area of similar size in Britain does alder buckthorn grow more abundantly than at Wicken Fen. Whenever any part of the area is left to itself, this and other shrubs form dense thickets known locally as "carr." Control measures are necessary to keep the carr within bounds.

Over the green algae, the outspread waterlily leaves, the

blooms of the yellow flags bordering stagnant pools along the way, we watched filmy gnats and black caddis flies dancing. Water striders skated over the surface film of Drainer's Dyke and Wicken Lode. And from the overhanging sallows, shaggy with the filaments of their windborne seeds, shining bits of willow fluff drifted down to float on the brown fen water. In old books you may read how, in ancient times, a physic brewed from willow twigs was administered "to drive out the folly of children."

The gnat, the caddis fly, the water strider are but a trio among an estimated 5,000 kinds of insects living at Wicken Fen. Entomologists have collected there 130 species of water beetles, 737 kinds of moths and butterflies, and 1,075 species of land beetles.

A century ago, on spring and summer nights as many as half a dozen large white sheets, supported by poles and illuminated by the glare of acetylene lamps, could be seen strung along the length of Wicken Lode. From among the swarms of moths attracted to the lighted sheets, collectors chose the rarer species. In the records of one old-time entomologist there is a note about a long-sought butterfly, a Camberwell Beauty—the mourning cloak of our American fields and woods—which he found sunning itself on the path before him at Wicken Fen. To which is added: "Did not capture it, it being Sunday."

The most admired of all the fen insects undoubtedly is the swallowtail butterfly. Generations of local cottagers have kept "cots," the chrysalids of the swallowtail, on mantels in order to enjoy the beauty of the perfect, newly emerged adults. In the late 1940's this most famous insect of Wicken Fen disappeared entirely. It was considered extinct in the area. None were seen for years. In 1955, however, swallowtails were re-introduced from the broads of Norfolk. They have since spread and multiplied.

For me, the paths we followed that day led among new

bird voices. The small winged fauna of the carr called and sang mostly unseen. I could visualize the wrens that scolded as we went by, but no mental image came to mind when we heard the warble, brief and metallic, that is the whin-chat's song. Once, after listening to the accelerating tempo of the song of a reed bunting, we saw the handsome male, with its black head and black bib above a collar of white, dart from the twilight of the thicket to perch on a bush-top twig in the full brilliance of the sun. From the distance, over and over again, we caught the mellow notes of a cuckoo and, nearer at hand, a dozing, dreamy, almost purr-ing sound—as though the calling bird were nodding on its perch—the voice of the turtledove.

Two diminutive birds of the carr, the willow warbler and the chiff-chaff—both greenish olive-brown, both exactly the same size, birds that are almost indistinguishable to sight—have entirely different songs. Occasionally we heard the small descending song of the willow warbler. And many times, in many places, we paused to listen to the dry, end-lessly-repeated phrases of the similar-appearing chiff-chaff. It is the first warbler to arrive in the British Isles in spring, the last to leave in fall. Some years it reaches Devon as early as February 14. "To those who mark the progress of the year by the song of birds," Grey of Fallodon wrote, "the first hearing of the chiff-chaff is the beginning of a new stage."

The main part of its song consists of a monotonous repe-tition of "chiff-chaff, chiff-chaff," the whole sounding like a ball being batted back and forth in a game of table tennis. Like our chickadee and killdeer, the bird calls its name. The "chiff" and the "chaff" are in different keys, the latter a step lower than the former. Weeks before I first heard this song, the warblers had built their nests, delicate little domed structures with the entrance on the side.

The square mile of wetland over which we wandered on

that afternoon in May was part of the original tract allotted
to one of the fourteen Gentlemen Adventurers. Until the
present century Adventurers Fen, adjoining Wicken Fen
on the south, also remained untouched. Then it fell victim
to two World Wars, each with its accelerated demand for
agricultural expansion. As we looked down on its drained
land, already lower than Wicken Fen, Gerald Humphrey
called my attention to blackened stumps, ancient and long-
buried, now brought to light again by the subsidence of the
fields.

In 1952, following the ending of the Second World
War, the area was returned to the control of the National
Trust and joined to Wicken Fen. Water has since been
channeled back to form a large mere overlooked by a reed-
thatched observation tower. Within a week after the flood-
ing took place, more than 250 ducks, including half a dozen
species, established themselves there. In time it is expected
that this mere on old Adventurers Fen will swarm with
waterfowl, affording a further glimpse of conditions as they
used to be.

chapter 23

HOME
OF THE
BEARDED TIT

We were now in the month of June. Swirls and currents and rip tides of seaside visitors flowed down the streets and along the sidewalks of Great Yarmouth, on the Norfolk coast. We found a room, at last, facing the sea, at the old Royal Hotel, which Charles Dickens recalls in *David Copperfield*. Down all our corridor, rooms were named for characters in his novels. I threw open the window overlooking the water. From the sidewalk below rose a woman's voice in that deathless complaint of seaside resorts:

"It seems such a long time till dinner!"

To fortify ourselves, Nellie and I bought a bunch of dark grapes from a woman at a stall in the open market. After a debate about whether the metal hook that had supported the bunch should be removed before or after the fruit was weighed, we wandered among stalls bearing such signs as: "Noted Chip Potatoes" and "Underwood's Noted Tripe Saloon." Around us jellied eels, pork pies, scones, plants, fruits, china, lobsters, cockles, mussels, and winkles vied for customers.

240

Perhaps it was the argument over the metal hook. At any rate, something brought to mind the eighteenth-century English scholar who silenced the abuse of Billingsgate fish-wives by thundering the single epithet: "Parallelopipedon!" Eating our grapes as we came back to our hotel, we reviewed the rich lode of vituperation that lies all untapped in that unlikely source, natural history guidebooks. Simply employing the names of two wildflowers and a shellfish would produce:

"You false hellbore You viper's bugloss! You wart-necked piddock!"

Twenty miles in space and three centuries in time from the scene of these ruminations—at Norwich, in the seventeenth century, to be exact—a busy physician with wide-ranging interests devoted his spare time to the study of natural history. Like that of the later Gilbert White of Selborne, his aim, revolutionary at that time, was to study living creatures instead of relying on what others had written about them. This pioneer physician-naturalist was Sir Thomas Browne. The fame of his classic meditative and philosophic volumes, *Religio Medici* and *Urn-Buriall*, written in a stately literary style rich in imagery, has overshadowed his accomplishments in the field of natural history. Yet the latter were of sufficient value to warrant publication, more than two and a half centuries after his death, of a volume of his *Notes and Letters on the Natural History of Norfolk*.

In the days of Browne and White, days of quieter life and simpler problems, the great upheavals of the outer world seemed occurring far, far away. No hourly bulletins on television, no extra editions of newspapers, disturbed their placid studies. This remoteness from great events is sensed in the writings of these naturalists. White lived in the time of the American Revolution, yet no mention of it appears in *The Natural History of Selborne*. Similarly,

Browne, in those momentous days when the Royalist cause
was nearing its downfall, was making known his inquiries
into popularly held beliefs such as whether swans sing before they die, whether the Phoenix and the Griffin ever
really existed, and whether the right and left legs of badgers
are equally long.

It is Browne who is usually credited with introducing into
general use the name "broads" for the wide and shallow
bodies of water, the "broad waters" or "broadings," that
are a feature of the lowlands of eastern Norfolk. Number-
ing between forty and fifty, they vary in size from two to
500 acres. In all, their waters cover about 5,000 acres.

Inland from the coast, on succeeding days, we traveled
through this region of ditches and canals, of old windmills
and flat meadows. White sails moved across the green landscape above invisible boats that followed unseen water-
roads, the broadland canals. The sky was intensely blue; the
air transparent and shining. This is the land that so often
appears in the paintings of Cotman and Crome. Each year,
during vacation months, it attracts as many as 100,000 visitors.

At first, as Browne's term implies, the extensive water
tracts of eastern Norfolk were believed to be merely the
broadening of old river beds. In recent years, however, a
new and more surprising explanation of their origin has
been substantiated by the geological explorations of Dr.
J. M. Lambert and others. Their evidence reveals that the
broads are man-made, produced by the peat-digging of the
ancient Saxons. Without forests, Norfolk, in earlier days,
depended exclusively on peat for fuel. Widespread beds,
laid down over a period of thousands of years, were worked
almost continuously for four centuries. How vast was the
demand for this fuel is indicated by the fact that, in a single
year in the fourteenth century, the priory of Norwich
Cathedral alone consumed 400,000 turfs.

Unlike the Channel coast with its abrupt headlands and cliffs, the eastern part of Norfolk slants gently toward its meeting with the North Sea. Nine centuries ago, when extensive peat digging began in the area, the land was ten feet higher than at present. In the fourteenth and fifteenth centuries, as a result of great storms and the sinking of the land, the sea invaded the depressions left where peat had been extracted. Later, barriers were built up by the waves, cutting off the salt water, and the broads became fresh.

Of them all, the largest—and the most interesting to the naturalist—is Hickling Broad. We came to its shore at the village of Hickling, a dozen miles or so northwest of Great Yarmouth. Before us extended a sheet of water a mile and a half in length. Over most of this expanse the depth is no more than four or five feet. In places the bottom is deep with oozy mud. But large stretches of the bed are solid and paved with gravel. I was told that a man of average height could walk, with his head above water, over hundreds of acres of this gravelly bottom.

In the natural history of England, the reed beds that rim Hickling Broad and cover its islands are famous as the place where the bittern and the bearded tit made their dramatic comeback after virtually being given up as lost to Britain. Until about a century ago, the bittern was one of the commonest birds of the region. It was the habit of marshmen to have a bittern for dinner each Sunday. In 1843, fen shooters near Hickling Broad killed between twenty and thirty of these birds in one morning. Year by year, the bittern became more scarce. By the late 1880's its booming call was gone from England. The usual explanation given for its disappearance is the draining of many marshes. But, as David A. Bannerman points out in the sixth volume of his *Birds of the British Isles*, the destruction of the bitterns in winter by shooting had a far more serious effect upon their numbers.

Almost a quarter of a century went by without a single bittern being reported from the wetlands of Britain. When Conan Doyle was writing *The Hound of the Baskervilles*, at the turn of the present century, he had one of his characters speculate that a strange and terrifying sound coming from the night on Dartmoor might be the call of that "very rare bird—practically extinct—in Britain now," the bittern. Then, on a July day in 1911, among the dense phragmites of a small island in Hickling Broad, Miss Emma L. Turner and James Vincent, head keeper at Lord Desborough's Whiteslea Estate at Hickling, discovered the nest of a bittern. That was the beginning of one of the brightest chapters in British bird protection. Under the administration of the Norfolk Naturalists Trust, all of Hickling Broad is now a sanctuary. Here the bittern, protected from hunters, has increased until, in 1954, nearly sixty were recorded booming around the edges of this one broad. In the succeeding years, it has spread back to former nesting grounds in other parts of England.

For eleven years after the bittern's return to Hickling Broad, Miss Turner studied and photographed the bird, both winter and summer. This remarkable woman was one of the pioneers of bird photography, the recipient of the Gold Medal of the Royal Photographic Society, one of the first women elected a Fellow of the Linnaean Society, a Fellow of the Zoological Society, and one of the first honorary lady members of the British Ornithologists' Union. After Richard Kearton introduced her to bird photography, Miss Turner spent part of each year at Hickling Broad. She built a houseboat, named the *Water Rail* after the first marsh bird she ever photographed. In it she spent as much as three weeks at a time alone, anchored at the edge of mosquito-infested reed beds, enduring hardships, exposure, and fatigue, carrying on her photography and, as she said, "picking up the gossip of the birds." To her, as she wrote in that book of charm and substance, *Broadland Birds,* they were "the most elusive of all the beautiful things which make life a joy." They remained the chief interest of this self-taught authority on the birds of the shallow Norfolk broads until her death at Cambridge in 1940, at the age of seventy-four.

Close to the spot where her houseboat first slid into the water on March 18, 1905, Nellie and I met George Bishop, the warden in charge of the Hickling Broad National Nature Reserve. A sturdy, fine-looking man with an engaging smile and a ready sense of humor, he proved to be the possessor of a wide range of varied and accurate information about the wildlife of the broad.

As we followed him down a dusty cinder road to the reserve headquarters, Whiteslea Lodge, we passed two men cutting sedge and stacking it in piles beside the road. From the beginning, a source of income at the reserve has been the harvesting of sedge and the reeds of the phragmites, *Phragmites communis,* for use in thatching. Both are highly prized and always in demand. The cutting of the reeds, usually winter work, is done with billhooks and scythes. On at least two occasions, in earlier generations, bitterns were accidentally mowed down and killed when they remained in camouflaged immobility among the reeds. When the phragmites are cut in midwinter, bearded tits often flit or hop about examining the ends of severed stems for overwintering insects. A century or so ago, the green reeds, cut in summer, were hauled south for use as litter in London livery stables. In places where the phragmites of Hickling Broad are left unharvested, their dense stands form the winter roosts of tens of thousands of starlings.

Bishop pushed us away from Whiteslea Lodge in a Norfolk punt, a low craft noted for its stability in rough water, yet having a draft so shallow it "floats on dew." Manning a long pole at the rear, he guided us down winding channels among the reeds and out into sunlit little bays where water beetles spun on the dark surface and dragonflies flashed past, hawking among the dancing gnats. For minutes at a time, all was still except for the soft plash of the pole as we advanced. At one point the punt slid through the beauty of a bay filled with mare's-tail water weeds. Norfolk marshmen have given local names to many of the wetlands plants, names that range from "apple-pie" for the hemp agrimony, *Eupatorium cannabinum*, to "halfpennies and pennies" for the frogbit, *Hydrocharis morsus-ranae*.

A little beyond the bay of the mare's-tails, we slipped into a narrow channel hemmed in by reeds. Here a number of pike—which in Hickling Broad may weigh as much as thirty-two pounds—had gathered. In panic they stampeded all around us. For two minutes or more, the large fish charged this way and that, shouldering above the surface, their tails sweeping whirlpools in the dark water, before they made good their escape.

Among the small islands of the broad, one stands out in memory. Yellow flags ran in a line along the water's edge and dangling masses of comfrey, some purple, some white, bloomed not far from an old thatched hut that links the present with Miss Turner's day. Anchored here, at Pleasure Island, she developed many of the negatives of her celebrated pictures of the broadland birds.

For the better part of that afternoon, we became invisible to the wildlife of the broad. We saw without being seen when on another island we observed the events around us from the interior of a small hut-on-stilts, a camouflaged hide or blind. Bishop led us up the weathered wooden steps at the rear. Carefully he closed the door—so that no bird's keen eye would catch movement against the light—before he opened the long horizontal slit of the observing window. For hours afterwards, sitting on a plank bench and looking out, we watched the activity of that sunny day taking place as though no human eye observed it.

Swallow Falls in northern Wales

Below us, winding in and out among the clumps of vegetation, a lapwing materialized leading four striped and downy chicks. A baby lapwing can run within an hour after hatching, and within twenty-four hours it can swim if necessary. These chicks, only a few days old, were continually in motion, continually coming upon surprises as they explored a whole new world at the water's edge. We saw one race around a rush clump, come abruptly to the end of land, apply the avian equivalent of emergency brakes, and halt at the last second before plunging into the broad. Small worms, insect larvae, and tiny mollusks formed the food sought by the foraging chicks. In a series of starts and stops and side excursions, this lapwing procession continued on out of sight.

Wherever the birds around us paused in their wading or rested at the edge of the shallows or preened themselves on a mudbank, their clear reflections appeared in the mirror of the still, dark water. In such images we saw the brilliant orange-red legs of the redshanks, the contrasting white and black and brown plumage of the ringed plover, the chestnut flanks of the shoveller ducks. Across the surface of this mirror stole the forms of passing terns, common and little. And there we saw reflected all the movements of a ruff—a particularly dark one, Bishop noted—as it carefully dressed its plumage on a small bar nearly awash with water.

Until about 1870 the ruff nested regularly in England. Now it breeds only sporadically. It is mainly a bird of passage, a visitor encountered most often along the eastern coast of Britain. At one time or another, almost every rare duck and wading bird on the British list appears at Hickling Broad. Once six posts rising above the shallows were all capped with glossy ibis.

Beyond the mud bar where the ruff continued its preening, a great crested grebe, the largest grebe in England, appeared, swimming steadily, a cluster of young grebes riding on its back. As we watched, one tumbled off. It swam be-

Malham Cove and the stream that flows from the base of the cliff

hind, paddling furiously, until it caught up and clambered aboard again. Over the reeds, over the water, over the islands, butterflies, some white, some the handsome black and yellow swallowtail, drifted by in the sunshine. At first glance, the latter gives the impression of being a smaller form of the familiar tiger swallowtail of eastern North America. In these early June days, this most famous of the broadland insects was still emerging from the chrysalis. The main period of emergence extends through May to mid-June. Bishop mentioned that he had followed an old custom of the region and had put a chrysalis or two on his mantel in order to have the pleasure of watching the colorful insects emerge. Among the broads, the swallowtails spend their days patrolling the marshes for the nectar of such wildflowers as ragged robin and marsh valerian, or seeking the milk parsley, *Peucedanum palustre*, on which they most frequently lay their eggs.

On one tiny islet, directly in front of us, the head of a nesting black-headed gull rose above the vegetation. In a quick descent, a dunlin alighted only a couple of feet away. Close together, the images of the two birds appeared mirrored in the water. The mate of the brooding gull paid no attention to the small shorebird. But when, a few minutes later, a pair of swans—one ahead, the other behind, with half a dozen woolly cygnets between them—paraded slowly by close to the islet, the gull rushed to an attack, screaming, diving close, threatening, strafing the unconcerned swans as long as they were near. In various places, floating on the surface of the broad, we saw white swan feathers. At that time, the population of these birds stood at about 200. It ranges, on Hickling Broad, from a low of about 100 to a high of about 400.

Once a heron, changing its position along the shore, flew past our blind. Among the broads, this bird is known as "Old Franky" because its call, uttered on the wing, resembles "Frank! Frank!" In the heat of that afternoon, the air was filled with the scent of wet reeds and exposed mud and decaying vegetation. Pouring forth a ringing, jumbled song as it descended into the phragmites, a sedge warbler parachuted down. Hardly had it disappeared when a larger bird, its plumage blue-gray above and transversely striped with white and dark below, slipped swiftly and silently into the reed beds. It was a female cuckoo intent on finding a nest, particularly one of its commonest victim here, a bird that nests in small colonies, the reed warbler.

In and out where the phragmites grew along the shallows, a mother coot threaded her way, trailed by two of her young. The day before, Bishop told us, there had been four where now there were only two. The others had fallen victim overnight to some predator. Other coot, in various directions beyond the curtaining reeds, revealed their presence by their curious strumming calls as though they were plucking low-pitched musical strings.

In earlier years, Hickling Broad was famous for its annual coot shoot. Some of "the best guns in England" converged on the broad and as many as 1,000 coot were killed in one day. At that time, a woman who was nearing eighty lived in a house overlooking the broad. Her special pleasure was making friends with waterfowl. Each day she fed as many as 100 ducks on her lawn. A large picture window permitted her to watch their activity while lying in bed. When the time of the coot shoot arrived, each year, it was her habit to lay trails of grain leading into net-enclosed areas. There she penned up the waterfowl that visited her regularly, keeping them from harm until the "best guns" were gone and the slaughter of the day was over.

We were on the open water again, returning to the lodge, when the most unexpected sight of that day appeared in the sky. Curving over the water, only a few hundred feet in the air, swift and clean-lined, a Spitfire monoplane approached like an apparition out of a heroic past. This was the aerial machine that played so large a part in England's stubborn battle with the Luftwaffe in those desperate early months of World War II. This particular plane is the pride of a Royal Air Force field, a dozen miles from Hickling Broad. Occasionally on fine days it is taken aloft. During war years, Bishop said, all the larger broads in Norfolk were filled with heavy upright poles and a maze of interconnecting steel cables sufficiently strong to wreck any enemy seaplane attempting to land.

More than once, that day, we heard within the dense reed beds the voice of a small, unseen bird. It reached our ears as a repeated "Ting! Ting! Ting!" It is a sound that has been described as resembling the single strokes of a bicycle bell. Bishop was reminded of two pennies clinking together. In those ringing notes, we were hearing a voice that is dramatically linked with Hickling Broad. It was the voice of the bearded tit.

This bird—which is not a true tit and is more aptly described by its old East Anglian name of "reedling" and even better by Charles Vaurie's suggested name of "bearded reedling"—virtually disappeared from Britain following several winters with record cold and snow and freezing fog. For years afterwards, nowhere in the British Isles except at Hickling Broad could a bearded tit be seen or heard. Here it made what seemed its last stand. Then the population slowly increased. By 1957 it had reached the highest point in 100 years. In a spectacular eruption, the species spread to other phragmites stands in many parts of England. The drama of this small bird's fight for survival, like the comeback of the bittern, was played on the stage of Hickling Broad.

Although we heard the "Ting! Ting!" of bearded tits ringing their little bells, first from one direction, then from another, only once that day did we catch a glimpse of one of the singers. Then a male—tawny-backed, with striking black moustaches and ash-gray head, a bird about the size of the song sparrow of eastern North America—rose briefly in a low, fluttering flight close to the plumed heads of the phragmites. Until then, the little bird's colloquial name, "reed pheasant," had been a mystery to us. Now we saw that its elongated tail and short, low flight gave it the appearance of a pheasant in miniature.

It was not at Hickling Broad, the place so memorably linked with its history, but farther up the Norfolk coast, beyond Cromer, famous for its Cromer crabs, that we saw the reedling at its best. Between Salthouse and Cley-next-the-Sea, the green of a level marshy lowland extends from the highway to the yellow line of distant coastal dunes. Happily for the teeming bird life of this expanse, it, like Hickling Broad, is a sanctuary under the administration of the Norfolk Naturalists Trust. It was in Norfolk that modern bird protection began in England and the Norfolk Naturalists Trust is the initial organization of its kind in Great Britain.

Everywhere we looked, birds were taking off and landing. The air, at times, seemed alive with them—coot in labored flight, lapwings veering wildly, marsh harriers quartering in the distance, redshanks, swift and twisting, black terns, airy and graceful on the wing. Scattered across the lower vegetation we could see the raised, alert heads of half a hundred nesting black-headed gulls. Farther out, we could make out a family of graylag geese and, where a clump of denser vegetation hid their bodies, the high-stretched necks of Canada geese, as wary here as we had seen them vigilant beside the Missouri River in the Dakotas.

Across these marshes of Cley, along one end, there extends an elevated path. It follows the grassy top of a long dike that traces a straight line toward the dunes. We were perhaps two-thirds of the way down this dike when we came abreast of a large stand of dense phragmites. Appear-

ing and disappearing along its edge, darting in and out of
the sunshine, small birds of the reeds came and went. Here
again was the reed bunting's black head and bib above the
white collar that I had first seen at Wicken Fen. Here we
noted the quick dartings of the rusty-brown reed warbler
and saw the white eye stripe of the sedge warbler shining in
the sun. And here, most exciting of all, we looked down on
the activity of the bearded tits. As we had wanted to see
the Dartford warbler in Hampshire, so, in Norfolk, we
wanted to see the bearded tit, to see it at leisure, at length,
in an unhurried view.

Our first sighting brought a quadruple thrill. A lively
band of four suddenly materialized at the edge of the reeds.
Chasing one another, performing acrobatics among the
vertical stems, repeating the small metallic note of their
calls, they dashed in and out among the reeds. Only one of
the four was an adult male. For a time it clung, peering toward us, its eye-catching black moustache-markings prominent on its gray face. Bearded tits almost completely reverse
their diets, summer and winter. In summer they feed
mainly on insects; in winter, mainly on seeds, particularly
the seeds of the phragmites. We saw the lively birds pause
here and there to peer intently at the canes and leaves of
the reeds or halt momentarily in their romping advance to
snatch up some morsel in passing.

Other males, farther on, were making their "pheasant
flights." Females popped out at the edge of the reed beds,
then disappeared again. And from the depths of the dense
stands, over and over, as long as we remained in the vicinity, the bright, ringing "Ting! Ting! Ting!" of other unseen
members of the colony reached our ears. At times we
caught the sound with difficulty amid the clamor of the
black-headed gulls and the commingled songs of skylarks
over the open pasture land beyond the dike. In those meadows, sheltered by the dunes, black and white met black and

white; oystercatchers wandered among feeding Holstein-Friesian cows.

To our south, across the highway, the land ascends steeply to Salthouse Heath, where the nightjar nests. Along the face of this slope run cultivated fields. Among them, from time to time as we returned along the dike top, we heard explosions and caught sight of small gray clouds of smoke drifting away. We saw no hunters. Later we learned that farmers in this region keep birds from their crops, especially where peas are grown for the canning industry, by using carbide drip devices that automatically set off explosions throughout the day. Birds conditioned by being shot at flee from explosive sounds, while cows which are not shot at ignore them. The grazing cows continued feeding, undisturbed by these periodic blasts. A cow is a huge animal. It requires much food. Eating is the paramount work of its life. When the German city of Aachen was under heavy Allied artillery fire, during the Second World War, a herd of Holstein-Friesian cows continued calmly grazing while the shells screamed overhead and exploded nearby.

"There are few places in England," W. H. Hudson wrote in *Adventures Among Birds*, "where you can get so much wildness and desolation of sea and sandhills, wood, green marsh, and grey saltings, as at Wells, in Norfolk." Our ascent of the curving coast beyond Cley-next-the-Sea brought us to this red-brick town and to the open land beyond where the road runs on to Holkham. The name Holkham should be linked in the mind of every reader with another name, Coke of Norfolk. In the same year that America declared its independence, Thomas Coke, Earl of Leicester, inherited 40,000 acres of land at Holkham. It was described at the time as so barren that two rabbits might be seen fighting over one blade of grass. By experiment and research, by consulting every expert he could find, Coke made the fields of this poor inheritance increase their yield tenfold. He is known as the father of English Farming. He introduced the growing of wheat. He improved the standard of livestock. Every British treatise on modern agriculture recognizes the value of his innovations. Coke of Norfolk was one of the quiet heroes. Yet his work did more to benefit his country—fundamentally—than did the activity of many a political leader or general, surrounded as they were with splendor and display.

Beside the high red wall that now encircles Coke's Holkham Park, we turned toward the sea where a long line of dunes, crowned by dark pines, parallels the shore. This was Hudson's "A Wood by the Sea." Walking on the soft, needle-cushioned path among the pines, following the ridge top more than half a century after Hudson last walked here, we glimpsed between the tree trunks the glitter of the sea and the yellow of the shore on one hand and the flat expanse of the saltings running inland on the other. A kestrel, "the windhover," hung on fluttering wings, facing the breeze, peering intently down at the open ground. The smell of sea and pines filled the warm air.

Just below, in a dense cluster of small willows, we heard again that warbler voice, the "chiff-chaff, chiff-chaff" that here sounded like the whetting of a knife. That bright sound brought with it, like a drifting cloud shadow over the mind, remnants of that somber, pensive mood that pervades some of Hudson's most eloquent and deeply felt pages—his chapter on "The Return of the Chiff-Chaff," subtitled "Spring Sadness," in A Traveller in Little Things. The land breeze freshened around us. The low crooning song of wind among the pines, that same wonderful music I remembered from pine winds of boyhood in the dunes of Indiana, increased above our heads.

When Hudson walked this way, his ear had been caught by the manner in which the barking of a dog on the beach had echoed among the dunes. On this day so long after, we were delighted to notice something of the kind. As we drew near the end of the pine plantation, where the ridge makes a sudden sweep to the left, we heard a cuckoo calling somewhere before us. The voice, echoing from the curving sounding board of the ridge, seemed magnified. The calling bird seemed shouting at the top of its voice, repeating its notes with greater volume than we had ever heard before. And something else we noticed. The call seemed more "cuk-cuk" than "cuckoo-cuckoo." We were noting, on this June day, what John Heywood, in the sixteenth century, had put into rhyme:

> "In April the koocoo can sing her song by rote,
> In June, of tune, she cannot sing a note;
> At first koo coo, koo coo sing still she can do;
> At last, kooke, kooke, six kookes to one koo!"

chapter 24

ROBIN
HOOD'S
OAK

What St. Francis of Assisi used to call "my brother the wind and my sister the rain" followed us around the upper rim of the Norfolk coast. On whipping bushes beside the road, early flowers of the dog-rose waved in the downpour. So rich in vitamin C are the red hips that replace the pink and white of these flowers that, during the Second World War, they were gathered by the ton to produce a rose-hip syrup that was employed as a substitute for oranges.

With screaming gulls always in sight, we circled the end of the Wash next morning. The wind and the rain were gone. Lincolnshire extended before us. We now were entering a new part of Britain—the upper England of Robin Hood's Sherwood Forest, Izaak Walton's River Dove, the high Yorkshire moors, the Lake District of the poets.

In Thomas Fuller's time, "for the waterfowl therein," Lincolnshire was known as the Aviary of England. The wetland of the fens then stretched up the coast and spread for hundreds of square miles inland. On this later morning, in place of those ancient marshes the drained land lay out-

spread in immense flat fields where men wielding hoes or
bending down with scratchers engaged in the long spring
battle against weeds. At times our road ran more than fifteen feet above the level of the farmland. Around us, as we
drove north, extended strawberries in white bloom, mustard
fields spreading away in acres of yellow, mile after mile of
tulip and narcissus rows, with square, stolid farmhouses of
brick spaced widely apart. Far in the distance we could see
tiny lines of Lombardy poplars rising beside remote drainage ditches

In those early days of June, towns all along the way were
clogged with traffic. A tide of vacationers swept across the
land toward the coast. We found it almost as hard to get
out of Boston, in Lincolnshire, in England, as it used to be
to get out of Boston, in Massachusetts, in the U.S.A. To
the north, not far from the birthplace of the John Smith of
the Pocahontas story, we stopped at Spilsby for a loaf of its
famous plum bread. As I waited my turn at the bakery, I
was impressed, as I had been in many parts of England,
with the extreme politeness of people there. Serving a
young woman, the owner asked:

"What would you like, please?"

"Four currant buns, thank you."

When she received the buns, the customer said:

"Thank you. And a loaf of white bread, please?"

"Thank you."

The bread was delivered. The customer responded with:

"Thank you very much."

This went on through a dozen or more thank-yous and
pleases until all the purchases were made. I added to the
number and left with a loaf of plum bread. Its "plums," we
discovered, were raisins and currants.

North of Spilsby the scenery altered radically. The flat
land of the reclaimed Fens sank behind. We rode up and
down higher and higher hills. In valleys below, the haw-

thorn—now past its prime in Devon and Dorset and Surrey and even along Shakespeare's Avon in Warwickshire—stood out in lines of white rimming the fields. Its blooming time, in this more northern zone, appeared still at its peak.

Small pictures of the Lincolnshire country return to mind. Once ahead of us we saw what we mistook, at first glance, to be a country graveyard filled with white head-stones. As we drew nearer we saw that sheep and lambs were lying down, evenly distributed across the grass. The lambs were woolly; the sheep were shorn. That often-quoted assertion in Laurence Sterne's A *Sentimental Journey*—repeated at least three times in the novels of Anthony Trollope—that "God tempers the wind to the shorn lamb" finds little in nature to support it. Moreover, as we saw here, it is not the lamb that is shorn. In England a lamb is called a lamb until it is about nine months old. It is more than a year old, usually fifteen or sixteen months old, before its first shearing occurs.

A paved highway that at times seemed laid out along the line of a taut string carried us south again from Brigg to Lincoln. This was the Ermine Street of the legions, what has been called one of "the most impressive stretches of Roman road in Britain." In his *The Decline and Fall of the Roman Empire*, Edward Gibbon speaks of such roads as these "whose firmness has not entirely yielded to the effort of fifteen centuries." An even more ancient roadway followed the edge of a limestone ridge just to our west. Winding southward from Scunthorpe, it first came into being as a trail of prehistoric men.

As we drew near Lincoln, we saw the cathedral, whose immense bulk of golden-tinted stone towers above the city, illuminated by the light of late afternoon. As at Salisbury and Wells, cathedral daws sailed around the lofty towers. Gray groups of young starlings hunted for food across the lawns. By now most of the first broods of the smaller birds were fledged and on the wing. But those supreme vocalists of the English spring, the male blackbirds, still sang on in the trees of the cathedral grounds. We had left the song of the wood thrush at home; we had found the song of the blackbird in England.

Hardly had we started out next morning when an open roadster sailed past us. In it was a man wearing a Sherlock Holmes hat. That insignia of a nemesis of crime seemed particularly appropriate on this day when we were bound for the Sherwood Forest of Robin Hood. As we rode along I made up a joke about a man who thought the highwayman said: "Your money or your *wife!*" Somehow that frivolous note seemed less funny to Nellie than it did to me. So our morning began.

Our route followed a rambling path south and west and north and east again. Once we passed a shop run by a butcher named Bloodworth. It recalled the numerous striking family names we had encountered in England—Halfhide, Hailstone, Rainbird, even an undertaker named Nightingale. Along our road, as down how many hundreds of miles of other roadsides, ran white banks of cow parsley. I remember Nellie's delight in this simple flower. Once when she gathered a head to examine the small blooms more closely, we rode for miles afterwards with its sweet perfume filling the interior of the car.

Somewhere near the Nottinghamshire border, we observed a rook struggling to rise from the edge of the road. It appeared to be trying to lift a load too heavy for its wings to support. When we drew abreast we saw the burden which it had dropped was a song thrush killed by a car. Not far beyond, all the treetops of a small grove were filled with the stick nests of the gregarious rooks. Our eardrums, as we slowed to a halt, were pounded by the raucous din. Turning and diving, alighting and flapping into the air again, swirled the black forms of half a hundred birds. We had seen rooks carrying sticks in Cornwall. We had seen them picking wool from thorny pasture bushes to provide lining for their nests. Here all the fever and excitement of a rookery in the spring still continued.

An odd thing has been noticed in connection with such nesting colonies in various parts of England, in France, in Germany and elsewhere. Among the droppings below the trees, the ground is sometimes littered with pieces of rubber. They are chiefly rubber bands and rings used on hermetically sealed bottles and tins. In one instance some of the strips appeared to have come from a toy balloon. The predominant color is red although some of the fragments are pink, others white, others blue and still others green. On occasions, bushes beneath the nesting trees are festooned with such pieces of rubber. In the early 1930's, when the trees of one rookery near Wakefield, in Yorkshire, were felled and the area cleared by fire, a smell of burning rubber pervaded the region. The rooks apparently pick up the rubber as food, mistaking the indigestible bands and rings for something edible.

Our progress, that June day, was one of starts and stops and turnings aside. We turned aside to Ancaster where quarries produce stone that is soft and damp, easily cut and carved, when it comes from the ground but that becomes hard when exposed to the air. Once before, on an August day in central Kansas, we had encountered similar rock. Buff-colored and called greenhorn limestone, it provided fenceposts on the treeless plains. At Ancaster the oolitic limestone comes from the earth in various colors, yellow-brown, pink, white, bluish, and mottled. It weathers to gray. In all such rock the moisture, called "quarry sap" or "quarry water," holds various minerals either dissolved or in suspension. As the stone dries in the open air, the minerals are deposited in the outer portions of the rock and it becomes tough and hard.

Another time we turned aside to see the town made famous by the medieval folk tale of The Wise Men of Gotham who, to avoid paying taxes, convinced messengers of the King they were imbeciles by trying to drown an eel, by planting a hedge around a thorn bush to imprison a cuckoo, and by burning down a barn to destroy a wasp nest. Later they could boast: "More fools pass through Gotham than remain in it." We passed through—ignoring the saying—and continued on our way.

Sometime after ten o'clock in the morning, we turned into a ridgetop layby. A station wagon was already there. On its tailgate a small portable heater was boiling water for mid-morning tea. While they waited, a whole family stood looking down into a golden valley, enjoying a dramatic natural scene. For, in Nottinghamshire, this was the high noon of the buttercups and the entire valley floor was carpeted with the wildflowers. Perhaps it was in a similar situation that Grey of Fallodon once observed: "The earth is full of wonderful things and I would like to dwell on two especially. One is the infinite beauty of the world; and the other, separate and yet inseparably connected with the first, is the power of man to perceive the beauty and to be moved by it."

I do not know exactly what we expected to find when we reached Sherwood Forest. Probably it was some dense, deeply-shaded Old World woodland with glades dark and lonely. What we actually found came as a complete surprise. Even in the time of the legendary Robin Hood, the forest was relatively open and sunlit. When Daniel Defoe was writing the third volume of A Tour Through the Whole Island of Britain, in 1726, he reported: "This forest is now given up, in a manner, to waste: even the woods, which formerly made it famous for thieves, are destroyed, so that Robin Hood would hardly find shelter for a week." Such shelter was further reduced during the First World

War when many of the remaining trees were cut down for fuel and wide areas were cleared for cultivation.

It was through Edwinstowe—with its Robin Hood Inn and Robin Hood Avenue and its tradition of being the place where Maid Marian and the outlaw were wed—that we came to the central part of the forest. Here, north of Nottingham and approximately half way between London and the Scottish border, we were close to the site of the Major Oak, that immense hollow tree where, folk history has it, Robin Hood and his men hid from the Sheriff of Nottingham. And what did we find? Instead of a wild and unfrequented forest, we found acres of varicolored automobiles jammed together in the open spaces. The blare of portable radios filled the air. People swarmed among the trees eating picnic lunches in the shade and in the sunshine. Ice-cream stands, carnival booths, even a merry-go-round, occupied the largest open space.

On this warm and sunny Sunday, after the raw cold of the winter and the chill of the Midland spring, men, women, and children had poured from the densely packed manufacturing towns, from Sheffield, Nottingham, and Manchester, into the open air. But their holiday had carried them from crowds to crowds; from the crowds at home, where they lived and worked, to crowds in the country, where they picnicked.

In the card catalogue of the main reading room of the New York Public Library, there are more than 100 titles listed under Robin Hood. This folklore hero, who no historian has been able to prove ever existed, whose only life may have been in romance and ballad, is, in fact, represented by more reference cards than such authentic historical heroes as Captain James Cook or the Duke of Marlborough.

He first appears in English literature as the outlaw of Sherwood Forest, Robyn Hood, in the fourteenth-century poem, *Piers Plowman.* Tales of his exploits grew, reaching their height in the ballads of Elizabethan times. He is commemorated by numerous place names: Robin Hood's Cove, Robin Hood's Cave, Robin Hood's Stride, Robin Hood's Chair, and the well called Robin Hood's Cup. Little John, Maid Marian, Allan-a-Dale, Friar Tuck, and other members of his band continued for centuries favorite characters of English ministrelsy. As King Arthur was the hero of the upper classes, so Robin Hood—the incomparable archer, the lover of the free life of the forest, audacious and adventurous, robbing the rich and giving to the poor—was the ideal of the common people during the time England was emerging from the Middle Ages.

Today Sherwood Forest, linked so indissolubly with his name, is about twenty miles long and between five and ten miles wide. For a time, that afternoon, we left the radios and the merry-go-round and ranged northward as far as Worksop. Once, in the heart of the forest, we came upon a large area of churned-up ground where army tanks had maneuvered in training exercises. Now and then we caught sight of venerable oaks possibly descending, themselves, from the Middle Ages. The most famous of all these ancient trees of the forest is the Major Oak, so called from a certain Major Rorke, an early writer on the region who expressed a special preference for this particular tree. Our desire to see it drew us back to the congested part of the forest near Edwinstowe.

When we asked directions, we were shown a broad path beaten by the feet of generations of visitors. It led a mile, we were told, to the tree we sought. That distance, however, proved to be a city man's mile, more nearly half a mile. Upwards of 1,000 persons made this same pilgrimage that day. Strung out as far as we could see, the straggling parade suggested some colorful posse combing Sherwood Forest for Robin Hood. Beside their owners, Scotties and poodles padded along the dry path, their feet sending up little spurts of fine gray dust.

"How curious it is," Nellie remarked, "that the dog is 'man's best friend,' and yet nobody wants to be compared to him. 'You dog!' is uncomplimentary. 'You cur!' is worse. Even referring to someone as 'a faithful dog' is a compliment nobody appreciates."

At times the path before us spread out to a width of as much as fifty feet. It extended like a boulevard through the forest. We passed long vistas where a scattering of dead oaks and slender white birches rose above brown acres of fallen, last-year's bracken. At this season, cavities in dead trees of the forest were providing nesting sites for numerous birds. The smallest tit in England, the diminutive coal tit, with its black crown and white nape-patch, flitted in and out of one nesting hole high in a long-dead stub.

Another weathered stub, close beside the path, rose like a totem pole. Its bark had fallen away years before and the sun and wind and rain had polished the wood beneath. From top to bottom the silvered trunk was decorated with the swirling patterns of the grain. It, too, contained a nesting hole. Here we added another bird to the life list of those we had seen, the colorful little redstart of Europe. For some time we stood watching this new species in its comings and goings. Throughout our trip, we were less interested in compiling a long list of birds than in becoming as well acquainted as possible with those we saw. The pair of redstarts seemed almost undisturbed by the passing parade of humans. Gray above, black of face and throat and white of forehead, with reddish breast and fiery chestnut tail and rump, the handsome male again and again appeared suddenly, alighted, and disappeared in the hole with forest caterpillars in its bill. The less colorful female lacked the white forehead and black throat. But both birds flashed the same flickering reddish tails that make so appropriate the colloquial name of the species: Firetail.

When we reached the Major Oak we found it surrounded by a throng of people. Most of them were gazing fascinated at its immense girth and at the size and spread of its gnarled branches. The English oak is the largest and longest-lived of British deciduous trees. Estimates place the age of the Major Oak at 1,000 years or more. Its hollow trunk, breast-high, is reported to have a circumference of more than thirty feet. Children and grown-ups alike were squeezing through a narrow opening to view the interior of the tree. When we looked up, we saw a maze of steel cables bracing its massive limbs. To slow down the processes of weakening and decay, sheets of metal covered holes and damaged places on the upper side of the branches. All around the squat form of this giant oak, everywhere beneath the spread of its branches, the ground was bare and packed hard by the feet of visitors.

We were gazing up among the branches, near the end of our stay, when Nellie caught sight of a small brownish bird of subdued plumage. It remained silent as it restlessly moved from limb to limb. We were about to dismiss it as an ordinary house sparrow when it alighted on a lower branch in a shaft of sunshine. There, as it twisted, peering this way and that, we saw its head was capped with chocolate-brown instead of gray. Then we picked out the black comma-shaped cheek spot. The bird we were seeing was the European tree sparrow, *Passer montanus*. Only once before, under far different conditions and in far different surroundings, had we encountered this bird. It was on a windy day in February where the Illinois River joins the Mississippi. We had stopped to sweep the skies with our binoculars in a search for bald eagles when a small dark bird alighted nearby. When we focused on it, we saw, in its highly re-

stricted New World range, our first European tree sparrow.
A single, relatively small area in the Midwest, centering in
St. Louis, on the Mississippi, is the only place throughout
all the North American continent where this introduced
species has survived and become established.

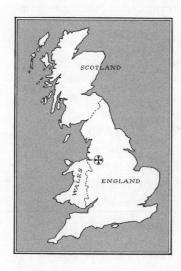

chapter 25

DOVEDALE

There is a path in western Derbyshire that threads a green valley, narrow and deep. It winds beside a stream, clear and gentle. The stream is the River Dove. The valley is Dovedale. This stream and this valley lie in the heart of the countryside that formed—in "such dayes and times" as he had "laid aside business and gone a-fishing"—one of the favorite haunts of Izaak Walton.

Rivers have many lives. The Dove, for most of its course from its origin high on the bleak moors of Axe Edge to its juncture with the River Trent, forms the boundary between Derbyshire and Staffordshire. For half a dozen of those miles, this boundary is traced by the deep-cut serpentine of Dovedale. The course of the stream also generally marks the western edge of the Peak District, the picturesque region situated at the lower end of the Pennine Chain, that backbone of hills extending down through northern England. Narrow valleys are numerous in the Peak District. But of them all the most famous, the most beautiful is Dovedale.

We came to it in bright sunshine on a June morning.
The path we followed descended to the stream where it
veers sharply to the west, blocked by the 900-foot-high bulk
of Thorpe Cloud. When we looked up the steep slopes of
this towering conical hill we saw silhouetted against the sky
near the top, reduced by distance to fly dimensions, the
tiny forms of grazing sheep and human climbers. Our path
wandered away upstream, clinging to the Derbyshire bank.
Beside us flowed the shifting currents of the stream; above
us rose, on either side, the tree-clad walls of the limestone
ravine. So transparent was the flow of the still unspoiled,
still unpolluted Dove that we could see, sharply defined,
the drifts of sand grains, the stretches of pebbles, the light-
colored rocks speckled with small, dark snails, the water
growths waving in the current. We viewed the bed of the
stream as through faultless glass.

A leisurely breeze blew down the valley that morning. In
each sheltered bay among the bushes, dancing midges rose
and fell. Where sunbeams spotlighted the larger swarms,
the insects swirled in glowing, diaphanous clouds. Mayflies
drifted on the breeze. They emerged from the shadows,
caught the sunshine, fluttered in gauzy radiance for a time,
then, their brightness suddenly extinguished, entered the
shadows once more. Living dangerously, a few alighted on
the surface of the stream, floated with the current, took
wing again. Others alighted, drifted—but did not take off
again. Instead, there was a swirl of water, the glint and colors of a trout, and the floating insects disappeared.

Below the white water where one cataract tumbled over
mossy rocks in Walton's stream, we watched the movements of a particularly beautiful trout as it stemmed the
current, slid effortlessly over the stream bed, threaded in
and out among the waving curtains of the water weeds.
Half a mile or so beyond, sunshine reflected into the
drowned cavern beneath an undercut tree on the opposite

bank. There we picked out the form of another, much larger trout. All told, we glimpsed nearly a dozen of these gamefish. The River Dove, three centuries after Walton's time, remains still one of the famous trout streams of England.

Such sights as these Walton knew; such scenes he cherished. And some of the pure and limpid quality of the stream that winds through Dovedale found its way into the pages of his classic book. When the first edition appeared in the spring of 1653, its advertisement presented it as: *"The Compleat Angler, or the Contemplative Man's Recreation, being a discourse of Fish and Fishing, not unworthy the perusal of most Anglers, of 18 pence price. Written by Iz. Wa."* It is the contemplative side of the book, its feeling and atmosphere, that have contributed largely to the fact that a new edition has appeared on the average of every two and a half years since it first was published. Generations of readers have turned to this volume for something more valuable than accurate science or expert guidance in catching fish. They have found in its pages the calm of a simpler, quieter world. "It would sweeten a man's temper at any time to read it," was Charles Lamb's verdict.

Although Walton spent most of his life in London, the book he wrote is concerned with things far removed from city life. To *The Compleat Angler*, as to *The Natural History of Selborne*, a special flavor is imparted by the depth and sincerity of that delight in simple things that characterized the lives of both Izaak Walton and Gilbert White.

The portion of the River Dove most intimately associated with Walton flows through Beresford Dale, a few miles upstream from Dovedale. Here, during some of his happiest days, he followed its meanderings with his friend, Charles Cotton, who, after the author's death, added to the fifth edition of *The Compleat Angler* a second part, on fly fishing. Cotton's birthplace, Beresford Hall, is now in ruins.

But his Fishing House, a square, single-roomed structure of stone, still stands on the riverbank, a memorial to these two friends who often rested there.

More than once as we wandered beside the Dove, the same thought recurred. How pleasant a place to be on a sunny day in June! The green of new leaves surrounded us. Wildflowers bloomed along the length of the valley. Probably only a small proportion of Britain's native plants grow here. But many we saw seemed of special interest. Along the edge of the shallows on several curves of the stream, huge, heart-shaped leaves massed together. Some of the stands were more than twenty feet across. This was the butterbur, the wild rhubarb or bog rhubarb, *Petasites hybridus*. The leaves, which appear after the flowers have bloomed, are dense with cottony white hairs beneath. Sometimes they measure more than two feet in width. It is from these large leaves that the plant's generic name arises. It is taken from *petasos*, the Greek word for a broad-brimmed hat.

The butterbur, found in moist soil and along streams, is one of the common plants of Britain, such a plant as one old-time botanist, intent on saving himself work, was wont to dismiss with such statements as: "It is so well known I will not trouble you with a description of it. My book grows big too fast." Or: "It is a plant so common that everyone who hath eyes knows it, and he that hath none cannot read a description of it if I should write it."

For us, the butterbur was another old friend in a new place—or, to be more accurate, an old friend in an old place. For Europe was its original home. It is one of that large number of botanical immigrants that crossed the Atlantic from Britain to America. There it has established itself in a range that extends from Massachusetts to Pennsylvania, and there it has acquired new colloquial names: umbrella-leaves and batterdock. In pioneer times the dried leaves of the butterbur were sometimes employed in what is described as "a particularly rank substitute for tobacco."

When, where, or how it first arrived on the shores of the New World nobody knows. Most of the immigrant plants reached America unheralded. Who can say, for example, how the common St. John's-wort, *Hypericum perforatum*, and the familiar butter-and-eggs, the yellow toadflax, *Linaria vulgaris*, reached the roadsides of North America? In a few instances, however, the time and place of arrival can be stated precisely. John Bartram, some 200 years ago, noted in a letter to an English correspondent the manner in which one of the common British thistles was added to the flora of Pennsylvania. "A Scotch minister," he wrote, "brought with him a bed stuffed with thistledown in which was contained some seeds. The inhabitants, having plenty of feathers, soon turned out the down and filled the bed with feathers. The seeds coming up filled that part of the country with thistles."

The Dovedale gorge, as we walked slowly along, narrowed and widened. Our path rose and fell. At times we were looking down at the river; at other times our way led close beside it. Since long before Walton's time, Dovedale has been famous for echoes. In one place where the walls of rock pressed close together and the river flowed between, a tangle of bushes clung half way up the opposite side of the ravine. From it poured the varied, trilling song of an unseen wren. Loud and clear, the music seemed magnified, tossed back and forth, caught in the valley, the sound tumbling about our ears.

Those who traverse the full length of Dovedale encounter curiously-shaped rock formations, caves, crags and pinnacles. They pass Raven's Tor, Tissington's Spires, the Twelve Disciples, the Shepherd's Abbey. They come to Reynard's Cave with its smaller cavern, Reynard's Kitchen. They find the Lion's Head extending out over the path, a jutting crag suggesting in outline the maned profile of a lion. Before Milldale, the walls of the gorge fall away, the valley opens out and the river scene becomes more tame.

As we returned downstream again, with the river beside us speeding up in foaming rapids and slowing down in placid pools, we rested beside a large undercut alder with its several trunks leaning out over the water. For nearly a quarter of an hour we remained there, diverted by the activity of three ducklings that followed a female mallard along the wilder edge of the opposite bank.

Their little procession threaded in and out among the overhanging vegetation. Everywhere they went, the downy young mallards snapped up small insects. They picked them from the water and snatched them from the air. In areas of special abundance, we saw them spinning like whirl-igig beetles. Several times they entered clouds of air-borne insects hovering just above the water. Then we saw them, with tiny wings fluttering and necks outstretched, almost leaping from the water as they snapped the flying food from the air around them.

One of the ducklings became so engrossed in catching insects, it let the current carry it away. Cutting sharply around sticks and water weeds, turning its head rapidly from side to side, frequently lunging ahead or at a veering angle, its bill opening and closing in quick succession, it continued its feeding. Before it realized that it was separated from the others, it had drifted nearly a hundred feet downstream. Skittering back over the water, it narrowed the gap and regained the procession which gradually worked upstream around a bend and was lost to view.

Less than thirty miles, airline, northwest of Dovedale, lies Manchester. With its more than 600,000 inhabitants, it is the fourth largest city in England. On a day when Nellie remained near the valley and added a new bird, the brownish garden warbler, to her life list, I covered that distance for a changeover—turning in our rented car to be over-

hauled and receiving another tuned-up Vauxhall in exchange. Our first car, light blue, we remember as "Bluebell." Our second, pale green, received when we were amid
the spring foliage of the New Forest, we named "Green-
leaf." The last of the trio, the car that would carry us to the
end of our trip, we called "Dovedale." At its wheel, buf-
feted and bewildered, lost among hundreds of intersecting
streets, I found my way out of Manchester with difficulty.
Revived by oatmeal cakes bought at Buxton and eaten in a
layby near the stone village of Chelmorton, I made my way
back to Dovedale.

Our first excursion in the new car carried us south
through Ashbourne, past the Green Man Inn where Samuel Johnson and James Boswell stayed, and over the Staffordshire border to the village of Ellastone, the "Hayslope"
of *Adam Bede*, where George Eliot's father, the hero of that
story, spent his youth. All around this village the pasture
fields were tapestries of green and white and yellow—rich
with grass and daisies and buttercups. One lamb—born into
beauty—lay by itself in the sunshine surrounded by wildflowers.

Among other flowered fields, a few miles away, we looked
between the bars of a high, spiked iron fence that seemed
formed of a thousand upright spears. Beyond, at the foot of
a gradual slope, Wootton Lodge formerly stood. Just a century before, in this secluded place, that sensitive and proud,
trusting and suspicious, greatly gifted and tremendously
handicapped man, Jean Jacques Rousseau, had written his
Confessions.

During the time he was a guest at the lodge, Rousseau
had visited Dovedale and the higher country surrounding it.
When we climbed, that afternoon, into this stony upland
bordering the valley, our road lifted us almost 1,000 feet
above sea level. As far as we could see across the harsh,
wind-swept highlands, the white lines of stone walls cut the

countryside into a vast jig-saw puzzle of irregular fragments. They wound in slow-curving serpentines. They angled in abrupt zigzags over the hillsides. They pitched in long, straight lines into the valleys. On far-away slopes, small squares and rectangles and looping lines, forming pens and pastures, ran like hieroglyphics across the green expanse.

Here we were in a modern Stone Age. All the works of man, the walls, the gateposts, the sheds, the low solid houses, were formed almost entirely of limestone. "Derbyshire peak" or "millstone grit," another stone of the region, has long been quarried at the lower end of the Pennines. It is famed for making millstones that for centuries were especially prized for grinding barley. Wherever stone was quarried we saw revealed the thinness of the outer layer of soil. On this limestone upland there was none of the ingratiating softness of a Devon or Hampshire. Everything was spare and hard. All was more sparse, less friendly to man.

However, throughout the land of the Dovedale region there was everywhere a kaleidoscopic interest: Milldale with its pack-horse bridge barely wide enough for pedestrians; the River Manifold flowing underground; Dove Holes where the bones of mastodons were discovered; the Illam Valley, said to be the setting of Samuel Johnson's *Rasselas*; Wren's Nest Hill, honeycombed with caves left from the lime workings of the Industrial Revolution; caverns famed for their "Dudley bugs" or fossil trilobites.

An early writer dismissed the beautiful gorge of Dovedale as "without any matter worth noting." It was not until the eighteenth century, with its awakening appreciation of wild scenery, that the valley came into its own. But two centuries passed and the last month of 1950 arrived before—with Dovedale as the main attraction—542 square miles of the Peak District were set aside to form the first national park in Britain. Almost one-half the population of England lives within fifty miles of the park boundaries.

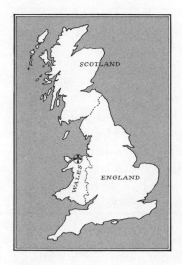

chapter 26

THE DIPPER
OF SWALLOW
FALLS

We climbed the heights of Axe Edge, skirted the spongy ground of Goyt's Moss, and, over the border in Cheshire, came to the Cat and Fiddle Inn. Sixteen hundred and ninety feet above sea level, it is said to be the highest licensed hostelry in England. No other human habitation stood in view. All around, like some Dartmoor of the north, the country rolled away in immense swells of somber land. To the south, between the headwaters of the River Dane and the gritstone heights of the Roaches, lay the eastern edge of that romantic region, the Green Knight's legendary hunting ground. For this still-wild country formed part of the setting of the old medieval poem *Syr Gawayne and the Grene Knighte*.

For a last time, Nellie and I looked back across Axe Edge toward Dovedale. Then, turning west again, we began a long, curving toboggan run down to Macclesfield and on to lower ground where the hollow plain of central Cheshire extends between the Pennines and the foothills of northern Wales. We had reached the land of Cheshire cheese, the county where the last wolf in England is said to have been killed in the fifteenth century, the home of the grinning Cheshire Cat of Alice's *Wonderland*.

No longer the leisurely *Cranford* of Mrs. Gaskell's novel, the town of Knutsford swarmed with Saturday shoppers. All the country around, the farms, the roads, the villages held a special significance for us. For it was in this countryside, in the fall of 1944, that our son, David, had been stationed before going to the European front where, at the age of nineteen, less than two months before the end of the war, during night reconnaissance patrol ahead of the American Third Army, he was killed on the Moselle River, in Germany.

In one of the last letters written before crossing the Channel, David had mentioned some lovely English village he hoped to see again when the war was over. Military restrictions forbade mention of its name. On this day, in the sunshine of another season, we drove for a long time among the villages of the Cheshire plain in the vicinity of Knutsford. In each we gazed about us. Were these the cottages, these the lanes, these the trees that, under conditions immeasurably different, had seemed so peaceful, so attractive to him?

In the parsonage of one village, a dozen miles from Knutsford, the village of Daresbury, Charles Lutwidge Dodgson was born on January 27, 1832. The world remembers him by a different name, Lewis Carroll, creator of Alice, the Mad Hatter, the Cheshire Cat, the Red Queen, the March Hare, and all those other inhabitants of an immortal *Wonderland*.

James Boswell, on his first visit to London, sought out the printer at Bow Churchyard where the stories he had read as a child were published long before Lewis Carroll was born. He selected his favorites and had them bound into a single leather-covered volume which he called *Cu-*

rious Productions. One winter day, at the Houghton Library, at Harvard University, I held this very volume in my hands. As I turned its pages I found on a flyleaf at the front of the book, in ink now more than two centuries old, Boswell's written record of the history of the volume. It ends with the words: "He who pleases children will be remembered with pleasure by men." Who more than the child born in the Cheshire village of Daresbury, the author of *Alice in Wonderland*, exemplifies the truth of Boswell's observation?

The soil was red, the rocks were red, the stone houses were red along the roads we followed south and west through Cheshire. The foundation of this land was Old Red Sandstone, rock we kept encountering in widespread outcroppings all the way from Devon to the top of Scotland. Beyond the Vale of Clwyd and the marches, or borderlands, of Wales, the open meadows of dairy country gave way to rougher land, to steeply tilted hillside pastures where sheep cropped among the heather. Nellie's rhyming conclusion: "Sheep and heather go together," held good all through the highlands of England, Wales, and Scotland. More than once, across some pasture slope, all the stiff twigs of the lower shrubs were decorated with tufts of pulled-out wool.

Far into the warm evening, from the market square below our window in Ruthin, that night, we heard the unfamiliar sound of a foreign language, the soft, lilting cadence of the Welsh tongue. But neither soft nor lilting was the clangor of a great bell on the fourteenth-century church nearby. Its sound, devoid of sweet or musical tones, struck like a physical blow. Clang after clang, it crashed against our ears with a kind of burly, domineering authority, a voice, not of reasonableness or persuasion, but of naked force. We wondered how the sound would alter if we were farther away, whether distance would subdue its brazen, strident quality and add those mellow tones that make the pealing of far-off church bells one of the most beautiful of man-made sounds.

Higher and higher before us, next morning, rose the mountains of Wales. In an earlier period, when Daniel Defoe saw in Derbyshire only "a howling wilderness," when Nature was viewed as "a damp, gloomy place where fowls fly about uncooked," a returning English traveler summed up Wales in the words: "a horrid spot of hills." But generations pass and ideas alter. Today, the mountains of Wales are recognized as one of the outstanding scenic treasures of Britain.

Along the valleys and up the slopes, that tree of the mountains, the so-called mountain ash, the rowan tree, was clad in white blooms. It thrives at higher altitudes than any other tree in Britain. All through the dark centuries of Norse and Celtic superstition, the rowan was linked with the God of Thunder, Thor. Its leaves and twigs and orange-red berries were believed to provide protection against witches and goblins and evil spirits.

In September when clusters of brilliant fruit have replaced the flowers, blackbirds and other thrushes quickly strip the branches of their berries. Paradoxically, this hinders not at all the multiplication of the rowan tree. Rather it contributes to it. For the seeds within the small apple-shaped fruit are sheathed in a leathery coating that permits them to pass uninjured through the digestive tract of the bird. In fact, seeds that have been swallowed by birds sprout more quickly than those planted by hand. Thus both bird and tree benefit—one from the nourishment of food, the other from hastened germination and more widespread distribution of its seeds.

We were in the presence of white again just beyond Bettws-y-Coed. This time it was the airy white of dancing foam tumbling down one of the most picturesque waterfalls

Low Nest Farm with Helvellyn rising beyond

in cascade-rich Britain. At Swallow Falls, the plunge of the torrent is more strikingly spectacular because its water fans out in lacy white over tilting rocks as black as anthracite. Among the uncounted thousands who had stood beside this cataract in prior years, one was George Borrow, who watched the water pitching down this same black descent nearly a century and a decade before. In *Wild Wales*, he notes that Swallow Falls derives its name "from the rapidity with which the waters rush and skip along."

Standing on a small promontory projecting out to one side and a little below the top of the falls, we remained absorbed in the active white and the passive black of the scene before us. We watched the moving skeins of water twining in and out among the rocks, joining, separating, weaving lacelike patterns of foam all down the face of the cascade. At its top, the rocks shattered the stream into fragments; below, in the depths of a dark ravine, the river reformed and flowed on as before. In one of the upper pools, a round mass of yellow-tinted foam, like a chiffon or angelfood cake, revolved endlessly in an eddy among the rocks. It seemed held there by a spell while all the other foam, white and shining, streamed away around and below it.

Above the roar of the water, Nellie called out:

"There should be a dipper here."

Hardly had I caught the words when a swift ascending movement above the cataract arrested my attention. Climbing steeply on short, whirring wings, a dark-backed, chunky bird was ascending the falls. It scudded low through spray above the tumbling water. Its form alternately disappeared against the background of dark rocks and reappeared against the white of the moving foam. This sequence produced the illusion that the bird was momentarily slowing down and speeding up in its ascent.

Near the top of the falls it alighted on a rock. We caught it in our glasses. Amid whirling spray and crashing water,

Hadrian's Wall, looking east from Cuddy's Crag

with its short, wrenlike tail cocked upward, it spasmodically bobbed and dipped in the characteristic movements that have given it such colloquial names as "bobby" and "the washerwoman." The sight brought back a memory of the wild Hoh River, tumbling down its rocky bed amid the rain forests of the Olympic Peninsula, and the related bird of similar form and habits we saw there—the New World dipper or water ouzel of western North America. That bird was clad completely in dark slate-gray, whereas this dipper of Swallow Falls, each time it lifted its head, revealed, like the flashing on of a light, the patch of a snow-white bib.

In its bill we glimpsed a small mass of green. Then in a swift, darting movement, the bird was gone. We swept the rock with our glasses for a minute or more before we detected its hiding place, a spray-drenched hollow filled with moss near the rock's lower edge. The accumulated moss formed the domed shelter or protective shell within which the dipper builds its cuplike nest of dry grass or sedge lined with leaves. The similar shell of the American dipper, with its low entrance hole, suggested to John Muir an old-fashioned brick oven or the hut of a Hottentot. At first the cup of the dipper's nest holds from four to six foam-white eggs; later, the fledglings, grayish-brown in hue.

Even before they are able to fly, nestlings sometimes take to the water. On several occasions, when nests have been disturbed, the young dippers have been seen dropping into the water and swimming beneath the surface. After being carried downstream for several yards, they scrambled out to hide among the rocks. Far more than was formerly realized, other land birds of many kinds have shown an ability to take to water temporarily. Some years ago, *British Birds*, the journal of the Royal Society for the Protection of Birds, published numerous reports concerning instances of the kind.

On the saltings of Canvey Point, on the Essex coast, in

February 1949, M. J. Ardley, while watching shore birds, saw a flock of some thirty dunlin take off at high tide and alight on rough water some six yards from shore. The whole flock remained riding the waves for a quarter of an hour. Then they lifted easily into the air and joined other dunlin on the beach. On the Dorset Coast, R. F. Coomber observed a kestrel descend into the sea about a hundred yards offshore. It floated there for about two minutes. Then, without apparent difficulty, it rose into the air from the crest of a wave.

On other occasions observers have seen birds as varied as the reed bunting, the song thrush, the willow warbler, the house sparrow, the mistle thrush, the starling, the redwing, the skylark, and the meadow pipit swimming without difficulty. Snipe have been observed on several occasions taking to the water. They rode "high like a gull" as they swam. Even so heavy-bodied a bird as a pheasant was seen by P. J. Chadwick and Bernard King, on a November day in 1952, alighting in a reservoir in Somerset, swimming for a time and then, facing the wind, lifting into the air again.

But of all land birds, the most aquatic is the dipper. Its whole life is associated with water. It is never found far from a lake or stream. Most often its years are spent in picturesque surroundings—beside highland becks and burns and tarns, along swift, white-water brooks, near mountain waterfalls. Only in severe winters, when hill-country lakes and streams are frozen, does it descend to sea-lochs, coastal bays, and the slower-moving watercourses of the lowlands. When a dipper dives, swims with the aid of its wings, and walks along the bottom of a stream, its course is often revealed by a line of rising bubbles. The seeming miracle of a songbird, without benefit of webbed feet, plunging beneath the surface of tumbling mountain brooks, remaining submerged without drowning, obtaining its food from the stream bottom, so impressed primitive men that they considered this bird among the wisest of all wild creatures. It was anciently held, according to *The Golden Bough*, that eating the heart of a dipper would give a man sagacity and would make him invincible in argument.

As we waited, the dipper of Swallow Falls reappeared as suddenly as it had disappeared. One instant the rock was bare; the next, it held the bobbing form of the bird. For only a moment or two it remained there. Then it went whirring away down the steep descent into the depths of the glen below, later to return with another billful of moss. Because of the lateness of the season—the dippers being generally early nesters—we wondered if the bird could be bringing food to the young rather than material for the nest. But our glasses clearly revealed that it returned each time carrying only the rich green of freshly collected moss.

In earlier times the dipper was accused of feeding on trout eggs. However, when modern scientists carefully examined the stomach content of these birds, they found that this widely held belief was without foundation. In fact, one of the favorite foods of these birds, the studies revealed, is the so-called "water flea," the small crustacean *Granmarus*, long recognized as one of the chief enemies of trout ova. Thus the feeding habits of the dipper make it beneficial instead of harmful to the prized trout streams of Britain.

The country beyond Swallow Falls—the wilds of Snowdonia, with 3,560-foot Mt. Snowdon as its hub—was known to the early Welsh as *Eryri*, the Land of the Eagles. It now enjoys protection as a national park. As we drove on, threading our way up long valleys, with firebreaks cutting thin, straight lines up the steep ascent of evergreen-clad slopes on either hand, the summit of Snowdon, the highest peak in Britain south of Scotland, towered in lofty beauty above the lesser mountains to our left. Among the passes we met once more the familiar warning we had seen on so many mountain roads at home: "Danger. Falling Rock."

Black-headed gulls increased in the valleys as we advanced. They emphasized our nearness to the sea. We came out on its shore about noon on Conway Bay, by Lavan Sands, at Bangor. With the high mountains behind us and the open land of Anglesey before us, we rode on among gale-bent trees to Holyhead. Since prehistoric times it has been the principal port in sea traffic with Ireland, seventy miles away. From this far-western point in northern Wales, we gazed south. We looked with regret toward the beauty of central and southern Wales, toward all that glorious sea and mountain country that the pressure of time prevented us from visiting. Then we turned back to Bangor and, with the Irish Sea on our left and the mountains of Wales on our right, followed the windings of the north coast eastward. In many pastures that ran down to the shore, sheep were rubbing themselves on vertical stones set up in the fields as scratching posts. Their activity, in effect, was a long process of buffing the surface of the stone. It might, in time, impart such a polish as we had seen on the glistening sides of glacial boulders that, for ages, had been used as rubbing stones by the wild bison of the North Dakota prairie.

Circling around the Sands of Dee, next day, back in Cheshire, we crossed the Wirral, that roughly rectangular peninsula that projects out between the estuaries of the Mersey and the Dee. It gave rise to an old description of Cheshire as lying "in the form of an axe, Wirral being the handle thereof." All across the north, we saw the sky smudged by the smoke of Liverpool. Side-stepping the sprawl of this port and manufacturing city, we worked our way into Lancashire. About one-thirty that afternoon, with a summerlike haze enveloping the land, we turned aside before St. Helens to visit the spot that in all of Lancashire interested us most.

More than a dozen years before, when we had crossed

America in a journey through autumn, we had encountered in many places—at Cape May on the New Jersey coast, along the Missouri River in the Dakotas, at the mouth of the Columbia River in the far northwest—the trail of one of the great pioneers of natural history exploration, Thomas Nuttall. Probably no other scientist saw so much of primeval America. Roaming alone in the wilderness in the early 1800's, he explored the region of the Great Lakes, paddled down the Mississippi, wandered through the untamed Indian country of the Arkansas, crossed the Rockies, reached the mouth of the Columbia, and sailed westward to Hawaii. No one else in the history of American botany added so many species to the lists of science as did this self-taught naturalist. He became Curator of the Botanic Garden at Harvard University. He produced basic books on American botany and ornithology. The scientific names of numerous genera and species of both plants and birds commemorate this early wanderer, and the oldest bird society in America, the Nuttall Ornithological Club of Cambridge, Massachusetts, is named in his honor.

In 1842, when Nuttall was fifty-six, an uncle bequeathed him his country place, Nutgrove, near St. Helens, on condition he spend nine months of every year there. Reluctantly he left the scene of his great accomplishments. On the eve of his departure he wrote: "I must now bid a long adieu to the New World, its sylvan scenes, its mountains, wilds and plains, and henceforth, in the evening of my career, I return, almost an exile, to the land of my nativity." During the last seventeen years of his life, he quietly tended his gardens, particularly his rhododendrons, at Nutgrove. There his adventurous career came to an end on September 10, 1859.

Rhododendrons were still in blue-purple bloom beside the red-brick house at Nutgrove when we turned into the driveway. Immense beech trees shaded the lawn. How many times, we wondered, had the eyes of Nuttall rested on their smooth-barked trunks, those eyes that had gazed at the trunks of sweet gum and ponderosa pine and trembling aspen amid the untouched forests of America, in days before the coming of the settler's axe? The beech trees, the rhododendrons spoke of Nuttall's time. But in other ways all had changed. The farm had been swallowed up by the expanding town. Additions in new, lighter-colored brick had increased the size of the house. In the intervening years, it had been transformed into a home for the aged. Perhaps a mile away, as we were leaving, we pulled up beside a field sheeted with the white of daisies. In the peculiar hazy light it seemed covered with dew or frost. Dateless, a scene that might have been spread out before us in another century, it, also, seemed a link with the Lancashire Nuttall knew.

On our way north to Preston, we rode on a superhighway through a land of houses and factories and smoking chimneys. Even in the most rural stretches we could see towns all around us in this Black Country of southern Lancashire. Before we turned to the east, toward the Yorkshire border, at Preston, our ride was enlivened by the discovery that only three miles to our right lay Houghton Tower, where the word "sirloin" originated. On a visit there, King James I, according to tradition, found a cut of beef so delicious he bestowed a knighthood on it.

The inland road that carried us toward Yorkshire's western boundary led through a region of mines, with raw patches on mountain slopes spreading like sores, past mills pouring smoke into the sky, through grimy villages imprisoned in the vise of deep ravines, where most of the sky and much of the daylight was stolen away. Near Todmorden we entered the West Riding of Yorkshire. We were in the county where my father was born, where he spent his childhood and from which he had emigrated to America in

1884, the same year John Burroughs published his natural-ist's impressions of Britain, *Fresh Fields*. For the first time in my life, I inhaled the air of this region of my ancestors. It was scented strongly with coal smoke.

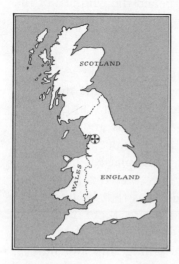

chapter 27

MALHAM TARN

Ravensthorpe. The name has a wild ring, a sound of the open air. I was a small boy in Illinois when I first heard of this Yorkshire village from which my father had come to America. In the intervening years my mind had conjured up the vague image of a lonely cluster of houses nestling on the high moors surrounded by crags and fells and swift-running becks. Now, after so many years, I rode, at last, into Ravensthorpe.

The first thing I discovered was that I did not know I was there when I arrived. For miles, that morning, in the region of Dewsbury, we crawled under a seemingly unending pall of smoke and mist. Huddled together along the way, grim under the sunless sky, stone houses rose dingy with soot. In the midst of one continuous line of houses, all connected together, many with piles of coal dumped on the sidewalk waiting to be carried inside, I slowed to a stop beside a pleasant-faced young constable and asked how to get to Ravensthorpe.

"Ravensthorpe?" he answered. "You're in Ravensthorpe."

We looked around. Everything belied the wildness of the name. Beyond the houses, woollen mills and other factories poured smoke into the heavily polluted air. The leaves of trees hung dejectedly, tarnished and blighted by airborne soot. Except for the young constable, the people we saw appeared neither healthy nor happy. Ever-present in the air was the heavy smell of coal smoke. Here was that grim paradox of all industrial countries—meanness and poverty at the very centers where great wealth is produced, wealth that is drained away to other more congenial places.

And this was Ravensthorpe. This was the place from which my father had come. Glad I was that he had come.

Somewhere nearby, I wondered where, there must be an old stone quarry. I recall my father telling me of his small-boy's dream of going to sea on a sailing ship and how, at the age of only eight or nine, he used to climb to the top of lofty booms in a neighboring quarry to accustom himself to ascending high masts. Instead of a life at sea, he had found a life far inland in America. Instead of dealing with sailing ships, he had dealt with railway locomotives. I remember the smoking flares of the roundhouse at night where he worked, the ponderous turntable, the great engines he repaired. Remembering also the soot and smoke of the midwestern railroad town where I grew up, I wondered if my father, when he began working as a mechanic on the Michigan Central Railroad, had, in some subtle way, been drawn back to the kind of environment he knew in his youth.

In all this country around Dewsbury—the "Jewsbury" of Yorkshire pronunciation—we ran through other communities, each as smoke-stained as Ravensthorpe. Their images tend to merge together in smoke and mist. A few, like Ossett and Flushdyke, stand out through associations: Ossett where my father was born; Flushdyke, where, more than a century and a half ago, before her marriage, my grandmother had been instrumental in starting a church and, according to family tradition, was known as "The Angel of Flushdyke." Well before the present century began, another relative, a pioneer woman photographer, Amy Goodall, focused her camera in early morning light on a winding country road near Dewsbury. I still have a print of that scene, a simple and haunting record of the dewy freshness of dawn. I wondered if I could find the road again. But I knew I never could. And, in truth, that was my good fortune. For the memory was better than the reality. Without doubt, the intervening decades had witnessed the beauty of that country scene swallowed up beneath the murky advance of industrial development.

The night before, here in Yorkshire, we had had Yorkshire pudding with our roast beef. Now, beyond Ossett on our way to Pontefract, we made a lunch of another dish of the region. Pulling into a layby, we dined on small pork pies. That particular layby, where a skylark sang above a tiny strip of green among factories, stands out with special vividness in our memories. It was less the singing bird than something else—our nearness to Walton Hall—that impressed the scene upon our minds.

At Walton Hall there was born, on the third day of June, in 1782, that eccentric naturalist and explorer, Charles Waterton. And there, six miles from Ossett, in the very year my father was born, 1865, Waterton had died. Between those dates, the adventuresome career of this Yorkshire squire led him into innumerable bizarre experiences. He rode on the back of a South American alligator. He treated a sprained ankle by holding it under Niagara Falls. He climbed St. Peter's, in Rome, and left his gloves impaled on the lightning rod. A man of strong opinions, he always referred to Henry VIII as "Our Royal Goat."

Four times, in the primitive days of the early nineteenth century, Waterton penetrated alone into the perilous jungles of British Guiana to bring back specimens for museums. He was the first to give a detailed account of the life of the sloth. He was the first European to discover the secret of the manufacture of curare, the poison of the South American Indians. Waterton's delicate system of taxidermy was generations ahead of its time. And his adventures with alligators, jaguars, and boa constrictors have made his *Wanderings in South America,* first published in 1825, a classic thriller for armchair explorers for more than a century and a quarter.

At Walton Hall, Waterton regulated his life with a clock that had once belonged to Sir Thomas More. He slept on the floor of his bedroom wrapped in a blanket and with a block of oak for a pillow. Each morning he arose at three and lit his fire. Then he lay down again on his oaken pillow for what he called half an hour of luxury. His breakfast consisted of dry toast, water cress, and a cup of weak tea. In the afternoon, Waterton walked in his woods, usually carrying a bit of bread in his pocket for a favorite goose that waited for him at the end of a bridge. On days when he forgot the bread, he would say: "How shall I ever get past that goose?" Frequently he would hide in the woods until it went away rather than disappoint it. He read the same books over and over. One was Gilbert White's *The Natural History of Selborne.* Until he was past eighty, it was his habit to climb barefoot in the trees to watch birds and read Latin verses among the upper branches. Yet Waterton always maintained that he was the most commonplace of men. To him, his eccentricities seemed not eccentric at all.

In his day, the estate at Walton Hall comprised a lake of about thirty acres and a park, mostly woodland, of about 260 acres. This tract he turned into the first bird sanctuary in England. As early as 1818, he gave strict orders that no shot was to be fired in the park, no dogs allowed to roam in the woods, and no boats to sail on the lake during the nesting season of the waterfowl. Far in advance of his time, he believed that predators, hawks and owls and carrion crows, were necessary in maintaining nature's balance. To attract more birds, he dug a stream for herons to fish in, excavated holes in an embankment for sand martins, put out stumps for kingfishers to perch on, added aquatic plants for waterfowl, and planted dense clumps of yew and holly to provide cover and nesting sites. Around his whole estate he erected a high brick wall three miles long and from eight to sixteen feet high. Ten years' work and a total of $50,000 (£21,000) went into the construction of this protecting barrier. Waterton was wont to say that, as a teetotaler, he built the wall with the wine he did not drink.

And what of Walton Hall today? Great changes, we found, have overtaken it. The spendthrift son of the old squire had sold the estate to the family of the very soap boiler his father had long battled in court for polluting the air and water. Successive owners evinced little interest in the natural history that once delighted Waterton. The wildlife that teemed in this first of Britain's sanctuaries is now largely gone. But, as was the case with Nuttall's red-brick house at Nutgrove, which became a hostel for the aged, Waterton's large stone house at Walton Hall has found a worthwhile modern use. It has been turned into a maternity home.

That night we lay awake in a hotel room overlooking the railroad station and switchyards at Huddersfield. Passenger trains arrived with a metallic blaring of loudspeakers at the station. Freight trains, hauling coal for factories, dragging empty cars away again, halted and started and backed with the clash of couplings. During those sleepless hours, I recalled a woman in America whose house stood close beside a main-line railroad track. In spite of thundering express trains that shook the ground, she slept soundly. Then a widespread strike halted all traffic. The first night, she lay wide-eyed until dawn, unable to sleep in the unaccustomed quiet. We were dressing next morning when we heard our first clap of thunder in England. It came like a single roll of drums, dying quickly away.

The noise of switchyards, the smoke of factories, faded behind us next day when we climbed over the high moors on our way to Haworth. Surrounded by bleak highlands, with venerable houses running beside its steeply ascending cobblestone street, with its mossy graveyard beside the parsonage deeply shaded and overgrown, the hill town of Haworth seems only a step from the village Charlotte and Emily Brontë knew. The tiny books they produced as children, barely an inch square, are still a center of interest at the museum which now occupies the parsonage where they lived. But dominating the region is the lonely, windswept moorland that exerted such a powerful influence on the minds of these sisters a dozen decades ago. Remembering Emily's closeness to these solitary heights, Charlotte once wrote: "My sister Emily loved the moors. Flowers brighter than the rose bloomed in the blackest of the heath for her; out of a sullen hollow in a livid hillside her mind could make an Eden. She found in the bleak solitude many and dear delights; and not the least was liberty. Liberty was the breath of Emily's nostrils; without it she perished."

Wilder moors, more remote, lay on our way to lonely Malham Tarn on a subsequent day. We set out from that city of strangers, the Yorkshire spa, Harrogate. Almost everyone there of whom I asked directions replied:

"I'm sorry, but I'm only here for the day."

It was in the rambling Harrogate hotel where we stayed overnight that we noticed signs all along the corridor of our wing. They read: "Fire Escape Through Room 329." The number of our room was 329.

"At least," Nellie said, "we'll get waked up if there's a fire."

Across the River Nidd and by High Winsley to Pateley
Bridge. Up Greenhow Hill and over Bewerley Moor,
through Dry Gill and by Fancarl Crag to Grassington. Past
Skyhorns and Robin Hood's Well, Low Ox Pasture and
High Wind Beck to Arncliffe. So we reached the jumping
off place across the higher, wilder moors to Malham Tarn.

Just outside Arncliffe where, along Cowside Beck, we saw
our first yellow wagtail, we stopped to talk to a walker wearing heavy shoes and with a pack on his back, a bearded university student on a few days' holiday before examinations.
He spread his detailed map on the top of our car and studied it carefully. Yes, he said, there was a "gated" road to
Malham Tarn that appeared passable. With that encouragement we continued on. Up and up, climbing in low
gear, we ascended from the River Skirfare, out of the
depths of Littondale, to the vast green plateau of the West
Moor.

The primitive track we followed led toward Nab End
along the great chasm of Yew Cogar Scar. When we
stopped and walked to the edge of the gorge, our glance
plunged down the great dropoffs of the sheer walls into the
depths of the narrow limestone valley. Sheep, feeding along
the very lip of the abyss, lifted their heads to watch us.
Above these upland flocks, just as above the sheep of lowland pastures, lapwings veered in twisting flight. These
birds have been recorded at altitudes as high as 6,500 feet.
They have been clocked at speeds of up to fifty miles an
hour. And, as always on the moors, skylarks were everywhere. As we stood on the springy turf beside a darker
patch of bracken, one hung in the air directly above us. It
sang on and on, hovering in almost exactly the same point
in space, supported by its fluttering wings.

Farther away, larger birds of the high moors filled the air
with a long, sweet, bubbling trill, wild and beautiful and
carrying far across the open land. Over and over we stopped

to listen. This was a voice we were to hear far into the Scottish highlands, the voice of Europe's largest wader, the curlew. Here, there, over the moor, we saw the buffy birds gliding earthward on a long slant, riding on set wings, their downcurving bills outthrust, calling as they descended. Each time their song began and ended in a long-drawn, low-pitched whistle that reached our ears in a forlorn and lonely cry. At times the rolling trills broke out in a kind of clamor amid the green immensity of the moor. Because it chooses for its nesting place wasteland, unplowed regions, bogs and moors and heaths and sand dunes, the curlew was described by an old writer as one of the creatures that dwell in "The Land of God's Own Holding."

Where water cascades down from Darnbrook Fell, beyond Nab End, a stream has worn another, shallower valley in the limestone of the moor. On a series of switchbacks, we crept down one side and ascended the other. At the bottom of the ravine, sheltered from the wind, the stone buildings of a solitary farm huddled beside the beck. All around us the air swarmed with the diving, tilting, skimming forms of house martins. Their globular nests of mud occupied every inch beneath the eaves of all the buildings. Here alone in all those miles of open moorland was an appropriate place for them to nest. And here only on the moor did we encounter house martins. We were reminded of the far-spaced trees of the Oklahoma Panhandle where we had seen almost every branch supporting a bird's nest. Almost as much as the competition for food, the competition for nesting sites is a limiting factor in controlling bird populations. Here in this remote moorland valley we had come upon a dramatic instance of this basic rule.

Across all the rolling upland, ascending and descending the slopes, we saw high white sheep walls of limestone. They ran in lines and curves and zigzags. They wandered away as far as we could see. These miles of walls, often almost as high as my head, were the tangible evidence of what Herculean labors in the past; the visible creation of how many lives now gone! In our advance, we passed through at least fifteen of these barriers. This was the day Nellie opened the gates. Nearly every one, she found, was fastened in a different way. Some were held in place by chains, some by sliding bars, some by hooks. In the early afternoon, as the sky became increasingly overcast, we dropped down to the dark waters of Malham Tarn.

Roughly heart-shaped and about half a mile wide and five-eighths of a mile long, Malham Tarn is the largest lake in the West Riding of Yorkshire. The three Ridings—East, West, and North—into which this largest county in England is divided, incidentally, are a heritage of the Danish occupation of a thousand years ago. The area then was divided into three parts, or "Thryddings," a word corrupted into Ridings during the centuries since. Retained by a glacial moraine and bedded on Silurian slate, the tarn is situated in a land of caverns, echoes, and subterranean streams. The water that flows from its lower end quickly disappears into an underground channel leading toward the south. The Pennine Way, that famous north-country footpath, curves around the eastern side of Malham Tarn before it leads away up the map toward the Cheviot Hills and the Scottish border.

For a time, Nellie and I followed this trail on the white road that hugs the shore and winds in and out of a woodland of evergreens and deciduous trees. The chorus of birdsong was at its height; the blooming of wildflowers at its peak. We seemed once more in the Southern Appalachians in the spring. Carpets of flowers extended away under the trees, across the open spaces, along the road and beside the tarn. Where, originally, we had seen only a few blooms of the herb Robert beside a Dorset road, here we had a whole slope massed with the red stems, the geranium-like leaves, the five-petaled pink flowers. More than once we stopped beside the intense, entrancing blue of extended stretches of forget-me-nots. Down to the edge of the tarn poured cascade after cascade of buttercups. The shining white of ramsons, the demure white of wild strawberries, the silver, airy white of the seedheads of the coltsfoot rose among the familiar and unfamiliar plants. Beside this road we came upon our first Welsh poppy, with its yellow flower and yellow sap.

Among these interesting and unusual wildflowers, we met an interesting and unusual man. He came sauntering down the road, powerful field glasses slung around his neck. When he looked through them, we noticed, it was down the slope rather than up into the trees where the birds were singing. He was, we discovered when we fell into conversation with him, not a bird watcher but an orchid watcher. With his glasses he had recognized many a rare flower growing in places difficult to reach. His home was in the Thames Valley in the south of England and his lifelong hobby was botany.

The great discovery of his life had come on a summer day a few years before. For ten years he had haunted an area where a lost orchid, a plant that no one had seen for many years and that was thought to be no longer part of the British flora, once had grown. Then on that lucky day he had seen what he dreamed of finding. This flower that had been given up for lost was still alive. Recalling that moment of his discovery, he said:

"I nearly jumped up to the sky!"

Since that day, he has shared his secret with none but a few botanist friends at Kew Gardens. We were glad to note that he referred to the location of this lost wildflower, found again, a little vaguely as "near the Thames in Oxfordshire."

Below us in a rushy cove a little farther on, eight mallard ducklings darted and twisted and leaped, snapping up insects like the ducklings of Dovedale. Watching through our glasses, we saw that the air and water around them was swarming with the small winged creatures that provided their springtime feast. Beyond the young mallards, coot and tufted duck and crested grebe floated on the surface of the tarn. Above our road, dark wood flies whirled in a mating dance of spring. Everywhere the life of the season was vibrating, filling the air with sound, bursting into color. We advanced as through a magic place.

But overhead, as we advanced, the sky grew heavier. Gusty wind cuffed and pummeled the dark tarn water. By the time we came within sight of Great Close Scar with its limestone cliff dropping to the edge of the water, the first raindrops were spattering down. We made a run for a large linden, reaching its shelter just as the deluge began. Almost in the wink of an eye the air was full of gray lines of plunging rain. We stood as in a green cavern, largely protected by the foliage that roofed us over. For ten minutes the downpour continued. Then the rain tapered off, the short Yorkshire shower cleared the air, the sun shone again. We walked back along the road where dripping flowers now sparkled with droplets of rain.

The square stone building that overlooks the northern shore of the lake, Malham Tarn House, is now a scientific research center. It and the tarn and the surrounding estate of more than 3,000 acres form a National Reserve in the Yorkshire Dales National Park. Since 1948, the house has been leased by the National Trust to the Field Studies Council. As the Malham Tarn Field Centre, it houses a permanent staff of scientists who are engaged in a continuous study of the natural history of the area.

Looking around one corner of the house, a black and white dog watched us as we left. It was tethered to the wide porch that fronts the tarn. On that very porch, more than a hundred years before, Charles Kingsley had gazed across the lake while *The Water-Babies* was taking shape in his mind. That fairy tale is the first book I remember, the first I heard read aloud. By the time I was five, I must have heard it a hundred times. I wanted nothing else. "Once upon a time there was a little chimney-sweep and his name was Tom." From those initial words, I could quote whole pages, learned by heart, before I could read a single sentence. A favorite for generations, *The Water-Babies*, according to the historian G. M. Trevelyan, was chiefly instrumental in getting the reforms of the Chimney Sweeper's Act through Parliament in 1864.

The stone house at Malham Tarn was the original of "Harthover House" where Tom's adventures began. Kingsley was visiting a friend here when, by chance, the germ of the tale was planted in his mind. Two miles to the south at Malham Cove, the "Lewthwaite Crag" of the story, someone asked his opinion, as a naturalist, as to the source of dark, smudgelike streaks that run down the creamy limestone of the towering wall of rock. As a humorous reply, Kingsley volunteered that they probably were produced by a chimney-sweep sliding down the face of the stone. Just so, fleeing pursuit in the story, Tom descends the face of Lewthwaite Crag leaving, as Kingsley assured his readers, a long black smudge "that has been there ever since."

When we came in sight of this curved precipice of limestone, towering higher than Niagara Falls, it lay half a mile away beyond a checkerboard of sheep pastures. We descended a steeply pitched hillside and followed clear-running Malham Beck upstream to the base of the cliff. There its transparent water poured from the mouth of a mossy cavern, the whole stream, full-fledged, flowing from the base of the rock.

Looking upward along the face of the cliff, we saw the sweep and dive of house martins amid shining clouds of small insects hovering in the warm sunshine. Higher still, daws entered nesting holes in the rock wall. And, far above us, almost at the top of the 250-foot precipice, two small hawks, with vertical plunges and nerve-tingling aerobatics, harried a passing rook. Over the stream beside us, small May flies and stone flies wavered and drifted above the swift rush of the water. We watched one stone fly alight on the green plush of a mossy rock and creep down to the water line, apparently laying eggs. In *Proserpina*, John Ruskin describes these same green-clad stones of Malham Cove as "softer with moss than any silken pillow."

The life of the little brook, emerging mature from the base of the cliff, is compressed into a flow of no more than a mile and a half. Then it loses its identity in the waters of the new-formed River Aire. It was on a June day—as this was a June day—when Tom, miraculously changed in Kingsley's story into a water-baby, 3.87902 inches long, commenced his life among dragonflies and eels and otters as he journeyed down the brook to the river and down the river to the sea.

We followed the cliff-born stream as far as its first curve and its first waterfall. Forget-me-nots bloomed beside our path. All around us there rose the bleating of lambs. The voice of one came to our ears in a particularly high-pitched quaver. It's "baaa" was devoid of the "b." It reached us merely as "aaa." Before we turned away from the stream and climbed the hill and left the sheep behind, we had come to recognize the voices of a number of the bleaters. It was easy to believe that a shepherd, after daily contact with a flock, could identify, by voice alone, a majority of the individuals among the lambs.

Running north, riding toward the boundary of Westmoreland and the Lake District of Wordsworth and Coleridge, we glimpsed the stark heights of Ingleborough rising to our right. Reginald Farrer, explorer and botanist, had laid out the world's first extensive rock garden of Alpine plants at his home, Ingleborough Hall, nearby. There, too, he had set down, with one of botany's most eloquent pens, such moving volumes as *On the Eaves of the World*. I rode on remembering one sentence from that book, a sentence written during the darkest days of the First World War: "For the utmost griefs of beings, races and continents come and pass, but the beauty of a poppy-petal on an alpine fell, the child of a day at the mercy of wind and hail, that has its hour and passes also, continues immortally recurring through the ages."

Just before we descended into the valley of the Lune, almost exactly on the Westmoreland border, we witnessed an occurrence we saw but once in our British travels. Over rolling, open fields to the north, a straggling cloud of dark birds turned in unison, continually changing position in the sky. At first we took them for rooks. Only a few miles before, we had seen a score of such birds scattered across a cutover hayfield, combing the ground for insects.

Then overhead a lapwing sped toward the circling flock. Vaguely we wondered if it was a nesting bird intent on attacking the rooks *en masse*. I swung to a halt in a layby and we followed its flight through our field glasses. In the magnified view they afforded, we saw that all of the milling flock of nearly 100 birds were lapwings. Another assemblage, almost as large, was disappearing beyond a more distant hilltop. Gone was the wild, erratic twisting we had become used to in the flight of the single lapwing. In sweeping circles, the birds turned with wings beating rhythmically, with movements synchronized. So early in the season, before the middle of June, so soon after we had seen lapwing chicks at Hickling Broad, these birds were already flocking, already exhibiting that intense gregariousness that holds so powerful a sway in their natures.

Beyond we crossed over the River Lune and continued north to Kendal and Windermere, into that land of mountains and picturesque waters, the Lake District of the English poets.

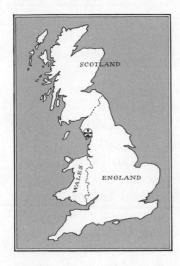

chapter 28

LOW
NEST FARM

We were riding toward Keswick when the sign loomed up beside the road. It appeared suddenly and unexpectedly, like something rising out of the remembered past:

"LOW NEST FARM. Good Tourist Accommodations."

More than 3,000 miles away, one evening beside the fireplace of a country home near Falls Village, in western Connecticut, Mark and Dorothy Van Doren had told us of spending a night at a farm in the Lake District of England, a place with the picturesque name of Low Nest Farm. We looked down the curve of the same descending lane they had followed to a stone house partly hidden by trees. Around it more than 100 acres of flower-strewn pastureland descended to the level of the valley floor with the heights of Helvellyn rising beyond.

Before the Armada sailed from Spain, before Shakespeare wrote *Hamlet*, before the grandfather of William Wordsworth was born, this Low Nest Farm was a farm. Its acres had been pastureland for half a century when the *Mayflower* sailed west over the ocean. They were two and a half centuries old when Lewis and Clark crossed the Rockies to the mouth of the Columbia River. For more than 400 years these fields have produced, in season, milk and cheese and wool. We turned down the lane. It was half-past five in the afternoon.

During the following half-hour, our attention was absorbed by a high nest at Low Nest Farm. From the window of our room at the head of the stairs we watched a black-and-white pied wagtail appear and disappear at a chink in the stone wall under the eaves. The bird arrived with insect food and left with empty bill. We took a step closer to the window, and it discovered us. Instantly it became shy and secretive. It fluttered toward the hole, then veered away. For a full five minutes it perched, its bill crammed with food, on the dead twig of a larch tree, tilting its black-crowned head this way and that as it eyed us, uncertain, instinctively wary, hesitant to reveal the position of its nest.

Birds, which, as James Fisher points out, have been in Britain at least 400 times as long as man, are most vigilantly on their guard at nesting time. Even when we moved well back into the room, the wagtail still peered in our direction. A gentle, steady rain began falling. The bird gave little shakes to rid itself of moisture. Constantly it uttered a small anxious note that sounded like "Tea-up!"

I pulled a lacy curtain across most of the glass and we moved even farther back into the room. Still the bird remained suspicious and uneasy. It flew up almost to the hole; then it seemed to remember at the last instant and swung away. A few minutes later it darted on a beeline for the hole, then zoomed up and alighted on the roof edge above it. There it leaned forward over the eaves, looking intently in our direction. It changed its perch, returned to the larch, then to the eaves, dropped to a shed roof, bobbed its tail, moved its head from side to side, altering focus. Thus minute after minute it presented the picture of indecision.

It had been away from its nest for more than twenty minutes when it alighted on the roof above the entrance hole, peered fixedly at our window for two minutes by my wrist watch, then, darting in a sudden downward arc, disappeared in the nesting hole. A moment later it was out and away, its feeding trips resumed.

The rain ended while we were eating a substantial country meal of roast beef, boiled potatoes, Yorkshire pudding, carrots, and whole-meal bread, with rice pudding and peaches for dessert, followed by crackers and Cheshire cheese. Outside, a glowing light lingered on after sunset, gradually paling into the long twilight of this northern county. Nellie and I wandered along a grassy path down the slope of the pasture fields. Beyond the wide valley of Naddle Beck, we saw England's third largest mountain, Helvellyn, rising high above the riggs, or lower ridges, around it. To John Burroughs, when he visited this part of the Lake District, Helvellyn appeared "like a great fat sheep with its flesh wrinkled." The most beautiful time of year here, we were told, comes later in the summer when the slopes are clad in flowering heather. Then the sunset light mingling with the color of the flowers clothes all the ridges with a radiance of varied and delicate hues.

Beside a gate where dog roses bloomed, we paused to listen to the distant concert of a thrush. As we stood there, the Low Nest farmer, Pettendrup, came down the path with his border collie, Bess, to bring home "the beasts" from the farthest pasture where cattle grazed. He stopped and for a time we talked of the intelligence of sheep dogs.

The finest animal of the kind he had ever known, he said, had died a few years before at the age of sixteen. It was named Fly. When ditching in the pastures, he would sometimes notice this border collie quietly cutting half a dozen sheep from the flock, maneuvering them to a certain portion of the pasture and standing guard over them while they fed. It seemed never to tire of exercising its special abilities. I remembered another collie that lived on an American farm. The high point of its day was bringing in the cows at milking time. So much delight did it find in this chore that at the mention of the word "cow," even in the middle of the day, it rushed off to the pasture and hurried the animals home to the barn. In consequence, it became standard practice on this farm to use the word only at milking time. During the rest of the day it was spelled out; a cow was always referred to as a "c-o-w."

Daybreak and the dawn chorus came early next morning. Long before five o'clock, we heard the singing of blackbird and song thrush, chaffinch and wren. House martins twittered about the eaves and the wild calling of shore birds passed overhead. Not long after five, however, the main chorus appeared to be over. The long day of the nesting birds had begun.

In the June dawn, in air soft and fresh and sweetly scented, I started down the lane. Dew covered the pasture grass. It sparkled among forget-me-nots beside the path. Even such a morning as this, I recalled, had appealed to the conventionally minded people of the Hardy poem ". . . as nothing other than Part of a benignant plan; Proof that earth was made for man." Sheep stood up and stretched as I approached, leaving darker patches where they had slept in the dew-covered grass. Twice along the pasture's edge, I came to thorn trees, each with its lower trunk clad in a pelt of wool left from the rubbing of the sheep.

From fields higher up the slope, where other pastureland forms a High Nest Farm, the stirring musical clamor of redshanks broke out again and again. Singly or in small groups, these gray-brown shorebirds went speeding overhead, the rising sun catching the bright orange-red of long legs thrust to the rear. During the middle of the last century the redshank nested regularly in but a single county in England,

Norfolk. Between 1860 and 1960, however, its numbers
have grown and its range has increased amazingly. Today it
is encountered throughout England, in Wales, among the
highlands of Scotland, on the Isle of Skye, and across Ireland.

Just beyond the gate where we had listened to the thrush
the evening before, two rabbits, fortunate survivors of the
plague that had swept across England, sat side by side amid
the dewy grass. Their noses twitched in the scented dawn.
Their long ears, almost translucent, glowed in the back-
lighting of the level rays. They watched my approach
through large, dark eyes. Then they bounded away, not in
panic but prudently seeking some safe and private hiding
place. For every healthy living thing in that June dawn life
seemed very good.

When I came back up the ascent of the lane, later on, I
met a solidly built Englishman, another overnight guest at
the farm. He was out in the dawn with a well-worn double-
barreled shotgun. He was, he told me, looking for rabbits.
He was soft-voiced, a dweller in one of the "new towns"
the government was building. We conversed pleasantly for
some time beside the gate where the rabbits I had watched
were now invisible. Then we separated. He went down the
lane with his gun—to come back, as I learned later, empty-
handed—and I went up the lane with my field glasses. We
parted, going in opposite directions—in more ways than
one.

Most of the night and all that day, a white cow in a field
close to the farmhouse bawled for a calf that had been
taken away "for the good of the milk" soon after birth.
This is an old, old sound wherever dairy cows are kept. It
was familiar to the ears of the unknown monk of the thirteenth century who wrote—in the verses beginning with
"Sumer is icumen in"—"Loweth after calf the cow." This
melancholy sound was around us during succeeding days

wherever we went among the valleys and mountains of this beautiful land. We heard it as we stood amid the circle of Bronze Age stones on Castlerigg. We heard it where we drank the pure, cold water descending from the heights of Skiddaw. And it was with us when we looked down wild and beautiful Borrowdale, where the discovery of graphite produced the first lead pencils, the "crayons d'anglais" of the sixteenth century.

Three counties share the Lake District: Cumberland, Westmoreland, and Lancashire. For generations the region has been compared to an immense cart wheel—the highlands of the central fells, the loftiest land of England, forming the hub; the radiating ridges the spokes; the valleys and lakes the spaces between. Within this area there are more than a hundred mountains, a score of passes, and half a hundred lakes. They range from the smallest and shallowest, Rydal Water, three-quarters of a mile long and a quarter of a mile wide, to Windermere, more than ten miles long and half a mile wide, the largest body of fresh water in England.

More than a century ago, William Wordsworth proposed that the Lake District be set aside as "national property" for the enjoyment of all. This suggestion has since been carried out. The area now comprises one of England's national parks. Another poet, Thomas Gray of the elegy in the country churchyard, played the leading role in first attracting attention to the beauties of the district. Gray, a timid traveler who was struck with horror at the wild appearance of Borrowdale and who embarked on the ferry across Lake Windermere only after he was blindfolded, published his *Journal of the Lakes* in 1775. It not only drew visitors to the region, but was largely instrumental in dissipating the popular belief that mountains were "horrid excrescences" to be avoided by lovers of natural beauty.

Although this area of mountains and lakes is the most

written-about region in England, it has not been over-praised. We felt no twinge of disappointment. Without doubt one of the loveliest parts of the world, it possesses the kind of simple charm that retains its hold after more spectacular and overpowering scenes have lost their appeal. It is the sort of beauty, Nellie observed, that you could live with forever.

Because the wind from the west, sweeping in from the Atlantic, meets the mountains laden with moisture, the rainfall in the Lake District is the heaviest in England. The annual average is more than 100 inches. The wettest spot in Britain is around Seathwaite. There the yearly average rises to 150 inches. Much of the beauty of the lake country is due to the moistness of its climate—the greenness of its hills, the luxuriousness of it plant growth, the richness of its fern-banks and wildflowers. Rhododendrons thrive here as they do on the misty slopes of the Great Smoky Mountains of southeastern North America.

Those who have read Dorothy Wordsworth's *The Grasmere Journal* will recall the frequency with which she and her brother, William, started for walks in the sunshine and returned home in the rain. But in the Lake District local showers are the rule; general rains the exception. The weather varies from valley to valley. The rains come and go. And the intervals between are often filled with beautiful weather, sunshine and drifting, fleecy clouds. As an old shepherd once responded when told that a fine day seemed in prospect: "Aye, it'll be fine between the showers." Nellie and I soon learned to expect at least half a dozen kinds of weather in the course of a lake-country day.

We met them all during the hours of a rambling, eighty-mile swing to the west and south, to the lower tip of Cumberland and back across the upper end of Lancashire to Coniston Water and Windermere. Under brooding skies we came to Cockermouth, the village where William and

Dorothy Wordsworth were born. In gathering mist we met black-headed gulls flying among rounded dunes near Seascale. Rain pounded down when we ate our lunch beside an embankment bright with the pink-purple spikes of blooming foxglove. And the sun was full on Duddon Sands when we reached, at low tide, the vast estuary at the river's mouth.

Often in our travels we have turned aside miles out of our way to visit some spot because of its picturesque name. So we followed a country road to the small Dorset village called Ryme Intrinseca. So we passed closer to Feather Bed Rocks on the Durham coast. And so, on this afternoon, beyond the River Duddon we turned south toward the Vale of Deadly Nightshade. It lies near the tip of Lancashire's upper peninsula, south of Dalton-in-Furness, where the painter George Romney was born.

Our descent into the vale, steep and twisting, was bordered by mossy woodland. Vapor clung among the treetops and the smooth-barked trunks of the beeches gleamed with moisture in wan, crespuscular light. Deadly nightshade still grows in the vale close to the crumbling red-sandstone ruins of Furness Abbey. This stonework dates from the twelfth century, and these fallen skeletons of buildings formed at one time one of the richest and most powerful of the abbeys of England. We were turning away when we noticed our first guelder-rose, the circular mass of its curious blooms composed of an outer ring of sterile white flowers enclosing numerous small scented and fertile inner ones. Linnaeus, in the eighteenth century, gave it the scientific name *Viburnum opulus*, for the guelder-rose is not a rose but a viburnum.

The mist lifted and the sun shone on old stone walls often shaggy with polypody ferns as we ran north to Penny Bridge. But before Coniston Water and Hawkshead, the village where William Wordsworth attended school, the clouds darkened again. And a deluge was beginning when we made a rush for the seventeenth-century farmhouse at Hill Top, near Sawrey, on the Lancashire side of Lake Windermere. Bought partly with royalties from *Peter Rabbit*, this was the home Beatrix Potter left to the National Trust. It is now maintained as a museum.

With the rain drumming on the farmhouse roof, Nellie and I spent a nostalgic hour among the original paintings of pictures we remembered from childhood. We were but two among 10,000 or more persons who, each year, are drawn to this country cottage above the lake through its association with one of the enduring classics among books for children. As we moved among mementos of the author's life, we thought of all the great suns of literature, all the lauded characters of impressive novels, that have sunk from sight while Lewis Carroll's March Hare, Kenneth Grahame's Mr. Toad of Toad Hall, and Beatrix Potter's Peter Rabbit have shone on undimmed through successive generations of the young.

The next day dawned with more misty Ossian weather. But clearing skies and morning sunshine soon imparted to the distant mountain slopes the appearance of crinkled green velvet—the nap of the velvet being grass and bracken. That day, at Keswick, we dined at the Royal Oak where memorial windows depict literary figures connected with the Lake District. We ate in one corner between windows devoted to Wordsworth and Ruskin, each with a landscape, a quotation, and the figure of the author in stained glass. Outside, set in one wall, a bronze plaque commemorates famous guests at this venerable hostelry. One of these was John Peel, "the colorful hunter," hero of the folksong "D'ye ken John Peel?" Beyond the Skiddaw Forest to the north, in the village of Caldbeck, his grave is set among the Cumbrian fells over which he hunted.

According to one contemporary writer, John Peel "seems

to have come into this world only to send foxes out of it."
For fifty-five years—including the whole first half of the
nineteenth century—he followed his hounds, often on foot,
often from twenty to thirty miles in a day, along the crags
and over the upland moors. Only a few weeks before he
died, on November 13, 1854, at the age of seventy-eight, he
was out with his dogs ranging over old familiar hunting
ground by Bassenthwaite. The fame of John Peel, "with his
coat so gay" and his hounds, Ruby, Ranter, Ringwood,
Bellman, and True, lives on through the rousing song written by his Caldbeck friend and neighbor, John Woodcock
Graves. Amid the same wild fields that were crossed and re-
crossed by the hounds of this implacable pursuer of foxes,
foxes still survive. One had raided a chicken yard less
than a mile from Low Nest Farm a night or two before.

Roads we followed over the mountains and through the
passes descended again and again to the shores of sparkling
lakes. We came to Derwentwater, from which Samuel Taylor Coleridge derived the name Derwent which he gave to
one of his children. We stood by Bassenthwaite amid great
banks of lady ferns. The "seed" of these ferns, it was once
believed, made the bearer invisible and caused buried treasure to glow with a bluish light on midsummer's eve. Near
Ullswater—probably Wordsworth's favorite lake, where he
was inspired to write his ode to the daffodils—we remembered the adventurous life of one particular bird, a
lapwing that was ringed, or banded, here in 1927. Not long
afterwards it was carried by a great westward-moving storm
across the North Atlantic. Far from the Lake District, it
ended its life in Newfoundland. There it was shot by a
hunter and the ring recovered.

Among the lakes I believe we spent the most time at the
least extensive of them all, charming Rydal Water. The
pink of dog roses and the cream-white of the flat flower
clusters of elder bushes leaned out over the edge of the lit-

Cataracts among the mountains of Scotland

tle lake. Ascending from rosettes of downy leaves, spikes of the wild foxglove rose waist-high beside our path. White clouds drifted overhead and moved in reflection across the still water. But here, too, were human visitors amid this quiet scene, Sunday picnickers from the city arranging folding chairs, tuning up the volume of their portable radios, unfolding their newspapers. One rueful sight encountered in their wake was fifteen stalks of wild foxglove broken off to form a bouquet and then tossed aside as litter along one of the paths to the water.

In the village of Rydal Mount, on the shore of this lake, William Wordsworth spent his latter years. Here he died. However it is another lake, Grasmere, the almost circular body of water half a mile to the west, that is most deeply identified with the poet's work. For eight years he made his home at Dove Cottage close to the edge of Grasmere. Here he produced many of his greatest poems. This cottage, with its low ceilings and recessed, leaded windows, was originally built more than 300 years ago as a roadside inn. Its name comes from the dove that appeared with an olive branch on the inn sign. We came to it—one of the world's most visited literary shrines—in the midmorning of a day of hazy sunshine.

At Dove Cottage Wordsworth's sister, Dorothy, kept her famous *Grasmere Journal,* containing such entries as that on a January day: "Wm. wasted his mind in the magazines" and those recurring notations of the spring: "William stuck peas." Sticking peas, I learned, is putting upright sticks in the ground for pea vines to ascend. An open space beside the cottage entrance marks the site of the small garden plot where the sticking was done. In the adjoining Wordsworth Museum, redesigned from an old barn and housing manuscripts and memorabilia, we examined with intense interest pages of the original journal in which Dorothy, in a headlong hand, set down her entries.

Castle on Lindisfarne

The annual rent at Dove Cottage in Wordsworth's time was seven pounds. In those days of "simple living and high thinking" one of the occupations of fall was preparing rush lights against the winter darkness. Rushes were gathered beside Grasmere, the green outer skin was stripped away, and the central pithy rod soaked in mutton tallow. Holders kept the rush lights upright and burning at one end or clamped in a nearly horizontal position and burning at both ends. The light shed by a burning rush could hardly have been much more than that produced by a wooden match, and at the end of an evening lighted in this way the low-ceilinged rooms must have reeked with the smoke of burning tallow. My eyes smarted at the thought of it. Understandably useful must have been the poet's eyeshade, which is preserved among the relics in the museum.

"The loveliest spot that man hath ever found"—so, in his poem A *Farewell*, Wordsworth describes that "little Nook of mountain-ground," the garden-orchard that rises steeply behind the cottage. There he and Dorothy set out ferns and mosses, wildflowers and shrubs and fruit trees. We found the garden much as it was in their day. All the plants mentioned in Dorothy's journal have been reestablished here. Steps of rock still lead up to the small terrace where the poet often worked. As we climbed those steps that morning, we stopped to examine an unfamiliar fern with comblike fronds. It was our first hard fern. Although it is found throughout Britain, somehow we had missed it all along the way, finding it at last in this garden the Wordsworths had created.

When, the following day, we regretfully turned to the east and looked back upon this land of lakes and fells and green hills for a last time, we left with one long hope unfulfilled. Somewhere in Cumberland, we had heard, an old gravestone bears those noble and often-quoted words: "The wonder of the world, the beauty and the power, the shape of things, their colors, lights and shades; these I saw. Look ye also while life lasts." We never found the stone. We never found anyone who had seen it or heard about it. But many of those of whom we inquired—like the travelers Thoreau, in *Walden*, queried about the hound and the bay horse and the turtle dove he had lost—seemed as anxious to discover it as we.

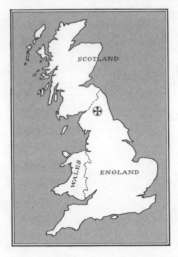

chapter 29

THE
GREAT WALL

On the other side of England, in days that followed, we cut in a wide curve across the Plain of York, up through the dark, damp woods of the Yorkshire Wolds, down along the coast and back to the Great North Road. Beyond Wetwang and Fridaythorpe we were enveloped in one of those dense, blinding fogs known in the North Country as a sea-fret.

When we crept in beside a fuel pump in the country, the owner suddenly loomed up out of the mist. He observed:

"If the wind would change to the west, in ten minutes all this sea-fret would be gone."

But the wind held steady. That bringer of rain and fog and chill weather, the villain of British meteorology, the Purple Wind of the old Celtic seers, the wind from the east, blew in over the cold waters of the North Sea. "When the east wind blows," Voltaire wrote, "Englishmen despair."

Those groping miles up the eastern side of Yorkshire return in dim and shadowy memories. All the multitudinous tide pools of the mile-long oolitic reef of Filey Brigg passed invisible to our right. Unseen on a fogbound moor stood the monument marking the birthplace of Captain James Cook. In a long procession, gray shapes and vertical lines beside the road strengthened into bushes and fence-posts. More than once we passed beneath some overarching tree, its top lost in the cloud that lay on moor and coast. Years before Nellie and I had driven the length of the Maine seaboard in a three-day fog seeing virtually nothing. We seemed repeating the experience.

But the fog was gone and the sun shone bright on the Great North Road the day we turned up this historic highway once trod by Roman legions, once followed by fast mail coaches between London and Edinburgh. A little after noon we were sitting in a layby, sampling for lunch six different kinds of scones I had bought in a village pastry shop, when a small railroad car mounted on rubber tires and transformed into a camping caravan went rolling by into the north. Riding in the same direction, we ascended through Durham, once described as a vast lump of coal with a million and a half people living on it, and crossed the boundary into England's uppermost county, Northumberland. Before Newcastle-upon-Tyne we swung to the west along a wide and fertile valley.

As the Mississippi River dominates the farmland of western Illinois—its presence felt although it lies unseen beyond the horizon—so all along the lower Tyne Valley the Roman Wall, Hadrian's Wall, the greatest memorial to the Roman Empire outside of Rome, dominates the countryside. Off there to the north, beyond the river, beyond the low farmhouses scattered across the green landscape, beyond the grazing sheep and the cattle lying in the meadows chewing their cuds, the line once followed by this ancient wall paralleled the farther edge of the valley. From sea to sea, stretching for more than seventy miles across the narrowest part of England, running from near Newcastle-upon-Tyne in the east to beyond Carlisle in the west, it crowned the natural fortification of the ragged escarpment of the Great Whin Sill.

This prehistoric intrusion of molten lava extends its hard basaltic rock over hundreds of square miles of northern England. Just beyond the Tyne it lifts into a series of towering cliffs reared vertically against the north and sloping gradually toward the south. Rising and falling, winding along the edge of the precipices, Hadrian's Wall extended in an enormous serpent of stone across the broken landscape. Today only fragments remain. But they reveal the staggering magnitude of the undertaking achieved in the space of four years more than eighteen centuries ago.

We came to the highest remnant of this "grandeur that was Rome" in a foreign land near Winshields Crag. Here the wall ascends to 1,230 feet above sea level. Looking to the east from this high point we could see the rises and dips and turnings of the wall as it linked the great bluffs together, running along the sheer drops of six separate crags within our view. All the dressed blocks of its gray stone had been fitted into place by the hands of men living in the second century A.D., during the golden age of the Roman Empire.

On his grand tour of conquered lands, the Emperor Hadrian had reached Britain in 122 A.D. To close the frontier against the untamed and warlike tribes of the mountainous north, he ordered the construction of a wall from the North Sea to the Irish Sea. This barrier was planned to be about eight feet thick and so high that the top would be beyond the reach of a man standing on another man's shoulders. Essentially it was a fortified sentry beat, an early-warning system designed to detect and check hostile advances before they could gain momentum toward the south. Night and day for more than two and a half centuries, Roman soldiers patrolled the path along the top of the barrier.

When we climbed to this path, the same stones that had supported those frontier sentinels less than two centuries after the birth of Christ supported us. The same wild sounds—the calling of the curlews, the voices of the skylarks, the sweet rolling trills of the redshanks—that came to their ears also came to ours. The same vista of far hills extending away into Scotland, met their eyes and ours.

Directly before us the wall and path dropped steeply into a valley or nick. Later that morning as we were toiling up the ascent on our return, the mounting thunder of an approaching Royal Air Force jet reverberated in the valley. The dark arrowhead of the delta-winged craft hurtled overhead. Its shadow flicked across the wall, spanning this barrier of the Romans in an infinitesimal fraction of a second. With diminishing sound and contracting form the machine streaked away, leaving us pondering on what creations of the future, manned by what sort of human beings, would flash over this Roman Wall in the thirty-seventh century— after the lapse of another interval equivalent to that which had passed since these stones were first laid down.

As many as 10,000 soldiers manned the length of Hadrian's Wall. Small forts called milecastles were spaced a Roman mile apart, and seventeen larger forts held the main concentrations of the legions. Just south of the course of the wall a modern highway keeps to the line of the old military road along which supplies were transported to the forts. We were following it toward Housesteads, or Borcovicium, the great five-acre fort commanding the ridgetop above Knag Burn Gap, late that afternoon, when we pulled up beside a stretch of marshy lowland. Above a scattered flock of black-faced, hook-nosed sheep a brownish bird was plunging in a series of oblique dives.

The bird was a snipe, the same *Capella gallinago* we

knew at home. On each of its steep descents there carried over the boggy ground a drumming, quavering sound that, in England, has given the snipe the common name of "the heather bleater." During these plunges the bird's outer tail feathers, widespread, vibrate in the wind. Because of their peculiar shape and structure, they continue to vibrate as long as a certain speed range is maintained. One scientist, experimenting in a laboratory, found he could produce the quavering sound at its average pitch by subjecting the feathers to a speed of 37.5 miles an hour. The lowest speed that would set them vibrating proved to be 24.2 miles an hour. The highest speed at which the feathers would produce the characteristic sound was 52.3 miles an hour. At 60 miles an hour, the experimenter found, the inner webs of the swiftly vibrating feathers began breaking down.

At the Housesteads parking field, a little farther along the road, we followed with our eyes a field path that climbed steeply ascending pasture land for half a mile to the sprawling ruins of the fort and the finest remaining section of the wall. We decided to return at leisure the following day. But the next day dawned with rain threatening and I came back alone. Hardly had I started up the path when the lowering sky grew lighter, the clouds broke, the sun shone, and the ever-widening panorama around me became dappled with light and shadow.

Looking back, I saw a rural postman lean his bicycle against a post, carefully fold his raincoat and place it on the seat, take off his hat and put it on top of the coat, and then, with a few letters in his hand, begin the same climb I was making to deliver mail to the National Trust headquarters beside the fort—a round-trip walk of a full mile to make a single delivery. We fell in step. He had other places along the route, he told me, that were even farther from the road.

"In winter," he added laconically, "it can be rough."

Near the headquarters building at the top of the climb, we could see the owner of a parked automobile rushing about, waving his arms, trying to drive away half a dozen black steers milling about his machine. As though bewitched, the animals were trying to lick the paint.

"Their tongues are like sandpaper," he complained as we came up.

This singular propensity in cattle, a craving for paint and other harmful substances, is a paradox in their lives. Calves sometimes die from lead poisoning after licking paint from buildings. Similarly, cows have died from cleaning out the residue in discarded paint cans. Perhaps the salty taste of the lead is an attraction. In America when the wild black cherry, *Prunus serotina*, is felled, prussic acid concentrates in the foilage as the leaves begin to dry. For some reason such leaves have a special appeal for cattle. Many have died in consequence. It seems curious that in such a life-and-death matter no instinct warns them of their peril. Perhaps the fact that cattle swallow large quantities of food rapidly and only later bring it back for a thorough chewing reduces their chances of detecting what is harmful.

For a time I wandered among the ruins of the immense fort where once a thousand soldiers lived within the protection of walls from twelve to fourteen feet high. Here stones still bear scars where Romans sharpened their swords, and sills show ruts worn by cart wheels thirteen centuries before Columbus crossed the Atlantic. Where, at the northern edge of the fort, Hadrian's Wall follows the very lip of a stupendous cliff, I climbed a series of projecting slabs of rock that ascended like a flight of stairs to the path at the top. The upper surface of each was hollowed out by the wear of centuries of tramping feet. Looking down over the edge of the wall, I saw pasture fields far below at the base of the cliff. Gazing into the north, I viewed the outspread land as from an airplane. Turning east and west, I observed the slender line of the wall winding away across the immensity of the open landscape. In the words of an old writer, from this viewpoint you see the Roman Wall "riding over the high pitches and deep descents, wonderfully rising and falling." I rose and fell with it, that day, as I explored the path along its summit.

With my lunch—a golden delicious apple—in my pocket, I set off toward the west. For a time I was surrounded by the trees and the moist shade of a small copse. Red campion bloomed among the bracken and the grove echoed with the bright songs of chaffinches. From the heights of Cuddy's Crag, beyond, I could see, nestled in the green of the rolling landscape to the north, the pale blue of those lovely lakes, the Northumbrian lochs. On one I could distinguish the tiny forms of floating swans and a Lilliputian boat where two men were fishing. From another, Greenlee Loch, Caw Burn flows down to Haltwhistle Burn and slips beneath the Roman Wall to join the Tyne. Hundreds of feet below me sheep cropped across the nearer pastures. Lambs scattered over the green were leaping, prancing, sleeping, nursing. Wherever I went along the edges of the cliffs their bleating rose to my ears.

Once as I looked down I saw a kestrel—swift, sharp-winged, with delicate shadings of grays and reddish-browns—shoot past below me in a long, slanting dive. At other times I peered down from above at jackdaws following the face of the cliff or alighting on the narrow ledges. Mine was a fresh, exciting viewpoint, that of a lofty soaring bird. So in sunshine, rising and descending and turning with the course of the wall, breathing the pure, exhilarating air of the high country, I continued on my way.

For more than a dozen centuries Hadrian's Wall was used as the great quarry of the region. Ancient farmhouses and walls and farm buildings were constructed of blocks of stone the Romans had prepared. Part of the monastery that housed the Venerable Bede was made of stones taken from Hadrian's Wall. Thus, in the course of time whole sections of the barrier have disappeared. I had finished eating my apple when I came upon workmen repairing a damaged portion at the edge of another nick or valley. A friendly brown-and-white border collie, which had come with them, adopted me. As I began retracing my steps, it raced ahead and frolicked back; when I petted it, it twisted and rolled until it seemed about to throw itself off the cliff.

During my return I stood for a long time on each successive crag-top. It was the tremendous view to the north that first held my eye. Then my gaze was drawn downward to the activity below. Wherever I looked, I encountered something of interest. Minute white butterflies, hundreds of feet below, traced erratic courses over the green of the meadows. Starling flocks, viewed from above, swirled and veered and dropped to a landing in the grass. I could see skylarks below me shooting up, hanging in the air and dropping to earth again. Sounds as well as sights reached me from a new direction. To hear the singing of the larks ascending from below instead of pouring down from the air above was a stirring experience. Everywhere across the sheep meadows, on either side and all along the wall, skylarks sang. Their music went on and on as I returned to Housesteads. It continued under darkening skies, with the sun gone, with a downpour imminent. No leaden light, no threat of storm, quenches the skylark's fire.

Beyond the ruins of the fort, where the wall winds away into the east, it tilts downward in a steep descent into the narrow valley of Knag Burn. All across the floor of this valley irregularly shaped rocks thrust their tips above the close-cropped turf. These weathered points form the singing perches of the wheatears. I saw the males, with gray backs, black masks and striking white rump-patches, flying from rock to rock. These birds of the open, treeless country are found throughout the British Isles. They breed in the Alps up to 6,600 feet, and their range extends well into the arctic. There is one record of wheatears nesting in the same place in Caithness for sixty-two consecutive years. On occasions the birds have made their nests in piles of peat, in old kettles and empty artillery shells and the warrens of rabbits. On the steppes of Siberia they frequently nest in the holes of ground squirrels. So long have bird and rodent been associated together that the birds, in effect, act as sentinels for the rodents. At a certain alarm note of the wheatear, all the ground squirrels plunge into the protection of their burrows.

As I watched these birds—called stonecheckers in Scotland—they occasionally burst into a modest warbling song. Samuel Johnson, in *Rasselas,* speaks of birds that "waste their lives in tuning one unvaried series of sounds." But far from unvaried are the actual songs of birds. The general pattern is the same; but many individuals produce their own slight variations. So it was with even so short a song as the wheatear's. To me it seemed to vary with several of the singers.

Another thing I noticed as I watched these gray and black and white birds under that lowering sky. The tips of all their perching rocks were covered with a dense layer of richly golden lichen. They stood out in bright contrast with the dull gray of the rocks and the green of the surrounding grass. Lichen platings of the sort are a familiar sight on the tundras beyond treeline in the arctic. An explorer friend of mine once told me that far out on the Great Barrens he could tell wherever a Lapland longspur had its singing perch by the brilliant growth of lichen on the rock. The droppings of the songbird stimulate the growth of these primitive plants. In the valley of Knag Burn I examined several of the rocks. Here, too, the droppings of the songbirds were scattered thickly on the lichen.

The first pelting raindrops of the oncoming shower splashed down as I regained the field path that descends the pasture slope to the parking field. Heading back toward our lodging for the night at Hexham, driving away in a pounding downpour, I met the rural postman again. He was clad in a streaming raincoat, pedaling stoically toward home at the end of his rounds.

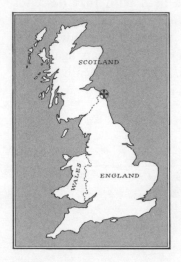

chapter 30

LINDISFARNE

Where the Northumberland coast nears the Scottish border, where the tide ebbs and flows about Dolphin Stones and over Fenham Flats, where the upper fringe of the Great Whin Sill tilts its volcanic rock above the waves, there rises, close to the edge of the North Sea, England's Holy Island, Lindisfarne.

In reality Lindisfarne is a part-time island. It might be called a ten-hour island. For only during about ten hours of every twenty-four is it surrounded by salt water. This occurs from approximately two hours before to three hours after each high tide. The rest of the time it is accessible from the mainland across the bed of a broad and shallow bay. In the words of a sixteenth-century report to the Crown, Lindisfarne "is scituate within the sea, and yit at every tyde of lowe water men may passe into the same on horseback or foote." A line of upright poles is still maintained to mark the course of the Pilgrim's Way once followed by ox carts and foot travelers, and now a low paved

causeway, passable when the tide is out, permits automobiles to cross the mile-wide bay in safety.

The tide was ebbing when we descended to the shoreline
a mile from Beal and took our place at the tail of a short
line of waiting cars. Before us the causeway was slowly
emerging from the receding waters. Beyond it rose the
sand dunes of the Snook, the end of the long westward-
projecting tail of Lindisfarne. Minute by minute glistening
mud replaced water in the bay. Both ends and last of all the
middle of the causeway lifted above the retreating tide. We
rolled ahead over the ocean litter strewn along its surface.
Seaweed bladders popped, shells crunched beneath our
wheels. We followed the edge of the tide line with sand
dunes on our left and on our right the wide expanse of the
bay bottom, redolent with odors of the sea, dotted with the
castings of marine worms, alive with the running forms of
shore birds. We paused to watch a short-eared owl quartering over the wind-blown bents of the dunes, at times hovering on beating wings like a kestrel. Then we climbed to
higher ground. We had reached that island of ancient
memories we long had wished to see.

This journey of hardly more than a mile across the Holy
Island Sands is like passing back through centuries of time.
Lindisfarne seems not only an island of land but an island
in time, a fragment of a remote era only partially connected
with the present, as Lindisfarne itself is linked only part of
the day with the mainland.

Its other name, Holy Island, is well deserved. For Lindisfarne was "the cradle of Christianity in the north," the
"mother of all the religiouse places in that part of the
realme." As early as 635 A.D., St. Aidan established a monastery here. In this remote spot early monks of the seventh
century produced one of the artistic treasures of the world,
The Lindisfarne Gospels. Now preserved in the British
Museum, in London, this priceless illuminated volume is

rich with intricate designs and interlaced patterns of birds and animals. And this is the island that is associated with the history of St. Cuthbert, onetime shepherd boy of the Lammermuir Hills, onetime Bishop of Lindisfarne. For nine years of his life this holy man, the friend of all wild creatures, dwelt as an anchorite, clad in skin leggings and garments of undyed wool. According to legend, eiders— still known in the region as "St. Cuthbert's doves"—fed from his hand and, in his lonely walks along the rocky shore, gray seals kept him company.

Nellie and I came to the last link with this ancient religious life of Lindisfarne when we stopped beside the ruins of an eleventh-century priory. Its redstone skeleton lifts delicate arches, wall fragments, and wind-worn columns against the sky. Beyond these remnants of the priory we could see the Pilgrim's Way stretching off across the shallows. Following it during other low tides almost eight centuries before, ponderous ox carts had hauled blocks of sandstone from quarries on the mainland. Through all the intervening years the winds of storms had scoured the surface of the stone. Swirling patterns decorated the face of the blocks where softer material had been worn away. We ran our hands over vertical columns, once heavy pillars, now reduced to mere pencils of stone.

Beside the priory ruins we paused before a white slab. It commemorates a thirteen-year-old boy with an unusual name who was drowned at Lindisfarne on the 19th of July, 1843. Much of the long inscription had weathered away but clearly legible were the words: "In Memory of Field Flowers, Son of Rev. Field Flowers, of Tealey Vicarage, Lincolnshire."

Wherever we walked about this ruined priory, surrounded by its brooding air of ancientness, we were treading ground that had been occupied by even earlier religious buildings. Time after time, in the centuries following St. Cuthbert's death in 687, the structures erected by the monks of Lindisfarne were destroyed by pagan marauders and Danish pirates. *The Anglo-Saxon Chronicle*, in the phraseology of the day, describes those troubled times under the year 793: "Dread prodigies appeared in Northumbria, and miserably terrified the people; that is whirlwinds beyond measure and lightnings: and fiery dragons were seen flying in the sky. Upon these tokens soon followed great famine and a little after that, in the same year, on the 6th day of the Ides of January, the heathen men miserably destroyed God's church at Lindisfarne, through robbery and slaughter."

Toward the end of the ninth century, under threat of a new invasion, the monks fled to the mainland. They took St. Cuthbert's coffin with them. There followed seven years of wandering, a pious odyssey in which they carried the coffin from town to town. At last, with the simple garments associated with his ascetic life replaced by silken robes bordered with cloth of gold, this St. Francis of the North, this friend of eider and seal, was given a final resting place at what is now the cathedral at Durham.

In the channels of the bay—out where terns were halting in the air, hovering with widespread tails, then plunging to hit the water with a splash—the silent tide was beginning its return. At first it crept stealthily in. Then it speeded up, spread out, righted the stranded boats where they lay heeled over on the mud. The sawing wash of the tides at Lindisfarne sometimes deposits in the shallows and on the shore small, round white plates, with a hole in the center. They are known as "St. Cuthbert's beads." Such segments of crinoids, primitive marine animals sometimes referred to as "sea lilies," are said to have formed the beads St. Cuthbert told in his rosary.

Another gift of the tide resulted, one year, in a spectacular concentration of waterfowl in the bay. During the abnormally cold winter of 1941–42, a 12,000-ton grain ship from Canada ran aground on Goldstone Reef and broke in two. Its cargo floated into the bay. Thousands of tons of wheat spread across Fenham Flats. For months afterwards this feast attracted a vast number of waterfowl drawn from a wide area along the coast.

You will notice if you glance at an enlarged map of upper Northumberland that the shape of Lindisfarne suggests a cleaver. The sandy portion terminating in the Snook represents the handle, and the rectangular main portion of the island, about a mile wide and a mile and a half long, the head. At the ruins of the priory we were standing at the western end of the lower shore, corresponding to the cutting edge of the cleaver. Looking to the east along this shore we could glimpse between the priory's crumbling walls, at a distance of about three-quarters of a mile, a castle rising high above the water's edge on a titanic pedestal of basalt. Like a story-book stronghold it towered above its surroundings, a castle as a castle should be.

This was our impression from a distance. It remained unchanged when, close at hand, we stared up at the solid stonework that lifted its walls and battlements far above the tide line and the green pasture fields that spread away inland below it. Built in Elizabethan times when the harbors of England were being fortified, this Lindisfarne Castle was originally known as the Fort of Beblowe—Beblowe being the local name for the mass of basalt that, in the northernmost emergence of the Great Whin Sill, forms its foundation. Among the various early governors of this fort the most famous was a certain Captain Robin Rugg. He was celebrated for his immense bottle nose, for his hospitality to strangers, and for his letter to King Charles I, complaining of arrears in pay, in which he signed himself: "The Great Commander of the Cormorants, the Geese and Ganders of These Hallowed Lands." In 1903, after centuries of neglect, the castle was bought by Edward Hudson, of

Country Life. With the help of the famous British architect, Sir Edwin Lutyens, he restored it for use as a home. Since 1944 it has been under the administration of the National Trust.

Where we stood at the base of the castle crag, a small brownish bird with striped body, dark, slender bill and gray outer tail feathers, flitted about with food in its bill. It watched us intently, repeating over and over a sharp note of concern. We were seeing our first rock pipit, the only British pipit with outer tail feathers that are gray instead of white. Somewhere nearby among jumbled rocks were hidden its nest and nestlings.

It was our good fortune to arrive on the island on the one day of the week when the castle is open to visitors. We climbed the steeply rising cobblestone ramp that ascends along its southern side and reached the lofty entrance door. Amid the long corridors and low-ceilinged rooms with their deeply recessed windows, we seemed exploring the interior of some vast ship of stone. From one window we could glimpse distant hills and dunes on the mainland rising miragelike above a low-lying layer of haze. Because the sea fret and the salt spray hasten rusting, the iron fittings of every window were coated with layer after layer of black paint.

Among the heavy ancient furniture with which the castle is now supplied, we were shown a massive four-poster bed of early Flemish design. Sliding panels at the head and foot opened on hidden compartments, those at the head for secreting jewels, those at the foot for holding firearms. Uneasy must have been the slumber of the wealthy who retired to such a bed at night. Today, the caretaker's wife told us, dwellers in the castle lie awake on nights in June not because of jewels to guard but because of the noise of the "mollymawks," the fulmars that nest on the cliffs below.

Years before, riding among migrating gray whales off the

coast of southern California, Nellie and I had ceased whale-watching to observe a fulmar. It followed our boat, swinging from side to side, soaring on rigidly extended wings. Now, a continent's span and an ocean's span away, we saw for the first time this oceanic wanderer on its annual visit to land. On this day and the following day we enjoyed the rare privilege of observing these far-ranging pelagic birds on their nesting grounds.

As we came out of the chill interior of the castle into the sunshine again and descended the ramp, these gull-like gray-and-white birds, with bull necks and stubby, tube-nosed yellow bills, slid by above us, wonderful soaring machines riding on the faintest updraft. They are slightly smaller than a herring gull and slightly larger than a black-headed gull. In the air, fulmar and gull can be told apart instantly by the wings, arched in the gull, held straight out in the fulmar. Moreover, when moved, the wings of the fulmar have a faster and shallower beat.

For at least 1,000 years the name fulmar has been in use. It means "foul gull" and is derived from the fact that these hardy birds, wintering at sea, are abroad in the foulest weather. They even scavenge among the icebergs and over the pack ice of the arctic. Carl Linnaeus gave them the scientific name of *Fulmarus glacialis*; arctic whalers called them "mollymawks." Members of the shearwater family, they spend most of their lives at sea, wandering over the northern waters of both the Atlantic and Pacific.

Hour after hour we watched these birds in flight around the castle, over the ruins of the ancient lime kiln farther to the south, above the green of sea moss and the gray of clinging limpets and the russet and olive of mounded sea-weed at the low-tide line. At times one would line up on us and come in low and straight, sweeping directly overhead. Each time one of the fulmars passed above us we observed how its tail altered position and shape in flight. Among these birds the tail muscles are exceptionally well developed. They twist and warp the tail feathers to assist in banking and fore-and-aft stability. Several times, as we looked up, flying fulmars alighted above us on the ledges of the castle cliff. Each time the wings, still stiffly outthrust, appeared to shake violently from front to back, slowing down their speed. The effect seemed to be the same as that produced by the last-minute fluttering of a settling gull or the tilted-back braking stance of an alighting gannet.

All of the fulmar nests we saw occupied ledges on the sheer, inaccessible northern side of the castle crag. Such nests, except in extremely rare cases, contain a single egg. Particularly large, it represents about 15 per cent of the total weight of the bird that laid it. In this connection it is interesting to note that the largest and heaviest egg of all living birds—that of the ostrich—is the smallest in proportion to the body weight of the bird itself, only about 1½ per cent.

As we walked below the castle, from all across the upper face of the cliff came the harsh calling of the fulmars. At sea, except when feeding, these birds are rather silent. It is when they reach land during the annual breeding period that they become vociferous. At this time the calls of the fulmars affect different hearers in different ways. James Fisher, in his classic study, *The Fulmar*, collected descriptions of the sounds as reported by various writers over a period of nearly two centuries. To one listener, the bird seemed giving "a rolling grunt"; to another, "something between the cackle of a hen and the quack of a duck"; to a third, a sound "like a squeaky door blowing to and fro"; to still another, "a deafening cackling and jabbering." To us, at Lindisfarne, in all the calls we heard, the dominant characteristic was a harsh and grating quality.

This sound reached us everywhere in the vicinity of the castle. It also came from the waters around the island when, for a time, we followed the shore, walking on the close-knit turf of the sheep meadows, springy beneath our feet and sprinkled with the small white flowers of the now-familiar English daisy, a name that has descended from the more poetic Old English designation: "the day's eye." From small bays—bays that had collected flotsam from the sea: a dead dolphin, a swan, a cormorant, a battered metal drum that rose and fell among the stones with a hollow clang like the slow tolling of a bell—eider ducks, with bobbing rafts of dark ducklings, edged away and, once, more than 100 gulls, in a shimmer of gray-and-white wings, black heads, and crimson legs, rose from some rich source of food.

Out from shore on the tide currents, buoyant as corks, riding high in the water, small clusters of fulmars drifted by. Facing the current, they were carried rapidly backward. We could gauge the speed of the swiftly running tide by the drift of the fulmars. As each newcomer alighted, a chorus of harsh calling broke out. Before such a bird settled down, it usually sailed without a movement of its wings, soaring on and on, often only a few inches above the water, sometimes for several hundred yards.

In sharp contrast to this floating, buoyant flight of the fulmar is the charging take-off and the beeline drive of the male eiders. Offshore among flashing sparkles on the waves we saw compact groups of these waterfowl, flying fast and low, the contrasting black and white of their plumage making them as strikingly beautiful as snow geese in the sunshine. For power and speed on the wing, the male eider is probably supreme among ducks. During a gale in the Outer Hebrides when the wind rose as high as ninety miles an hour, Colonel R. Meinertzhagen watched birds taking off and trying to fly. Most were carried away like bits of paper. Only the male eider was able to hold its own or slowly forge ahead.

Such flight, of course, consumes a tremendous amount

of energy, while the effortless soaring of the fulmar can continue hour after hour with a minimum of effort. Aloft far at sea it is one of the most graceful and efficient of aerial creatures. Not only is it a "wave-slope soarer" *par excellence,* making use of the updrafts produced on the windward side of waves, but it appears, at times, to approach the dynamic soaring of the albatross. This type of flight makes use of the differences in wind velocity at different levels above the sea. The bird acquires momentum by descending steeply with the wind in a higher, swiftly moving stratum of air. Then in a lower, slower-moving stratum, it turns head-on against the wind and climbs back up again, regaining its lost altitude. Joel Carl Welty, in his *The Life of Birds,* aptly compares the process to "a man hopping off a moving bus and using his bus-acquired momentum to run up a slope at the edge of the road." This the bird repeats endlessly, remaining aloft with only a slight expenditure of energy.

When Richard Perry was studying the wildlife of the island over a period of seven years, before publishing his *A Naturalist on Lindisfarne* in 1946, he compiled a list of 256 species of birds that had been recorded at some time in the area. It included such rarities as the hoopoe, the rose-colored starling, the black-browed albatross, and Pallas's sandgrouse. But for us it was not the rarities but two regular visitors to the island that interested us most. These were the fulmars and "St. Cuthbert's doves," the eiders.

Both these species have increased in numbers in recent times. The fulmars have benefited from the rise of modern trawler fishing, in which the catch is gutted at sea and the offal cast overboard, thus adding to the amount of food available to the birds. And the eiders have multiplied since the nearby Farne Islands have been set aside as a nesting sanctuary. On their breeding grounds, a curious habit of the female eiders, when suddenly frightened away by some intruder, is to squirt vile-smelling excrement over their eggs. The odor is so revolting that dogs turn aside. In the far north, it is believed, this may serve the purpose of protecting the eggs from arctic foxes.

Several times before we left Lindisfarne on our final day, we attempted to count the number of fulmars around the nesting cliffs below the castle. But it proved virtually impossible. The birds appeared and disappeared. They circled the pedestal of rock. Sometimes, nine at a time, they slid, flat-winged, back and forth along the face of the cliff. We ended by estimating the number at roughly half a hundred. In recollection we still see these soaring birds of the castle cliffs. For us Lindisfarne, Holy Island, will always return in memory also as the Island of the Fulmars.

When the tide runs out across the Holy Island Sands, the speed with which the bay empties is influenced by the direction of the wind. A wind from the north delays it; a wind from the south hastens it. On this evening the moving air came from the southeast. Even so, the retreat of the salt water was prolonged and unhurried. We saw people pacing impatiently up and down beside their cars. Some looked ahead through field glasses. It was after seven-thirty before the first car went through. Crossing the bay to turn up the coast toward Berwick-upon-Tweed—now in the final miles of our northward travels through England—we could hear, far out on the causeway, the sweet chiming of skylarks: larks on the island behind us, larks on the mainland ahead.

chapter 31

THE PALMS
OF SCOTLAND

On the morning of the twenty-first of June, driving north from Berwick-upon-Tweed, we crossed the Scottish border.

Summer and Scotland came together. It happened—without our planning it that way—that the day we left England and entered Scotland was the day we left spring and entered summer. Sampling "Berwick cockles"—shell-shaped mints that have been produced at the mouth of the Tweed since 1801—we turned west across the border country toward the Debatable Land, the Mull of Galloway and the Atlantic side of Scotland.

We had been on the road no more than half an hour when we descended into a dip among green hills where a clear-watered stream winds through the village of Ednam. This small Roxburghshire community, forty miles south of Edinburgh, is still rural, still unspoiled more than two and a half centuries after that eleventh of September, in the year 1700, when it became the birthplace of James Thomson, the author of that pioneer nature poem of such far-reaching influence, *The Seasons.*

335

The Seasons was the precursor of the poems of Wordsworth and Cowper. It was, as we have seen, the great in-
spirer of John Clare. It was the first book W. H. Hudson
ever owned. In far-away Argentina, it stirred his earliest
interest in the natural history of England. Down through
succeeding generations, Thomson's poem has continued
to "sing the glories of the circling year."

From the back of our car, I extracted a small leather-
clad volume. Its yellow cover was scuffed and stained.
Nearly a century and a half had passed since this pocket-
sized copy of Thomson's poem was new. The book had
ridden with us on all our long trips through the seasons of
America. It had crossed the Atlantic on the *Statendam* to
accompany us through Britain. Now under an ash tree,
beside the stream Thomson knew as a boy, in this village
of his childhood, we read again the old, familiar lines of
"Summer."

Around us the heat of the day was rising. The voices of
wood pigeons echoed hollowly from the treetops. Now and
then one swept across the road in arrowy flight. Daisies
whitened the fields, elders bloomed beside the stream, and,
springing from the moister soil like mammoth rhubarb
plants, the butter-burs spread their enormous heart-shaped
leaves. Beside this same swift-running stream, this quiet
country village had also produced—93 years after Thomson's birth—the famous hymn-writer, Henry Francis Lyte,
whose works include *Abide with Me*.

All along the border roads leading west from Ednam, we
heard the same sound repeated, the harsh, complaining
calling of new rooks. Coming north, we had run through
the whole cycle of the nesting of these birds. In Cornwall
we had witnessed the opening scene in this annual drama,
rooks carrying sticks to their nesting sites. Here in lower
Scotland we were in the midst of the last action, the curtain scene. The young birds, a whole new generation of

rooks, were launching themselves into the air, trying their wings, breaking home ties. Copses were filled with their discordant clamor. In the corner of one field near Kelso a score of the black birds had settled on a haystack. It appeared thatched with rooks. We saw the fledglings being fed in new-mown fields and along roadsides colorful with the purple-blue masses of meadow cranesbill. Of the making of new rooks there seemed no end.

Some twenty years ago, an investigating committee of the British Trust for Ornithology made a two-and-a-half-year study of these birds. It revealed some surprising facts about their numbers. For the whole of England, it showed, the average density of rook nests was eighteen to the square mile. For Scotland the figure was thirteen and for Wales twelve. During the period of the investigation, from February 1944 to September 1946, the total population of adult, breeding rooks in Britain was put at between 2,750,000 and 3,000,000.

Past other rooks scattered over furze-clad slopes, past lapwings twisting above cropping sheep, past curlews whistling their long-drawn notes over the open hillsides, we continued on. In the hours of that morning we were spinning the initial strands of that webbing of memory which now, for us, spreads over Scotland.

For a time, a lone black-headed gull soared beside us, riding updrafts where the wind vaulted over a sheep-wall. Wherever we went, along the coast or far inland, we encountered these gulls. Their rapid multiplication during the present century has been one of the most dramatic changes in bird life in Britain. During the Second World War, the eggs of these gulls formed an important source of food in England. From one colony, more than 72,000 were collected in a period of six weeks without producing any noticeable reduction in the breeding population. The birds had laid again in about two days after a single egg was taken from the nest. No doubt the versatility of their habits and the omnivorousness of their appetites have aided these gulls in their swift rise in numbers. In screaming clouds, we saw them following farmers cutting hay, dropping down to feed on insects among the new-mown grass.

And, it seemed to us, wherever we came to sheep pastures in Scotland we also came to lapwings. Once we saw four diving and zooming in a running attack on a border collie which had wandered too near a nesting site. In some parts of the Scottish lowlands, lapwings are still disliked because, three centuries ago, the clamor they set up when their nesting territory was invaded led to the discovery of Covenanters hiding in the fields during the religious persecutions of the seventeenth century.

Another reminder of unhappy years along this borderland—the region of night-raiders and mosstroopers—is found in some of the deep, southward-leading valleys that penetrate into Northumberland. During the centuries of the border wars between England and Scotland, raids and counter-raids laid waste the farms all down these valleys. To move the sheep away from the path of the night-raiders, it was the custom in those days to drive the flocks into the hills before darkness fell. For so many overlapping generations of sheep was this procedure followed that the habit is said to have become ingrained. Even today, I have read, in some of these narrow valleys the sheep begin, of their own accord, moving to higher ground when evening comes.

As your eye travels west along the boundary line between England and Scotland on a map of Britain, you come, as you approach Solway Firth, to a sudden jog. The boundary veers abruptly northward before it swings west again. Within the included area—between the rivers Sark and Esk in the storied Debatable Land which changed hands innumerable times in the border wars—lies the Solway Moss. It was in the region of this great morass that, in

1542, the troops of Henry VIII gained a decisive victory that played an important part in bringing centuries of border warfare to an end.

Beside the River Esk we wound for some time through woodland before we emerged into the open country where once the moss lay outspread in treacherous miles of almost fluid mud and decayed vegetation. Today much has been reclaimed as farmland and in only a few places is peat now dug. But, as we crossed the expanse of the former bog, we encountered one living link with those older times and older conditions. A snipe passed us flying straight and low, the same bird that received the attention of the Scottish parliament in the year 1551, when the price of a "snype" was set by law at two pence.

The sunshine had deserted us and rain was falling before we reached the farther edge of this historic tract. Other rain, descending in a succession of torrential storms in the autumn of 1771, had produced, during a night in November, a strange, almost eerie natural disaster at Solway Moss. Along its southern edge, at that time, a cultivated plain dotted with cottages descended to the River Esk. Although the great quagmire occupied a slightly higher elevation, it lay behind a wall of earth thrown up by generations of peat diggers. As the rainfall accumulated in the spongy, semi-fluid mass behind the wall, pressure mounted on this rude dike. About eleven o'clock on the night of the sixteenth of November, 50 or 100 yards of the dam gave way. An enormous mass of mud began moving out over the plain.

"Some of the inhabitants," says an old account, "through the terror of the night, could plainly discover it advancing like a moving hill. One house after another it spread around, filled, and crushed into ruin, just giving time to terrified inhabitants to escape. Scarce anything was saved except their lives—nothing of their furniture, few of their cattle.

Those who were nearest the place of bursting were alarmed by the unusual noise it made, others not till it had entered their houses, or even, not until they found it in their beds." Dawn revealed more than 200 acres buried beneath the still-advancing mud. It overran hedges and filled hollows to a depth of more than thirty feet. Although no human lives were lost, thirty-five families were dispossessed in that one night. For weeks afterwards the mud of Solway Moss flowed like lava down the slope. Its leading edge reached the Esk, turning the water black and driving away salmon. Months later lumps of earth and vegetation, carried out to sea from the disaster, were cast up on the Isle of Man.

With the rain increasing, that afternoon, we splashed along streaming roads, seeing little, until we stopped at Dumfries for the night. In Dumfries Robert Burns spent his last years, and near Dumfries, at Ecclefechan, Thomas Carlyle was born. When Ralph Waldo Emerson first visited Carlyle in 1833, he rode along the country roads in such a rain as ours. He could hardly see beyond his horse's head and reflected in his journal: "The scenery of a shower-bath must be always much the same."

In rain we started out next day. The downpour soon slackened and stopped. But trees continued to drip, and new-mown hay lay soggy in the fields as we rounded Wigtown Bay with its wooded points, its wind-warped trees and sandy beaches—the coastal scene that Carlyle always maintained was the finest view in Scotland. Villages were now gay with color, their stone cottages with walls of white or yellow and doors and window-casements of red or blue or green. Along the roadsides, on the way to Stranraer, workmen wielded curious double-handled scythes as they mowed weeds. That night we stayed beside Loch Ryan, in Stranraer, at North West Castle, originally the home of the arctic explorer Sir John Ross. Our window looked out across the wind-ruffled water where gannets, flashing black and white against a darkening sky, dived for fish.

What the Cornish peninsula is to England, Wigtown's western peninsula is to Scotland. Its tip represents the southernmost point in the country. Riding down this peninsula next day, we were, on this Atlantic side of Scotland, hardly twenty-five miles from Ireland and only forty miles from Belfast. Near Drummore, I remember, we met a woman leading on long leashes nearly a dozen beautiful pale cream-yellow greyhounds. At the far tip of the peninsula, at the Mull of Galloway, legend has it, those shadowy people, the Picts, made their last stand. The credibility of this account, it must be admitted, gains nothing from one version which has the last Pict leaping from the cliffs clutching to his breast the recipe for making heather ale. As we came back, cows were returning from pasture and, every few miles, we stopped to give them the right-of-way. Some were strikingly marked, black in front and rear, with a white belt around the middle. They represented Galloway's most picturesque breed of livestock, the famous "belties," whose origin, acording to the official history of the breed, "is lost in the mists of time."

Both England and Scotland are divided, so far as climate is concerned, less into north and south than into east and west. The east side of Britain tends to be more chill and harsh; the west side more mild. This is the direct result of the Gulf Stream, that warm river of the sea that leaves the Florida Straits with a flow of 100,000,000,000 tons of water an hour. At the end of its long sweep up and across the ocean, its dispersing waters reach the western coast of Britain in the North Atlantic Drift. Nowhere is its warming effect more dramatically revealed than in the palm trees of Scotland.

We came upon our first palm at Stranraer. Its fronds

were flailing about in the wind, with a dry clashing rattle, at the top of a twenty-foot trunk. We were to see other palms on the coast opposite the Isle of Skye. They are found even as far north as Ullapool, almost to the border of Sutherland. A dozen miles south of Stranraer, the famous Logan Gardens are lush with semitropical vegetation. Here flourish Australian tree ferns, palms from China, and the tall cabbage palms discovered in New Zealand by Captain Cook. Yet if you follow the latitude of these gardens around the globe, you find it runs across Labrador, Hudson Bay, the Aleutian Islands, and Siberia.

Ascending northward up the Ayrshire coast, on a succeeding day, we seemed at times on the Pacific shore of upper California. Huge, dark, wave-worn rocks trooped out into deeper water beneath towering headlands. For half a mile at a time our coastal road was bordered with dense stands of ferns, as other ferns had massed along our way beside the Wye on the border of Wales. Green pasture slopes, slanting down to the sea, were ribbed like corduroy by the close-set, horizontal paths of feeding cattle. Up many of them a scattering of wind-flared trees ascended like climbing laborers bending low under heavy burdens.

Beyond Ballantrae we stopped at a little cove where the tide had fallen away. There we wandered among odd shapes of stone, great rocks that had been worn by the waves as blocks of salt are worn by the tongues of licking cattle. Among these rocks ringed plover ran over the shingle and oystercatchers probed for food among the matted seaweed or investigated shellfish at the edge of the low-tide water. On a number of occasions, both the long orange bills of the oystercatchers and the short, black-tipped bills of the plovers—as well as the bills of terns, redshanks, gray plovers, and knots—have been imprisoned as in a trap by the closing shells of cockles. Unless they are freed in time, the

Stacks and cliffs of Duncansby Head

smaller birds, unable to lift the shellfish into the air, may drown on the incoming tide.

Out at sea, Ailsa Craig, the island home of thousands of nesting gannets, lifted like an immense haystack, misty in the distance. It was still in sight when, not far from the coastal village of Dunure, we rounded a turn above Cory Bay and saw the road ahead dip in a steep descent. I lifted my foot from the accelerator. The car slowed to a stop. At the bottom we turned around and went back up the road. This time when I removed my foot, the car rolled on and on. It seemed bewitched. Unable to accept this complete deception of our senses, we rode back and forth several times. Various explanations have been advanced for this apparent turning upside-down of the effects of gravity on this enchanted hill, the "Electric Brae" of Ayrshire, where cyclists free-wheel up but have to pedal down. One, from which the spot derives its name, attributes the phenomenon to electro-magnetism. The true explanation is simple. An ordinary carpenter's level will verify it. The descent of the hill is an optical illusion. Such is the lay of the land that the road appears to go downhill when, in reality, it is ascending.

It was afternoon when, on the southern edge of Ayr, we came to "Alloway's auld haunted kirk" and the birthplace of Robert Burns. Every year visitors from far parts of the globe flock to Alloway to do homage to Burns. Signing the guest book in the white-walled thatched cottage which once housed the family at one end and livestock at the other, we noticed that among those before us, one had come from Australia, another from South Africa. The last to sign were fellow Americans, from Lansing, Michigan. That night windless rain fell on Ayr. At dawn, all across innumerable rose gardens by the sea, fallen petals carpeted the ground with red and yellow.

Cottongrass growing on Duncansby Head

Eleven times we ran through showers during that day of changeable weather when we made a 180-mile circuit inland from the coast. The rain was set on a hair-trigger. We averaged one shower for each sixteen miles along the way to Dalmellington, Thornhill, Biggar, Lanark, and Auchinleck, by Douglas Water, beside Loch Doon and along the upper Clyde. For long stretches we were in a land of lonely moors and tumbling burns, in sheep country where the turf, close-cropped and smooth-appearing, ran like moss up and over the great hills. During the seventh shower, we pulled to the side of the road and, with the drumming of the rain loud on the car roof above us, opened a plaid tin box and ate "petticoat tails," the famous shortbread baked at Ayr.

All the sheep we saw were unshorn. Their wool was dense and coarse. Apparently the animals here were being raised for mutton rather than for fleeces. In the late-June warmth among the Lowther Hills they were shedding large patches of wool. It lay in masses and tufts among the grass. Some had lost their coats from the upper parts of their bodies first. They resembled men bald on top but with a thick fringing of hair below. Still others had shed all their wool except for dense manes around their necks. They were sheep that looked like lions. Instead of wolves in sheep's clothing, we had encountered sheep in lion's clothing.

On red roads—Old Red Sandstone roads—late that afternoon, we turned west from Lanark toward Auchinleck. There in the stillness before another shower we followed the wet paths of an ancient graveyard. Somewhere among the mossy headstones of that dripping cemetery one marked the grave of James Boswell. Here, home from his Grand Tour, back from his London days, the sum of his restless, inquiring life written down, he had come to his final resting place.

"Oblivion," Sir Thomas Browne wrote, "blindly scatters her poppies." But none was for James Boswell. Oblivion has not engulfed him. He is more alive today—to all who have read his resurrected journals—more alive in all his vanity and weakness and nobility, than most of the people we pass with a casual greeting in daily life. In that multi-volumed record of his days, his zest for living continued on in the world after life, for him, was over. In a way that might well have delighted him, he is immortalized by an inn sign close by the cemetery. It reads: "Boswell Arms. Wines and Spirits."

For an hour or more, among the burial places of innu-merable Muirs and Dunbars, we searched in vain for the grave of Boswell. The cemetery was deserted. There was no one to ask for assistance. In spite of the darkening rain clouds, all the trees around rang with the singing of chaffinch and robin and blackbird. On the island of Corsica, 200 years before, Boswell had discussed with the patriot Pasquale Paoli the possibilities and advantages of understanding the language of birds and beasts. "I would say," Boswell con-cluded in his journal after the conversation, "that an ac-quaintance with the language of beasts would be a most agreeable acquisition to man, as it would enlarge the circle of his social intercourse." As we listened to the voices of the singing birds, we longed, as so often we had longed in the past, to enlarge, in this way, the "circle of our social intercourse."

It was in a different language, the silent language of light and grace and beauty of action, that a bird without a song left the most vivid impression that returns to our minds from Boswell's burial place. Except for one small spot of shining blue almost directly overhead, the rain clouds had drawn together. In this opening on a brighter sky appeared the graceful form of a kestrel. For a minute or more, amid those dark and somber surroundings, it hovered on lumi-nous beating wings, its widespead tail translucent, its body glowing in the light streaming from behind it. Then the clouds closed together and the rain struck us, cold and driving. But for a long time afterwards as we rode in the downpour we felt warmed and exhilarated by that passing glimpse of so shining a presence in the sky.

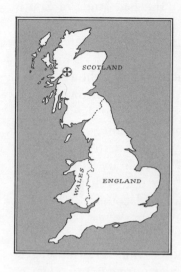

chapter 32

A THOUSAND
WATERFALLS

Docks. Cranes. Warehouses. The whistle of shipping. The rumble of lorries. The smoke of Glasgow. A forest of steel booms and mile after mile of flat-topped, soot-stained buildings. Then a ferry across the Clyde and an open way to the north. So we came, by the low road, to Loch Lomond.

For nearly twenty miles our way wound along the shore of the lake, the largest in Britain and one of the most beautiful in the world. Loch Lomond also is something of a geographical oddity—a large body of fresh water with an elevation of only 23 feet above the level of the sea and a distance, at its nearest point, of hardly more than a mile from salt water. Green were the ferns massed along the road and green the mountains that lifted steeply from the shore. With its summit 3,169 feet above the wind-ruffled lake, or 3,192 feet above the sea, Ben Lomond dominates the heights. In our leisurely progress, we saw the beauty of the lake in changeable weather. We saw it in sunshine, in rain, in gusty wind, in mist. And here began our days of mountain cataracts—days that joined to old memories of rainbows at Niagara, auroras over the bad lands of South Dakota, a night of falling stars on the western plains of Kansas, new memories of the white beauty of waterfalls in Scotland.

Wherever we stopped, somewhere within sight a foaming cataract traced its descending thread or narrow ribbon, chalk-white or shining silver according to the shade or sun, down the steep plunge to the opposite shore. By the time we turned away toward Inveraray—not far from the place where Wordsworth stood while "The Solitary Reaper" sang her plaintive song "perhaps . . . for old, unhappy, far-off things, and battles long ago"—we had counted 25 waterfalls.

Once years ago, when I was descending with a friend in the elevator of a New York hotel, two other passengers engaged in conversation in some Slavic tongue unknown to me. It sounded impressive, important, perhaps a bit sinister. My friend understood the language. One had said:

"I think it looks like rain."

And the other had replied:

"And it rained yesterday, too."

Similarly, when we drove into Inveraray we found the burghal motto, as it stood in Latin, *Semper tibi pendeat halec*, had a momentous and exalted sound. Translated, it is reduced to the commonplace: "May you always have a catch of herring."

On the outskirts of this town, as we were leaving, a sign bade us a charming farewell. It read: "Haste ye back." The road ahead climbed in wide loops and twisting serpentines. It threaded through glens among the mountains. Nellie continued her count of waterfalls. At times in this rainy weather they were on all sides. They fell from cliffs and followed deep-cut grooves down the mountains. Some tumbled in shattered foam over naked rock, others dropped headlong between banks green with grass. They appeared just above us, rushing through the bracken, to pass beneath our highway. One, as it made its final drop, fanned out across a tilted ledge of brownish rock, weaving an intricate, every-altering pattern of foam-lace over the face of the stone.

In narrow, gorgelike valleys, with the mountain tops on either side hidden in clouds, we seemed moving down long rooms with green walls that tilted outward and a lead-gray ceiling that pressed low. But even in the semitwilight of such deep glens, we could catch the glint of moving whiteness where cataracts appeared as though descending from the clouds. Nowhere else had we ever encountered the beauty of falling water in so many forms except once. That was at the Thousand Springs of southern Idaho where a whole subterranean river reappears, bursting forth from the face of a high cliff, pouring from innumerable orifices to plunge 100 feet or more into the Snake River below.

Somewhere along our highland road we rounded a turn just as the clouds parted and saw spread out before us an immense valley extending away in sunshine. We counted sixteen separate cataracts descending the opposite wall of this wide glen. Their silvered furrows dropped down the green flank of the valley side, each in its own fashion, one writhing in smoothly sinuous descent, another dropping in veering zigzags, a third riding down in a long straight chute of falling water. Extending away for miles along the length of this valley wound the glittering serpentine of a river. It was collecting the flow of the cataracts and carrying it away toward the ocean. All that falling water, like all the creatures in *The Water-Babies* that went hurrying past little Tom when the river began to rise, might have been repeating the same refrain: "Down to the sea, down to the sea!"

On this and succeeding days, along the highland roads we followed, we continued to be collectors of waterfalls.

We came to recognize them in their various forms, in their species and varieties, so to speak. By the time we had reached Connel Ferry on the first day, Nellie's count had risen to 329. Here, across the mouth of Loch Etive, close to *Ossian's* "Falls of Lora"—rapids that, at low tide, fill the air with an awesome roar—stretched the steel spider-web of a long one-lane bridge. When we reached it we were confronted by a sign: "WARNING. Stop on red light. Ring bell. Wait for green light." I climbed out and pushed a well-worn metal button. Another sign read: "Speed limit four miles an hour." The light turned green and we crept to the other side. The tide was up, the Falls of Lora hushed. But all the way across we were surrounded by the forlorn keening of the wind in the steel maze of the framework.

Weaving back and forth along the edges of the lochs, we zigzagged toward the north. High mountains were always around us now, lifting and contracting our horizons. By the time we came to Ballachulish for the night, our tally of waterfalls had mounted to 400. The count continued to rise next morning when we turned up the lower end of Glen More, the Great Glen of Scotland that, with its chain of lovely lochs, cuts for almost 60 miles in an upward-slanting gash that follows the line of an ancient geologic fault. Of the 1,200 and more earthquakes that have been recorded in Britain, a large share have been caused by slips along this fracture-line in the earth's surface.

On the winding roads of the valley we found ourselves saying:

"This reminds me of a road in Pennsylvania." Or:

"There's a turn in New Hampshire like this."

In Scotland we discovered it was easy to feel that we were still at home.

Without seeing it, that morning, we passed the highest mountain in the British Isles. Ben Nevis, invisible behind low-trailing rainclouds, lifted its summit to a height of 4,418 feet above sea level. Not many miles beyond, at Invergarry, we parted company with the Great Glen and struck out on a fifty-mile run across the highlands to the west coast and the Isle of Skye. Our road, one of the high roads over the roof of Britain, lifted us into wide, treeless tundra country such as we had found at an elevation of 11,000 feet in the Rocky Mountains of Colorado. Here, in the more northern latitude of Scotland, we were meeting comparable conditions at or below 3,000 feet. High altitude and high latitude have similar effects on climate and vegetation.

Looking down from the lofty ridgetops, we saw waterfalls from a new angle. We viewed their descent from above instead of from below. They tumbled away from us instead of toward us. We rode among them at their very beginnings. Time after time we came upon some spring-fed stream just commencing its long plunge. Our eyes could trace its progress until, in its foaming descent, it reached some slender loch shining in the valley far below.

Our count of cataracts was nearing the 800 mark before we passed the clustered peaks of the Five Sisters and descended, among suddenly increasing bracken and foxglove, to the edge of salt water and the ferry-pier at Kyle of Lochalsh. Beyond the swift-running currents of a narrow channel rose the mountains of Skye. In James Macpherson's forged Ossianic poems, Skye was the home of Cuthullin, Chief of the Isle of Mist. It was the Winged Isle of the ancient Gaelic bards. It is the classic home of the bagpipe. The most romantic of the Western Islands, it is a land of mountains and mist and rain and tumbling cataracts. Boswell records that when he and Dr. Johnson were making their tour of the Hebrides in 1773 he saw in the space of a quarter of a mile on the Isle of Skye no fewer than fifteen waterfalls.

For us, wherever we went along the foot of the mountains, the rush of white water formed an important element in the beauty around us.

Almost all the roads of Skye follow the coast. They circle the island, rarely penetrating into the mountainous interior. Those mountains, the youngest and most dramatic in Scotland, lift in a towering skyline of jagged, saw-toothed pinnacles. Their blue-black gabbro rock is yet to be rounded, smoothed, its contour softened by long erosion. The peaks of the interior are almost inaccessible. They provide the most exciting and dangerous mountain climbing in Britain.

On the day we visited it, this misty isle was bathed in brilliant sunshine. The air was sparkling. Each mountain tip was clear-cut, sharply imprinted on the blue of the open sky. Along the coastal road that runs north to Portree, the island's largest village, we watched gulls fluttering down beside the low stone houses of crofters, or tenant farmers, to feed with the domestic chickens. I remember one house set below the road on a tiny bay beside a half-moon beach of pebbles with the deep blue of the Sound of Raasay extending away beyond it to a towering wall of ragged peaks. It seemed a perfect setting for one of the wild and poetic tales of Fiona McLeod.

The long ridgelike summit that overlooks Portree and its harbor bears the name of Fingal's Seat. Fingal, King of the Isles of the West, was the great hero of Gaelic legend. Edward Gibbon, in *The Decline and Fall of the Roman Empire*, speculates on the possibility that it was he who, in the second century A.D., led the victorious army that defeated the Romans of Emperor Severus when he made his last, unavailing attempt to subjugate the Caledonians. In Macpherson's poems it is Fingal's son—the warrior-bard Ossian—who sings of "the deeds of the days of other years." From his seat on the eminence above Portree, Fingal, according to legend, directed a vast deer-drive in the valleys below in which 6,000 animals were killed in a single day. Hours of slaughter and days of battle—these form the subject matter of most of the "tales of the times of old" in Ossian's song.

Along the coast we kept encountering men digging peat. They used slender, squared-off shovels. The brown turfs, in little piles and long mounds, lay drying in the sun. To a non-digger on this sunny day, with larks singing overhead and with shining clouds drifting by, this work seemed one of the most pleasant occupations in the world. Several times we stopped and walked out over the peatland. Saturated sphagnum moss filled the wet hollows, and clumps of dark rushes rose among the white drifts of cottongrass. Once where flocks—shedding their wool—fed among the mounds of peat, we saw other sheep maned like lions.

Beside our road, in the sunshine, wild thyme bloomed, and bell heather. Once more we examined the comblike fronds of the hard fern, first met beside Dove Cottage in the Lake District. Now and then we saw a dipper with its peculiar whirring flight skimming low above some mountain stream foaming down its course. And always the waterfalls! We added more than half a hundred to our count between Kyleakin and Portree.

In the sunset as we waited for the ferry to carry us back to the mainland, we lamented that ours was but a taste of all the picturesque wildness of Skye. We longed to stay on for weeks. But the days were slipping away. June was over. July had come. We had a sense of time running through our fingers. Yet about all these final days in Scotland there was something of that added sweetness that characterizes those latter days of autumn that we call in America Indian summer.

In viewing the events of our lives that continually stream to the rear, we are convinced, in our minds, of the wisdom of savoring the fruit at its moment of ripeness, the flower in its time of perfume and beauty, the bird at its best, of enjoying each moment and letting it go. But still, in our heart of hearts, we are never completely reconciled to the transient nature of our pleasantest experiences. We dream of golden moments that will not recede into the past. We regret the necessity of our passing on in time and leaving such moments behind. We are, as Maeterlinck put it, the passer-by who never wants to pass.

In the lingering twilight at the end of that day we came to the charming fishing and crofting village of Plockton. Its single curve of stone houses nestles behind a sea-wall in the shelter of a promontory, facing a small bay. Sailboats with red, yellow, and white sails drifted in a variable breeze. They rode on Atlantic water. For this placid bay joins an extensive arm of the sea, the North Minch. In earlier times sailing vessels built at Plockton were famous all along the western coast of Scotland.

From the dormer window of our room, far into the evening, we looked down on palm trees and pampas grass growing among rose gardens at the edge of the bay. On this mild summer night, people below us, some clad in kilts, conversed in Gaelic. Each Sunday at the Plockton church, services are held in Gaelic at noon and in English at five o'clock. Across the bay the bulk of a gray castle stood out against the green of precipitous slopes behind it. Long after dark, after the moon had risen, even after midnight, we saw small glowing rectangles of yellow, lighted windows high in the castle, bringing life to the immense structure of stone. We went to sleep at last with the perfume of peat smoke, one of the great emotion-stirring scents of the world, drifting in our open window.

Perhaps it was three o'clock in the morning when we were awakened by the musical voices of shore birds, a dawn chorus rising and intermingling, then dying away again. Less than an hour later a blackbird broke into the first song of its long, long day. Before noon, Nellie and I had retraced our path over the highlands and resumed our northward-leading journey up the slant of the Great Glen. For more than 20 miles along its upper end, our road bordered narrow Loch Ness. Nowhere is this slender lake more than a mile and three-quarters wide. But because it occupies the chasm of an earth fracture along the ancient geologic fault, its waters have great depth. At one point they descend 751 feet below the surface.

The Loch Ness monster? We did not see it. That is, we did not see it unless a winding path of wind-ruffled water moving along the glittering surface of the lake was the monster emerging from the depths. Some scientists, in fact, have suggested that such trails, seen on misty days, may have given rise to the much-publicized tale. This, I realize, presents no difficulty to the true believers. To them it is not a gust-trail being mistaken for the monster; it is the monster being mistaken for a gust-trail.

Midway up Loch Ness a dramatic change took place beneath our feet. The hard schists and other metamorphic rocks of the mountains gave way to Old Red Sandstone. Meadows and grain fields opened up around us. It is the eastern portion of Inverness-shire that is most fertile, most cultivated, and most settled. In this Scottish shire, as in America, the west is wilder, the east is tamer.

But even after we had left the harder rocks behind, waterfalls continued. At times, instead of roaring down in torrents, they fell in gauzy spray, drifting downward like fine rain. Our count of cataracts had reached and passed the 1,000 mark when we stopped to examine a ragged line of yellow flowers running beside the road. Nellie leafed through *The Oxford Book of Wild Flowers*. The roadside plants turned out to be the common cat's-ear, *Hypochaeris radicata*. Relatives include the smooth cat's-ear and the spotted cat's ear. All are members of the great *Compositae* family.

Nearing Inverness, at the upper end of the glen, we rode

past an extensive field of oats over which a multitude of black-headed gulls swooped and fluttered. They were snapping up insects on the wing. Some twenty years ago, the omnivorous appetites of these birds came to the aid of the oak woods of Perthshire. During the summer a severe plague of caterpillars infested the trees. In large numbers, black headed gulls appeared, attracted by the feast. They penetrated far into the woodlands, picking caterpillars from the leaves, snatching them from the ground, hawking among branches to collect larvae dangling at the ends of their silken threads.

In the same part of Scotland another, more complicated, instance of the interrelationship of wild creatures was once reported by J. Arthur Thomson, of the University of Aberdeen. The owners of estates, annoyed by injuries inflicted on young trees by squirrels, formed squirrel clubs and set a price on the rodent's head. "After a period of squirrel-slaughter and some jubilation thereat," Thomson wrote, "a cloud began to rise in the sky. The wood pigeons were multiplying worse than ever, and the farmers, at least, said with no uncertain voice that they preferred the squirrels. An imperfect understanding of the web of life had left out of account the notable fact that squirrels destroy large numbers of young wood pigeons." This story, set in different surroundings and with a different cast of characters, is familiar around the world wherever man has interfered with nature's balance.

That great arm of the sea, the largest firth on the Scottish coast, Moray Firth, opens out beyond Inverness. On its shore Hugh Miller, the humble quarry worker who lived to become President of the Royal Physical Society, met his earliest adventures with the fossil fishes of Devonian seas. Hugh Miller was one of several men who, from modest stations in life, made real contributions to the natural science of Scotland. At Banff, farther along the coast, a shoemaker, Thomas Edward, in his spare time added twenty new species to the list of British crustaceans. And at the top of Scotland, at Thurso, it was a baker, Robert Dick, who assembled the first extensive herbarium of the plants of his northern region.

The hundredth day of our trip, following a night at Dingwall on Cromarty Firth, found us accompanying the coast upward toward the topmost county in Scotland, Caithness. In Inverness and Caithness the "ness" means "headland." As we went north birches increased. But they were not the straight and slender white-barked trees we knew at home. Most we saw were bent and twisted. Gradually the trees retreated into sheltered hollows, leaving the hill slopes to heather, golden broom, and wiry furze. In places we passed great bracken stands with immense ferns rising almost as high as Nellie's head. And always on our right, as we wound along the high roads of the coast, extended the interminable glitter of the North Sea. Unlike the gray, muttering waste we had first glimpsed on that rainy day at Dunwich, it now lay outspread rich in greens and purples and dark and beautiful shadings of blue, its surface alive with dancing spangles of reflected sunshine. Once we passed a bay of swans where more than a hundred of the white birds had congregated.

Increasingly as we advanced the country resembled frontier land. The widely scattered stone cottages fitted so perfectly into the scene they seemed no more foreign to their surroundings than a moldering log sinking into a forest floor. Elsewhere now the country houses were of the same design, with large fireplace chimneys and solid windowless walls at either end. From top to bottom, the end of one cottage was covered with deer antlers. Another was decorated with a vine trained in the shape of a large green heart. Slate had become the commonest roofing material. When occasionally we encountered a cottage with thatching, heavy stones weighted down the roof. Every barn we saw in this northern section of Scotland had a skylight in its roof.

Across the Caithness boundary, where we stopped to make a lunch of two small beef pies, we noticed how the hills were flattening out. The vast undulating plain of Caithness, a plain of Old Red Sandstone, characterized by deep peat bogs and tundralike open land, "the home of every wind that blows," stretched before us to the upper rim of Scotland. At its far northeastern corner, below the crags of Duncansby Head, the surging currents of the Atlantic and the North Sea meet.

More and more as we proceeded, the stone walls of cottages and farm buildings were blotched or overlaid with golden-tinted lichen. It mottled the exposed boulders. It extended over the great sea cliffs. It seemed the natural paint of this north country. Beside one cottage close to the sea two immense whale ribs formed an arch at the entrance to a garden path. The bones had lost their bleached whiteness. From end to end they were plated with the gold of the lichen.

So, on these final northward miles, the beauty of falling water was replaced by the beauty of lichen. No longer were cataracts around us. But whenever we recalled the preceding days of our wandering ascent through the Highlands, it was the memory of a thousand waterfalls that bound our travels together.

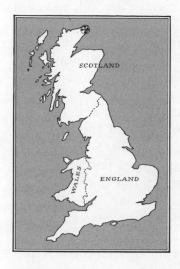

chapter 33

SEA-BIRD CLIFFS

"A desolate wilderness." "The bleakest corner of Scotland." So the land about Duncansby Head has been described. Coming north through England and Scotland, we had been warned we would find it without trees, without mountains, without picturesque scenery. It would be grim and bare, dreary and monotonous. But to us, when we climbed onto the immense headland that lifts more than 200 feet above the sea in the extreme northeastern corner of upper Scotland, it seemed none of these. Treeless it was. Open it was. But even tundra land, in its own way, may be beautiful. It may be picturesque. Every type of natural country has its own appeal. For us the high green moors of Duncansby, at the northern rim of mainland Britain, were as attractive as were the rolling downs of Sussex, at its southern edge.

Advancing across the undulating expanse of the open land, under the width of the sky, on the green turf, dense and elastic, our feeling was far from one of oppression. It was, rather, one of expansion, of freedom. Nothing closed us in. We walked in a land of far horizons. Our reaction was the same we had known so often in the wide spaces of the American west.

Overhead the skylarks sang—just as skylarks sang above us at Land's End at the beginning of our northward journey. Here, in July, as there, in March, the birds poured out the ecstasy of their song, rising and hovering and descending again, hour after hour. Around us there also arose another sound that had accompanied us all the way from Cornwall. This was the bleating of lambs. Scattered over the headland in small flocks, sheep moved slowly, cropping the grass. This led to an amusing incident close to the beginning of our walk.

Almost the only people we met that day were a man and a woman with a woolly white dog on a leash. We came upon them standing at the edge of the sheep meadow. Until we were only a short distance away we were not entirely sure whether we were seeing a white dog or a pet lamb. Nor were we the only ones confused. A hundred yards away, a cluster of a dozen sheep stopped feeding, raised their heads, and stared intently. Then they all broke into a run. Ranging themselves in a semicircle around the fluffy white animal, they examined it inquisitively. For several minutes they remained staring, silent and motionless. Then, their curiosity satisfied, they all turned and ran away.

Among the grazing sheep of the headland, a pair of oystercatchers had established their nest. As soon as we drew near, one gyrated around us, swerving and diving and giving the loud, shrill "gleep" of its call as long as we were in the vicinity. Some years ago, seventy miles to the west of Duncansby Head, in a rushy pasture beside Loch Inchard, in Sutherland, a ewe and her lamb were observed near the nest of other oystercatchers. The ewe settled down to chew her cud with her head almost above the nest. The male bird immediately went into action. Flapping its wings and pecking the nose of the sheep, it attacked repeatedly. The ewe arose, turned around, and settled down again. She was in almost exactly the same spot but with her tail instead of her head toward the nest. This satisfied the oystercatcher. The attacks ceased. Apparently it was the animal's head, not its tail, that represented a threat to the nesting bird.

Hour after hour—nourished by a pocketful of currant scones on which we munched from time to time when we grew hungry—we sauntered over the headland and along the cliffs. A wind from the sea labored over the green billows of the land. It swept around us, clean and fresh, strong with the invigorating smell of salt water. We inhaled deeply. Far in the distance, beneath a dark cloud, a gray sheet of rain descended. This was the northern summer. Around us a pink flush ran over the green slopes, the tinting of the sea thrift. And all across the moors and peat bogs, in patches like drifts of snow, waved the countless flags of the sedge we know as cottongrass. Over the cottongrass, over the sea thrift, over the rises and hollows of the headland, curlews passed on pointed wings, their long bills downcurving, their wild, sweet cries, a sound high, forlorn and lonely, carrying far over the green expanse around us.

We had gone perhaps a mile when we surprised a curlew family at the edge of a stand of cottongrass. The little group consisted of three long-legged, woolly young birds crowded between two parents, one on either side. Almost as soon as it hatches from the egg, a young curlew can run about. In one instance, one was found two miles from the nest two days after hatching. Immediately when they caught sight of us, the two older birds separated. One sought to distract our attention and lead us away. The other remained with the young. Watching the latter birds, we saw them tack this way and that. We saw them take advantage of every tuft and other obstruction. We saw them work gradually farther and farther away. In the end, all the birds disappeared from sight behind an especially dense and extensive stand of cottongrass.

On the wind, as we drew near the cliffs, came a multitude of strange voices. They intermingled into a shrill uproar, rising from an invisible source. With mounting excitement we approached the brink. For on these towering heights of Duncansby Head we were to witness something new to our experience.

The Old Red Sandstone, of which Duncansby's precipices are mainly formed, has been calculated to extend to a depth of more than 16,000 feet in Caithness. At the base of the great palisades that rise more than 200 feet above the water, the sea, through centuries of time, has nibbled in calm, gnawed in storm, battered in gales. The race of tides when gales are blowing makes these waters among the most perilous in the world. During one great storm in the 1860's, shattered waves shot up the face of the precipices and deposited a debris of small rocks and even fragments of the wreckage of vessels on the headland above.

This long wearing away by the violent sea has left the rugged coast pierced by great chasms with vertical walls. One, the Long Goe of Gloup, penetrates the rock of the headland for 100 yards. Another by-product of erosion are the needles or columns of stone that lift precipitously out of the sea close to the face of the cliffs. Some rise as high as 200 feet. From the old Norse word the Vikings used, *stakkr*, these isolated columns on the Caithness coast are known as stacks.

Our imagination had hardly prepared us for what we saw when we peered over the edge and our eyes followed the sheer drop of the cliffs and the vertical walls of the stacks to the sea far below. We were gazing into a vast city of birds, more densely populated than Edinburgh or London. Like the ascending floors of a skyscraper, the layers of sandstone rose up the face of each cliff. And all these multitudinous ledges were clothed from end to end with nesting sea birds. The mingled sound that had reached us on the wind was now magnified to a deafening din. We found we were forced to shout to make ourselves heard. In the spring and early summer of the year, while millenniums passed, this scene of sound and animation we were seeing for a first time had been recurring here at the edge of the sea.

With guttural undertones, the grating uproar never ceased. Whenever we changed our position along the cliff edge, alarmed herring gulls came flying toward us. They swooped low, wheeling, sometimes riding sidewise on the wind, uttering harsh, staccato screams as they went by. Looking down, we saw the nest of one in a well-protected spot where the ledge above projected out over it like a porch roof or an awning. A young bird occupied it, fluffy and gray with darker splotchings on its head. Over large portions of some cliffs the reddish rock was densely sprinkled with the snowy white of kittiwakes. The nests of these gulls appeared evenly distributed all along the ledges. The fact that all were about the same distance apart was no accident. It had been determined by the pecking distance of the birds.

Long since, however, squabbles over nesting spots had ended. The *status quo* was established and the sea birds had settled down to the serious business of brooding eggs and rearing young. All down the cliffs there was a constant coming and going; birds took off and birds arrived. Kittiwakes, the inky triangles of their wing tips showing, plunged in steep descents from the ledges or made their fluttering returns. Fulmars occasionally scaled by. And from a thousand places at once, the buzzy, beelike flight of razorbills carried them down and away toward their fishing grounds.

These members of the auk family were probably the most numerous birds on the nesting cliffs. We saw them, black of back and white of breast, sitting upright like miniature penguins, packed closely together on the ledges. When we swept our glasses over the finely crinkled surface of the sea outspread below, we saw floating birds, thousands upon thousands, mainly razorbills, scattered over the water. Some were drifting swiftly, carried by the powerful currents where Pentland Firth merges with the North Sea. Using their wings to propel them and their trailing feet as rudders, razorbills are strong and active underwater swimmers. One observer, looking down into a clear sea pool, saw the submerged birds, on occasions, twist over and, with their white breasts uppermost, swim rapidly for some distance on their backs.

Normally razorbills lay but one egg, which they incubate for more than a month. At the time of our visit, the eggs had hatched and the nestlings crowded the ledges. Drawing near was the great dramatic night of their lives. Most young birds leave the nest only when they are fully developed and ready to fly. Razorbills are an exception to the rule. They are still covered with down and their wings lack flight feathers when, in a spectacular mass exodus, usually during the hours of darkness, they plunge from the cliffs in a descent to the sea. Vibrating their tiny wings, they seek to break their fall. Some strike the water and immediately dive and swim away from shore. Others tumble down on the rocks, bouncing off, usually unharmed, protected by their dense coating of down and their thick layer of fat. The next morning the ledges that teemed with young razorbills the evening before are nearly bare. The adults, waiting below, convoy the descending birds out to sea. For some time afterwards they are still fed and protected by the older birds.

Among all this swarming life of the sea-bird cliffs, for us, the most interesting occupied the upper portions of the stacks and precipices. There, where patches of vegetation extended down the steep slopes like green rugs thrown over the disintegrating rock, the ground was riddled with the burrows of the puffins. In northern Scotland the colloquial name for the puffin is "Tommy Norrie." While the razorbill nests on the bare rock of the open ledges, "Tommy Norrie" seeks the shelter and seclusion of a burrow. Although a puffin stands only about eight inches high and is smaller than a domestic pigeon, its large bill and strong webbed feet make it an efficient excavator. On the island of Skokholm, R. M. Lockley found puffins had burrowed two or three feet into weathered and broken-down sandstone. When a solid bit of rock is encountered the tunnel bends sharply in a detour around it.

Somewhere, I believe in *A Naturalist on Rona*, F. Fraser Darling compares a gathering of puffins to a gay garden party. We never tired, that day, of watching the red, blue, and yellow bills, the black and white plumage, the bright orange feet appearing and disappearing at the entrance of the burrows. Almost every time one of the birds emerged into the light, it yawned, its abnormally large, laterally flattened bill splitting in the middle as the mandibles gaped widely. There is something of the appeal of a kitten or puppy or baby rabbit about the little puffin. It evokes the banal word "cute." It seems born yesterday. But closer scrutiny reveals a shrewd look and a self-confident air. It wasn't born yesterday, after all. In certain lights, the markings about the eyes—which are set well forward and provide almost binocular vision—give the puffin a worried look. With their short legs and stubby tails, the puffins of Duncansby Head recalled the cocky little ruddy ducks we once watched for hours along the dikes of the Bear River Refuge, in northern Utah.

On occasions, instead of digging their own tunnels, puffins will take over abandoned rabbit burrows. A few miles to the northeast of where we stood, on the low Pentland Skerries, two British naturalists one summer found a pair of puffins and a family of rabbits living amicably together in the same hole. The rabbits produced five young and the birds, taking turns, incubated their single egg for more than forty days. During the season when they are examining holes for possible nesting places, puffins sometimes make the mistake of entering chimney openings on headland cottages. At such times they frequently come tumbling down, sooty and disheveled, into the unused fireplaces.

For a long time one "Tommy Norrie" sat at the extreme edge of the cliff, looking down, seemingly lost in contemplation. Suddenly it toppled forward. Plunging head-first, it hurtled downward close to the wall of rock. Then it leveled off and slanted away in whirring flight. A hundred times we saw the colorful little birds take to the air in these almost vertical plunges. The ease of such a take-off is in sharp contrast to the difficulty with which a puffin becomes airborne when the seas are calm. For a considerable distance, like a laboring coot, it patters along the surface before it is able to lift free. The return to the cliffs, however, may be almost as swift and thrilling as the take-off. Speeding directly toward the wall of rock, the bird on such occasions tilts upward at the last moment into a rocketing zoom that carries it to the spot where it wishes to land.

When young puffins—the pufflings—are in the burrows, homecoming birds arrive with numerous small fish, usually whitebait or sand eels, carried crosswise in their bills. Sometimes as many as fourteen are transported in this way, the heads and tails dangling down on either side like silvery moustaches. Aided by a double row of backward-pointing serrations on the interior of the upper mandible, puffins are able to hold fish already captured while catching others.

Only four centuries ago, a curious subject for argument was whether puffins were birds or were, in reality, fish themselves. Konrad von Gesner, the Swiss naturalist, in his *De Avibus*, records of this species: "It is eaten at Lent because in a measure it seems related to the fishes. The English make the puffin a bird and no bird, or a bird-fish." In former times in Britain, puffins were sold as a table delicacy at three for a penny. Like the razorbills, as soon as the young puffins leave the nest they follow the older birds out to sea. From then on, their only contact with the land is during the breeding season. The story of these birds of Duncansby Head is similar to that of all the Atlantic puffins of the world, now estimated at 15,000,000. The greater part of their year, and all the bitter months of the northern winter, are spent in the winds and storms of the open sea.

Although, among this vast congregation of sea birds, it was mainly the puffins, the razorbills, and the kittiwakes that held our attention, we noticed other species come and go. A few were land birds. Eight jackdaws, flying together, dropped over the edge of the cliff. Starlings, carrying food in their bills, disappeared where they had appropriated some abandoned puffin burrow of the previous year. Once a lone pigeon, a slate-blue and white rock dove, tossed on the updrafts as it followed the face of the cliff as though in search of a nesting place of its own among the populous ledges. When our glance followed the cliffs down in a long plunge to the sea, we caught sight of cormorants bathing and, in a little cove where jagged rocks tore the waves into seething foam, a seal bobbing about eating a fish. Flying out to the stacks or skulking at the edge of the cliff, hooded crows prowled, alert for unguarded eggs. So bold are these gray-backed robbers they have been known to raid even the eyries of golden and sea eagles. Around one post close to the cliff edge, we found the grass littered with broken shells, mainly those of gull eggs. Apparently the post was a feeding perch of the marauding crows.

Several times that afternoon, we turned from the sound and excitement of a hundred thousand birds. Under the wide sky, with no other human being in sight, we wandered across the green headland. At first glance it seemed clothed entirely in grass. But a closer examination revealed that these high meadows are vast gardens of wildflowers. Short-stemmed plants bloomed in innumerable colors among the thick grass of the sheep-cropped turf.

Among them we recognized bog heather or cross-leaved heath, its whorls of four leaves making a cross when we looked down from above. Dangling in clusters were the tiny pinkish bells of its flowers. Here, too, were the yellow stars of the tormentil, one of the cinquefoils, *Potentilla erecta*. In older times, its roots were the source of a red dye and were used as a substitute for oak bark in tanning leather. In areas beyond the reach of the nibbling sheep, sea thrift bloomed on taller stems and here we saw the white-petaled daisylike flowers of the scentless mayweed or corn feverfew, *Matricaria inodora*. As is the way with our eyes once recognition comes, we began to see wildflowers everywhere. Of them all we remember best the orchids. The commonest was the hollow-stemmed marsh orchid, *Orchis strictifolia*. Although the color of its flowers ranges from purple through pink to almost white, all the clustered masses we saw on Duncansby Head were rich and velvety purple.

But always, after such excursions, we returned again to the lip of the great cliffs to sweep our field glasses along the teeming ledges of the nesting birds. Standing there at the edge of the seaward-facing headland, with the treeless hills rolling away behind us toward the south, with the broken line of the Viking coast extending off on either hand, with the vague outlines of the Orkney Islands receding before us into the north, we stood at the top of our long climb up the map of Britain. Land's End in the south; the end of land in the north—now we had seen them both.

The sun was still high but the day was far advanced when we came back across the moors with the crying of gulls around us. A dirt road, winding downward, carried us toward a small village huddling by the sea a mile or two from the headland. When we came out among its cluster of houses we had reached the destination toward which we had been moving ever since we turned away from the cliffs of Cornwall. We had arrived at John o' Groats.

chapter 34

THE NIGHT
OF LIGHT

Nine o'clock at night.
That is what my watch said.
Four o'clock in the afternoon.
That is what the sun indicated.
Surrounded by this daylight-at-nighttime, we stood on
the narrow strand between John o' Groats and Pentland
Firth. John o' Groats, like the Black Forest, the Western
Isles and the Great Dismal Swamp, has a name to stir the
imagination. This lonely, far-northern spot has drawn visitors as diverse as Thomas Carlyle and Andrew Carnegie,
members of royal families and travelers from as distant
places as New Zealand, South Africa, and the Orient. A
century ago it was the Mecca of tricycle and bicycle riders
as, today, it is the goal of thousands of motorists.

Our gaze swept over the sea, still sparkling in the sunshine; turned up to the sheltering heights of Duncansby
Head; swung back to the sunlit bulk of the John o' Groat's
House Hotel. Weathered by many storms, it—together
with a handful of houses and a couple of souvenir shops—

370

forms almost the entire village. Our upper window there overlooked the sea. The room next door held a couple from Rhodesia. Downstairs a maze of deer antlers surrounded the mirror in the dining room. There, each mealtime, a large dog, so dark brown it seemed black, accompanied one group and lay curled under their table while they ate.

Standing on the shell-strewn shore of this northern sea, we were almost nine degrees of latitude above Land's End. We were the farthest north, at the highest latitude, we had ever been. About 200 miles straight-line to the south lay Lindisfarne; about 400 miles Dovedale; about 600 Stonehenge and the White Horses. To Land's End the airline distance—the greatest distance between any two points in mainland Britain—is 876 miles. By the wandering, backtracking trail we had followed, that distance had stretched to more than 10,000 miles.

Close beside the hotel we saw, in the four-o'clock light, a small mound surmounted by a flagpole. It marks the spot where, legend has it, once stood the famous octagonal house of John de Groot. This transplanted Dutchman arrived on Pentland Firth in the early days of the sixteenth century. With the permission of King James IV of Scotland he settled in the shelter of Duncansby Head. At one time he maintained a ferry to the Orkney Islands, charging fourpence for a one-way passage. Relations settled near him, and by the time there were eight De Groot families, disputes are said to have arisen over precedence in seating at annual feasts. The conciliatory patriarch avoided dissension by constructing an octagonal house with eight entrances and an octagonal table where nobody sat at the head. In the intervening centuries, the name John de Groot became corrupted into John o' Groats.

All along the white strand beside the sea, the beach seemed formed primarily of broken limpet shells. But many other species of mollusk life contribute to the collection at the edge of the firth. The most famous of these northern shells are the "groaties" or "groatie-buckies" or "lucky-buckies," the product of one of the cowries, *Cypraea europea*. So delicate and beautiful are these shells of the Pentland coast that they are sometimes mounted in silver and worn as brooches.

The tide was down, the sea quiet. Angling out beyond the zone of shell fragments, serried ranks of black, layered rock tilted steeply upward into the jagged reefs or skerries that are exposed at low tide. We saw them now, ragged-edged, glinting in the sun, sprinkled with limpets and buffered with slippery masses of seaweed. Cautiously I worked my way out over the precarious footing among their saw teeth. In one place I stopped to examine a small sea snail with a shell tinted a pale, delicate shade of green. Everywhere on the rocks and in the tide pools the flattened cones of limpets, often mottled with soft shadings of gray and brown, clung tightly in place. Idly I tried to pry one loose, with no more effect than if I had been attempting to pry off a portion of the rock. So tenaciously do these mollusks cling by suction that tests have shown it requires a force of as much as sixty pounds to break their hold. As inhabitants of the surf zone, they are well adapted to absorb the shock of battering storm waves. The pounding water slides over each low shell, pressing the limpet against the rock, increasing rather than lessening the strength of its grip.

Although this shellfish is one of the most primitive and ancient of snails, it possesses abilities that still baffle scientists. Aristotle, more than twenty centuries ago, noticed that these mollusks leave their regular resting places and wander about to feed at high tide. After scraping from the rocks the tiny algae that form their food, they make the return journey. The homing instinct that guides them is still an unsolved mystery. How strong that instinct is was demonstrated, some years ago, on the coast of California. Across the path of a returning limpet, Dr. W. G. Hewatt filed a groove in the rock. The shellfish reached the edge of this confusing depression and halted. It remained there until the next high tide. Then it moved along the groove, circled the end, and completed its homeward journey, settling down in the precise spot it had previously occupied.

All up and down our beach of shells, under a sun that sank so slowly it seemed standing still in the northwestern sky, a pair of nesting ringed plover flitted before us, uttering soft and anxious cries. Looking out over the water, we watched an oystercatcher cross the path of the sun, then turn and come sweeping in to alight at the black edge of the reef. Along the shore, where stranded seaweed lay among the shell fragments, pied wagtails hunted for food. These hardy little birds are among the earliest migrants to arrive in Britain. Many brave the winter cold. Even in Scotland they sometimes congregate in winter roosts that may contain as many as 500 birds. When we stood still listening we heard from the vicinity of the hotel the harsh chirping of house sparrows and, inland from the sheep fields, the music of larks. Fainter, but still distinguishable to our ears, was the distant screaming of gulls. We saw them across the water to the north. They swirled in a shining cloud about a fishing boat that plowed slowly homeward to Thurso.

The water this boat traversed in the calm of that evening, the Pentland Firth across which John de Groot's ferry sailed three centuries and more ago, is famed for its sudden changes, its violent currents, its races and rocks and whirlpools, its gales and treacherous reefs. In sailing days, ships under full canvas, driven by the wind, sometimes moved backward in the grip of the swiftly running currents. At other times vessels were carried forward into the very teeth of the wind. The tide race in spring has been known to reach a speed of as much as ten knots. In the annals of seafaring tragedy, the Cliffs of Hoy, the Boars of Duncansby, the Pentland Skerries and the Men of Mey accounted for innumerable wrecks. Flood tide sets the sea to boiling around the rocks called the Boars of Duncansby. Ebb tide produces the same effect around the Men of Mey. On many a farm along this coast, in the time of sailing ships, gates and fences were made from wreckage collected on the shore.

A league away toward the sun the island of Stroma lifted its low, rounded form above the level of the water. Across its green fields ran a scattering of gray stone houses. All this northern coast, as well as the offshore islands, feels the moderating effect of the last remnants of the Gulf Stream. Although we were in the latitude of the northernmost tip of Labrador, only occasionally in winter does the mercury dip into the twenties. Even during the gales of January and February, snow rarely accumulates to any depth. And it soon disappears owing to the salty air. Receding into the north like low waves of land, the Orkney Islands faded into the distance. Even after ten o'clock, the nearer masses were clear-cut, lighted by the sun that now neared a horizontal band of slate-gray clouds outstretched above Stroma.

Twenty yards from shore the surface broke and the round, gray head of a seal appeared. It held something red and white in its jaws—the torn body of a large fish which it began leisurely to eat. While it floated there, tearing out chunks of flesh as it fed, another smaller seal surfaced nearby, swam about, dived and reappeared, but always kept its distance. No sooner had the seal and its prey become visible than gulls came flying. A dozen or more hovered around it, fluttering, wheeling, screaming, ready to plunge down and snap up whatever scraps were left floating from the feast.

From time to time the seal, as though tiring of the attention of the birds, would dive and swim beneath the surface

Red deer stag beside Loch Broom

to reappear at another point and continue its feeding. Each time the gulls, following its movements under water, flew with it so that it emerged with the birds hovering above it as before. The sight recalled from the back of my mind two wartime stories of plans to put gulls to work. Toward the end of the First World War a suggestion considered by the British Admiralty was the systematic release of garbage from submarines cruising below the surface. Gulls would thus be trained to follow submarines, associating them with food. In this way they would reveal the presence and movement of German U-boats. In the Second World War, during a naval inspection, Winston Churchill is reported to have asked:

"Do you see anything peculiar about that ship? No gulls around it!"

The ship in question was one of the dummy vessels used along the coast to deceive the enemy as to naval strength. No one, and consequently no food, was aboard. So it attracted no gulls. Afterwards, according to the story, garbage was dumped around such imitation warships so they could no longer be recognized by the absence of the birds.

The seal, beyond the end of the black reef, took a long time consuming its fish. It was an Atlantic gray seal, larger than the common seal, the other species found along the British coast. Zoologists estimate that 36,000 of the approximately 50,000 gray seals in the world are found in waters of the British Isles. The life story of each begins in the early autumn when the pups are born. Gray seals are gentle animals and, as F. Fraser Darling points out in A Naturalist on Rona: "There is no creature born, even among the great apes, which resembles a human baby in its ways and its cries more than a baby gray seal." So rich is the milk of the mother seal—its fat content being about 50 per cent, almost ten times that of cow's milk—that the young grow ex-

The light-filled night at John o' Groats

tremely fast. They gain about three pounds every twenty-four hours. In less than a month they are ready to start their independent life in the sea.

That life is aided by a number of special adaptations. When a seal dives, it has been reported, its heartbeat is reduced from the normal 150 a minute to 10 a minute. This is believed to be a safeguard against too rapid consumption of oxygen. On occasions seals have been timed on dives that lasted for nearly a quarter of an hour. Most amazing of all is the gray seal's ability to sleep under water. R. M. Lockley, looking down into clear, tranquil water from cliffs on the west coast of Wales, observed the procedure closely. Most of the animals slumbered on the bottom, but some slept upright in gently swaying water. At intervals of from five to ten minutes, they rose to the surface, apparently without fully awakening and usually without opening their eyes, breathed deeply between ten and fifteen times, then drifted downward again. Once when he observed two emerge simultaneously, Lockley saw them bump together. They awoke with a start and recoiled from each other. But soon they closed their eyes and sank into their underwater siesta once more.

Along the coast of Caithness both the common and the Atlantic gray seals breed in wave-eroded caverns beneath the cliffs. When John de Groot settled here, the wolf and the wild boar still inhabited the region. They survived in Caithness until the seventeenth century. In succeeding years the land has become tamer. But the sea—that ultimate wilderness—has gone onward the same, little changed by all the centuries, virtually untouched by man. This was the same firth, the same horizon John de Groot had known. The Viking ships that sailed the waters of this coast left no impression on them. They greeted our eyes just as they had greeted the eyes of the Picts, those ancient people who came to this northern land no one knows when or from whence and whose only link with the present is the primitive cairns and prehistoric relics they left behind.

By now the sun had reached and gradually sunk behind the cloud bank over Stroma. Exactly when it touched the earth's horizon, when the actual sunset came, we could not tell. That event was hidden behind a curtain of glowing and tinted clouds. But judging by the light in the sky, it must have been well after eleven o'clock. Only 150 miles to the north, beyond the Orkneys in the Shetland Islands, the midnight sun is visible on the longest day of the year. On the mainland of upper Scotland, at that time, people sometimes play golf and tennis matches by light reflected from the sky. If at John o' Groats we had not reached the Land of the Midnight Sun, we had come close to the Land of the Midnight Sunset.

Not long after the clouds obscured the sun, as we were looking toward Duncansby Head, from the top of the slender white column of its lighthouse a stab of light struck us. The revolving beacon had begun sweeping its long beam full circle over the land and water. Off in the Orkneys other lighthouses sprang into action, flashing their lights on and off like fireflies in the night. The tide had turned under the lingering sunset and now was coming in. We could catch the sudden gleam of white water breaking on the rocks of distant reefs.

In dimmer light, along the beach before us, we saw the pale running forms of the ringed plover materialize and vanish, become visible against the dark rocks, lost in the whiteness of the broken shells. Once a wheatear, its bill full of food for nestlings, alighted on a stone, then darted to the top of the beach embankment and disappeared. After ten-thirty at night it was still feeding its young. The rate of growth of such nestlings is speeded up by the increased daily intake of food resulting from the greater number of hours of daylight in the north.

Even when the hands of my watch neared midnight, we could make out objects around us well enough to recognize the white-rayed flowers of the scentless mayweed and clumps of the purple comfrey we had seen at Hickling Broad. Pale moths fluttered past or hovered above the plants. Little spots and dabs of white shone out among the vegetation—the froth masses of the froghoppers. We came upon a round, banded land snail clinging to a leaf, then upon another and another. We discovered them all around us on the stems and foliage of the weeds. The activity of the night—even on this night without darkness—was following its normal course.

Long after we had climbed the stairs to our room, long after midnight, we gazed out our window at the still-glowing sky and the sheen of tinted light reflected on the water. At 2:30 A.M., the zenith of the heavens was still flushed with the red and orange of sunset hues. All night long, with no other ilumination than that from the sky, I could read headlines in the *Scottish Daily Mail* and could distinguish among Roger Tory Peterson's illustrations in our field guide the puffins and razorbills and other seabirds we had watched on Duncansby Head. Before 4:30 A.M., daylight had almost come.

"Darkness and light divide the course of time." So, in the seventeenth century, wrote Sir Thomas Browne. But here in this night that rounded out all our northward travels through the British spring and early summer days, this light-filled night at John o' Groats, time had flowed on undivided.

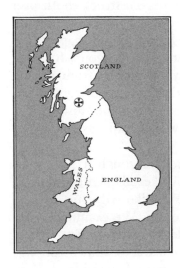

chapter 35

TIME
OF THE
ROSES

Toward the end of every journey our thoughts turn toward home, as toward the end of every winter they turn toward spring. Riding south from John o' Groats, we found ourselves longing for the calling of killdeer when we watched lapwings flying over the open fields. We pictured the great conifers of America when we encountered the Scots pine. We remembered the wild flowers of another continent when we passed pink-purple foxgloves or red poppies running beside the road. We understood the homesickness for that other world that John James Audubon noted in his journal when, alone in London, he watched a wild duck winging its way over the great city. So remembering the hills and valleys of home, we descended through Britain's beautiful and varied landscape.

Our drift southward from John o' Groats, that highest point of our travels, was a gradual retreat, like a tide ebbing from its flood. At first we followed the sea west, by Dunnet Head and the Castle of Mey, through Thurso and past the silvery sphere of Dounreay's lonely atomic-energy plant.

379

Then, beyond Bettyhill and Tongue, we struck south over the northern highlands, riding for half a hundred miles on one-lane mountain roads where white diamond-shaped signs surmounting poles marked the frequent turnouts for passing. As we swerved into one, a skylark shot up from a patch of dust where it was bathing. Larks are particularly fond of such baths. No sooner had it risen from the dust than it burst into song. For it singing was literally as natural as breathing.

All across the highlands we rode through a harvest of peat. Sometimes running in lines like dilapidated walls of brown stone, sometimes heaped up like wigwams or haycocks, the turfs were drying in the sun. We examined some that already seemed as hard as blocks of wood. Everywhere the harvest was going home. Here a tractor-drawn cart was piled high. There an aged woman, wrinkled and bent, leaning far forward to balance the weight, carried two or three turfs in a gunnysack on her shoulder. Mounds of peat were growing larger beside all the cottages we passed.

One afternoon on the broken coast of western Scotland, as we followed a road above tidal Loch Broom below Ullapool, we looked down on a large stone house set close to the water, a private dwelling that had been transformed into a hotel. It bore the name Tir Aluinn. So attractive was the setting that, on the spur of the moment, we turned back and found a room for the night. Big-game trophies decorated the halls, and statuary dotted the lawn that sloped down to the loch. Beyond the nearer mountains on the far side of the water, higher mountains rose to the west. In that wild country, between Little Loch Broom and Loch na Sheallag, F. Fraser Darling had carried on the fieldwork that resulted in his classic study, *A Herd of Red Deer*.

Our room faced in that direction. Looking out soon after dawn next morning, we saw a magnificent red deer, a stag from the mountains. But we saw it under circumstances unexpected and disconcerting. A clamor of gulls just out-side drew me to the window. In the yard below one of the kitchen help was putting down a large pan filled with left-over pieces of toast and scraps of bread. As she turned away, the swirling birds descended to feed. But almost im-mediately they rose into the air again. For the bushes nearby had parted. The head and great antlers of a stag had come into view. With stately tread the animal approached the pan, bent its head and, with the gulls screaming above it, began to eat. Piece after piece it chewed carefully and swal-lowed. When it was satisfied, it stood for a moment under the cloud of hovering birds. Then with antlered head held high, it moved away into the underbrush. Behind it the gulls dropped down to consume the remaining bread while jackdaws and house sparrows fed on crumbs around the edges.

At breakfast we learned the stag had first appeared as a young deer during a particularly bitter winter when food became scarce in the mountains. Accepting scraps put out from the kitchen, it remained near the hotel until the fol-lowing spring. Then it returned to the mountains. But when another winter arrived, it was back at Tir Aluinn. For four years now, each year with its antlers grown a little larger, it had come down from the higher country to spend the winter and stay on into the early summer beside the loch.

Sweeping now to the east, now to the west, we descended to Aberdeen, turned upstream along the Scottish River Dee past Balmoral Castle, wound southward through the Gram-pian Mountains. Reflecting that farmers' habits are much the same the world around—even in frugal Scotland—we passed a hay-baler rusting in one field, a last year's bale still in it green with sprouted grass. When we came to the twisting Devil's Elbow, in the Grampian Mountains, we found ourselves descending one foot for every five we advanced. In the valley beyond we stopped abruptly to watch for nearly a quarter of an hour our first red grouse, a female calmly sunning herself on top of a mound of heather hardly fifty feet away. The next day we were among cities, Perth and beautiful Edinburgh with its castle, like the castle of Lindisfarne, dominating the scene. Then we were below the Scottish border, beyond the Cheviot Hills, on the Great North Road once more.

Going south where we had gone north before, we saw everything at a later date, in a later season. The grain was higher. The lambs were larger. Almost before you can turn around, it seems, kittens are cats and lambs are sheep. We also traveled through a later stage in the sequence of the wild flowers. Now we saw the lesser bindweed, *Convolvulus arvensis*, blooming in pink-and-white patches beside the road while, like white morning-glories, the trumpet flowers of the larger bindweed, *Calystegia sepium*, shone out among the higher hedges. A third twining plant called black bind-weed, but in reality a member of the dock family, *Polygonum convolvulus*, also had opened its minute blooms. That it is not related to the true bindweeds can be inferred from its manner of twining. As it climbs, it turns in a clockwise direction. All the true bindweeds turn counterclockwise.

When we had come north in the earliest days of June, we had seen a man beside a Norfolk cottage examining intently a yellow rose, the first bloom on his bushes. Now, as we returned in July, the tide of roses that annually sweeps over England from end to end seemed at its height. Red, yellow, white, pink, roses bloomed everywhere; roses with two tones, with delicate shadings, with velvety petals. Villages were filled with roses. Country dooryards were colorful with their blooms. All down residential streets in towns, on either side, yards were rich with gardens of roses. Even in the Black Country the grim aspect of the smoke-stained land was relieved by the brightness of the flowers. Paradoxically, it has been observed that roses thrive near the industrial cities of England. The sulphur in the air combats black spot, the destructive fungus disease that attacks the leaves of these shrubs. The time of the roses—this was the outstanding impression of our final days on the roads of England.

Traditionally no other people take more delight in their roses or find more pleasure and solace in their gardens than the inhabitants of Britain. There are, it has been estimated, 10,000,000 flower gardens in England alone. When we passed Nottingham, off on the horizon to our right, we were not far from the village of Caunton. There, from 1850 to 1887—until his appointment as Dean of Rochester, near Canterbury in Kent—the vicar was Samuel Reynolds Hole. Tennyson named him The Rose King. For it was this Nottinghamshire clergyman who instituted the first National Rose Show at St. James Hall, in London, in 1858. He was the first president of the Royal National Rose Society, now the largest horticultural organization in the world. And of all the books that have been written about this national flower of England, the one that seems to me unequaled in charm is that other-century volume, Dean Hole's *A Book About Roses*, published originally in 1869. At one time his manor garden at Caunton held more than 5,000 kinds of roses.

Descending through this rose-time of the year, almost 11,000 miles from our start, our last day on southward-leading roads brought us to Maidenhead, on the Thames, about 20 miles west of the heart of London. We looked down that evening on the dark, green-tinted water of the stream, on the coming and going of pleasure boats, on swans and cygnets sailing serenely along the banks, on a female mallard that tried again and again to lead three ducklings across the river among the moving boats. We saw everything through windowpanes speckled with the skins of diminutive may flies anchored to the outside of the glass. They all pointed upward like tiny minnows stemming the flow of a tranparent stream. The next morning, near London Airport, we turned in the last of our three cars. Behind us now were all the once-unfamiliar, now-familiar roadside signs: "Diversion Ahead"—"Dual Carriageway Ends"—"Filter into Straight Line"—"Roundabout"— "Slow. Loose Chippings Ahead."

Our trip, rich in villages and countryside, so far had been England without London. Now, after so long a time and so many miles on English soil, we entered the capital. There the complications of the present descended on us with a rush. In one headline, the *Times* reported that all planes of the American airline that was to fly us home had been grounded by a strike. In another it predicted that by nightfall every hotel room in London would be filled by visitors from abroad arriving for the World Cup International soccer competition. At the Westbury Hotel, on New Bond Street, in the heart of the city, my publishers long before had reserved us a room for three days.

"What happens," I inquired of the manager, "if the airline strike continues beyond three days? We won't be thrown out in the street, will we?"

"Oh, Sir," he replied, "We never throw anybody out of the Westbury. We just ask them to leave."

At the end of a troubled morning, all was serene. We were able to transfer our passage to a BOAC VC–10 for the flight home. With three free days ahead, we commenced enriching taxi drivers in an attempt to see the British Museum, the Royal Academy, St. Paul's Cathedral, Buckingham Palace, Foyle's bookstore, and all the innumerable other places we wanted to visit in London. We came to crowds waiting outside 10 Downing Street, crowds waiting around Buckingham Palace, crowds collected near the

Houses of Parliament. In contrast to wilder scenes, to nature in Britain—which we had crossed the Atlantic primarily to observe—we were seeing, at last, what most visitors come to England to see.

Varied memories return from those crowded days. I remember a wood pigeon that flew low above the street in front of us all down one side of Regents Park. I remember a homesick oil-field worker from Oklahoma on his way to Iran who appeared vastly cheered by the voices of two Americans who had once been in Oklahoma. I remember coming suddenly out on Russell Square where, during the worst days of the Second World War, a British publisher had finally issued one of my books after courageously beginning again each time when first a bomb destroyed the plates for the illustrations at the engravers and then an incendiary bomb burned all the sheets at the bindery.

On our last free day we were joined by John and Lois James, who arrived from Woodstock. Foremost in our memories of that day together is our hour at Westminster Abbey. Nine centuries had passed since its founding by England's albino king, Edward the Confessor. Ten years had gone into washing the entire interior by hand in preparation for this nine-hundredth anniversary. Under its soaring arches and beyond its gold-plated altar area where successive British kings have been crowned, we found the marble statue of James Thomson. It climaxed the achievements of a life that began beside that wandering country stream we could now see so vividly in our mind's eye flowing through the lowland village of Ednam. We ended this *bon voyage* visit of our friends with a late tea in a room connected with a fine-food store where customers were being served by salesmen in long-tailed dress suits.

So the day ended that ended our travels through Britain. Behind us lay all our adventures in the springtime of another land. We reviewed in retrospect, before we finally fell asleep, the new birds, the new wildflowers, the new country we had seen. Our slumbers were intermittent that night, our last night on the eastern side of the Atlantic. We heard the deep-toned bell of Big Ben striking the hours of one and three and five.

chapter 36

THE
HIGH ROAD
HOME

We first saw Britain from the sea, low on the horizon, misty in the distance. We saw it as centuries of wanderers, the Vikings, the Danes, the Romans, the Normans had seen it. We saw it as the adventurous explorers, the Cooks and Drakes and Cabots had watched it rising before them at the ends of their voyages. We saw it as the roving naturalists, the Wallaces and Bateses and Nuttals, observed it at journey's end. We saw it as all those innumerable travelers, visitors to Britain from far parts of the world, had glimpsed it from the decks of infinitely varied ships, under numberless flags, over centuries of time.

We last saw Britain from the air. We saw it from the viewpoint of the gulls that have circled over all the ships of all the nations as they put out to sea. We saw it in parting as only those of the twentieth century have glimpsed it, from the window of a jet airliner, climbing steeply, leaving the land behind. Outward bound once more, this time traveling at three-fourths the speed of sound, we followed the high road home.

As we climbed aboard our BOAC VC–10 at London
Airport, we noticed a brownish bird hopping about, looking for crumbs, in the shadow of one of the outspread
wings. This house sparrow, for so long known in America
as the "English" sparrow, was the last bird we observed in
England. After that, the only sign of wildlife we saw was a
small fly that crawled about on the inside of our windowpane, an insect stowaway making the transatlantic crossing
with us.

The cliffs, the surf, the convoluted west coast of England,
the rocky offshore islands ringed with the white lace of
breaking water, drifted to the rear far below us. Then we
were over Ireland, its green fields threaded by a tangle of
wandering roads. An occasional momentary stab of light
shot up where some automobile windshield caught and
reflected the sunshine. Cumulus clouds, shining and immaculate, mushroomed up below us. Beyond Shannon the
cumuli dropped behind. The cloudscape altered. In the
more equable atmosphere over the sea, the airborne vapor
leveled out. For 2,000 miles, that day, its layer of white
formed the floor of our aerial world.

At times the cloud formation resembled polar pack ice,
heaved and broken, with windblown snow drifting across
the depressions. Again the clouds all streamed in one direction shaped by the transatlantic winds from the west.
For a long time one particular formation stood out as a
landmark—or a skymark. It resembled an immense white
comb with its teeth pointing toward Ireland. Sometimes,
flying in the sunshine, looking down from a height greater
than that of Mt. Everest, we saw small openings in the
clouds. They were as blue as the blue of "holes in the sky"
seen when looking up.

The joy that eighteenth-century Samuel Johnson found
in bowling along in a stagecoach is not multiplied by the
speed of the modern jet. Except for the changing panorama

of the clouds and glimpses of the sea afforded, at rare intervals, by larger gaps in the vapor, this high-level flying was uneventful and monotonous. Passengers read or slept. The main pleasure that breaks the sameness of such a trip is mealtime. Rushing through the sky, the thunder of the huge jet engines streaming away behind us, surrounded by the steady whisper of the gale tearing along our insulated, pressurized, streamlined cabin, we dined on roast beef, potatoes, carrots, peas, a salad, a roll, coffee, and strawberry shortcake with whipped cream. Hundreds of miles rushed by while we ate with relish. Never once did we see another plane above the clouds, never once a ship on the waves below. Ours was a lonely sky above the lonely sea.

As the hours dragged by, I leaned back remembering all our adventures in the Springtime of Britain. I recalled those first skylarks at Land's End, that day of rain amid the thousands of daffodils, the perfume of the hawthorn along Shakespeare's river, moonlight and the nightingale at Selborne, waterfalls shining on the Isle of Skye, and that night of light at John o' Groats. To while away the time I began jotting down a list of chapters—chapters you have already read—Adventurers Fen, Low Nest Farm, Archaeological Rabbits, Dartmoor in the Rain.

As we neared the rugged coast of upper Newfoundland the white sheet of the sea clouds was torn by violent updrafts from the land. The floating vapor broke up into innumerable varied, wild, and beautiful shapes. Between them we watched a vague, sprawling form, amoebalike, darken into Newfoundland's rocky island outpost of North America. Soon afterwards we caught sight of the first airliner we had seen. Its silvery, streamlined form, thousands of feet below, was heading for Europe. As we came down the New England coast, with tea and cakes reviving the passengers for disembarkation, rocky islands rimmed with the white of foam gave place to lower islands ringed with the shining yellow of sandy beaches. Houses multiplied. Towns drew closer together. With the communities of Connecticut and Long Island hurtling by, we curved out to sea, then came nosing down toward New York's Kennedy Airport, 3,456 miles from London. Where its concrete runways lie, Nellie and I, years before, had searched for short-eared owls. Then the whole area had been an abandoned tract called Idlewild.

In bringing the book of his travels in Britain to a close, John Burroughs, fourscore and more years before us, noted: "As we neared home the heat became severe." History now repeated itself. We touched the runway at Kennedy Airport in a record-shattering, mid-July heat wave. As our airliner slowed, the drag of the reversed jet engines braking its speed like a released parachute, I glimpsed a prairie horned lark flying up from beside the concrete. Thus two small birds bounded our ocean-spanning flight, the house sparrow of the Old World, the horned lark of the New.

Traveling with the sun, we had gained five hours of daylight during our seven-and-a-half-hour flight. By New York time, Nellie and I had been up since before one o'clock in the morning. This was our own longest day of the year. Beyond customs, my friend and publisher, Phelps Platt—whose voice I had last heard over the transatlantic telephone at Tunbridge Wells—waited with our car, the same white machine that had carried us on our 20,000-mile journey through winter. At his home in the country, near New Canaan, Connecticut, that afternoon, we slept for hours, drugged by fatigue and the sweltering day. We awoke to old familiar voices, the catbird, the towhee, the dog-day harvest fly wailing in the July heat.

The next morning we rode up the Connecticut Turnpike through a country of brooks and hills, through another, a New World "green and pleasant land." To my surprise, shifting back to driving on the right-hand side of the road proved no harder than for a bilinguist to speak in a second tongue. By sea and land and sky, by ship and auto and airliner, Nellie and I had traveled more than 17,000 miles when, in the far northeastern corner of the state, north of the village of Hampton, we turned down the lane at Trail Wood.

Once on a silver spoon I saw engraved: "The world is a book and he who stays at home reads only one page." We, who now had read other pages, realized that this is but partly true. At times when our tether holds us on one small bit of the earth's surface, we tend to feel that in this little area we are seeing only fragments of life. In reality we are touching threads that run around the world. The smallest foothold on the surface of the globe places us in contact with the whole world's unending web of life. There are no isolated fragments. There are only threads and links and segments. Nothing is alone, nothing is unrelated, all are linked together.

So we returned content to our white cottage under the high hickory trees, set among fields and woods, overlooking a brook, a pond, and a waterfall. For years to come we would compare and connect what we had seen with what we knew so well. We slipped into Trail Wood life as easily as a frog slips into the water of a summer pond. We had gained much by our experience. Our lives had been enriched by what we had seen. They also had been enriched in that peculiar way Thoreau had in mind when he wrote in his journal: "Only that traveling is good which reveals to me the value of home and enables me to enjoy it better."

INDEX

Route of
**EDWIN WAY
TEALE'S**
*Springtime
in Britain*

JOHN O'GROAT S

NORTH SEA

Lindisfarne I.

HADRIAN'S WALL

LAKE
DISTRICT

Tweed R.

EDINBURGH

Loch Lomond

Loch Ness

Isle
of Skye

ATLANTIC OCEAN